BOOKS BY TONI BENTLEY

Serenade: A Balanchine Story

The Surrender: An Erotic Memoir

Sisters of Salome

Holding On to the Air (coauthor, with Suzanne Farrell)

Costumes by Karinska

Winter Season: A Dancer's Journal

SERENADE

SERENADE

A BALANCHINE STORY

TONI BENTLEY

PANTHEON BOOKS NEW YORK

Library of Congress Cataloging-in-Publication Data
Name: Bentley, Toni, author.
Title: Serenade : a Balanchine story / Toni Bentley.
Description: First edition. New York : Pantheon Books, 2022. Includes
bibliographical references and index.
Identifiers: LCCN 2021041885 (print) | LCCN 2021041886 (ebook) |
ISBN 9780593316399 (hardcover) | ISBN 9780593316405 (ebook)
Subjects: LCSH: Serenade (Choreographic work : Balanchine). Bentley, Toni.
Ballerinas—Bolshevik—Russia—Biography. Ballerinas—New York (State)—
New York—Biography. Balanchine, George. Choreographers—New York
(State)—New York—Biography. New York City Ballet.
Classification: LCC GV1790.S47 B46 2022 (print) | LCC GV1790.S47 (ebook) |
DDC 792.8/2092 [B]—dc23/eng/20211020
LC record available at https://lccn.loc.gov/2021041885
LC ebook record available at https://lccn.loc.gov/2021041886

www.pantheonbooks.com

Frontispiece: George Balanchine 1938, New York World-Telegram and
the Sun Newspaper Photograph Collection (Library of Congress)
Photograph of George Balanchine on page 249 © Paul Kolnik

Jacket illustration by Erik Werner © Artists Rights Society (ARS),
New York/VISDA
Jacket design by Emily Mahon

For RSA

&

For the dancers of *Serenade*—
past, present, future

Momentary as a sound,
Swift as a shadow, short as any dream,
Brief as the lightning in the collied night
That, in a spleen, unfolds both heaven and earth,
And ere a man hath power to say, Behold!

—*A Midsummer Night's Dream*

CONTENTS

CURTAIN UP

||||||||||||||||||||||||||||||||||||||||||||||||||||||||||||||||||||||||||||||||||||||||||||||||||||||||||

The violins begin. It is 8:07 p.m. I know this because that is when the 8:00 p.m. performance starts. *Serenade* is always first. Always the opener of three ballets. The hors d'oeuvre, Mr. B would say, of the meal he served to his audience night after night in his restaurant, his theater of beauty. Five minutes earlier, our handsome stage manager Perry Silvey had called "Places, please!" This is the cue to take a last sip of water from the hallway water fountain beside the elevator, just beyond the backstage area. I wet my fingers and smooth down any remaining stray wisps of hair. Not a single one is out of place. It can't be. I rub a finger across my teeth to remove any pink lipstick that migrated over, and then smooth some Vaseline on my teeth. This way, if my mouth gets dry onstage, my lips won't stick to my teeth. That's a bad moment, liplessness.

I have just finished sewing, with big broad stitches in thick beige crochet thread and a large darning needle, the half-inch tips of my tightly knotted toe shoe ribbons inside the ankle ribbons. Not everyone does this: some just tuck them inside. I used to tuck too, but although I never had one come loose, the thought alone eventually became so worrying that I started sewing them in. It's not that your shoe would come off—that simply does not happen to a professional dancer; it's unthinkable—but that that little half inch of extra ribbon would protrude from your ankle and wreck the smooth line of

your inner leg and foot. And ballet is all about lines, if it's about anything. Tying our ribbons is a practical necessity, while sewing their
tips is an aesthetic one, thus they are of equal concern. The ends are
sewn in. Security.

We all flock around the rosin box like hummingbirds at a feeder.
Rosin on the heels of the tights to anchor the inside of the shoe,
then rosin all over the flat toe tip, the sides, the shank. Next girl.
Now the water bucket. A quick dip—about two inches deep—with
a flexed foot, shoe and all. Soaking the heel not only shrinks the
satin around the ankle for extra traction but also forms a sticky paste
with the rosin inside the heel of the shoe. And wrecks your tights.
Despite nightly washing, they become permanently hardened, dark-
ened at the heels, crunchy with embedded rosin.

Ready.

The shoes, the hair—a high, tight bun, no glitter, no tiara, no
pastel flower bouquets. We don't even wear the usual small stud
rhinestone earrings that we do for most other ballets, which shed
occasional sparkles as we move. *Serenade* is matte. (Never, in any ballet, do we wear personal jewelry that would distract, indicating one's
offstage life: onstage we are Other.) Then the costume: the tight blue
bodice, secured by invisible nude elastic straps, is shaped by vertical
princess seams, 360 degrees around, to cling to our slim torsos. The
matching blue tulle to the ankles has two translucent panels running
the full length of each leg in front.

Madame Karinska, the Russian costume designer, is cunning
and elegant in equal doses. I can see her in her chic navy Chanel suit,
hair in a permanent wave, though not yet perhaps in the lavender
hue it became later, and Mr. B in his jacket, cowboy shirt, silver tur-
quoise bracelet, and cravat circling his neck though slightly askew,
chattering in Russian over tea from her silver samovar one afternoon
in the costume shop on West 59th Street. It's 1952.

They are like two imperial Russian aristocrats discussing the latest Fabergé egg in an atelier by the Neva. She is showing him the
blue tulle that has just arrived from Paris. It's the first time she's
been able to get fabric from France since the Second World War
ended. Yards and yards of it, covering the cutter's table and spilling
over onto the floor. He is gathering it in his hands and then letting
it go, to see how it moves. The way he gathers us, his dancers, and

Dancer Lisa de Ribere smoothing out her tutu
before the curtain rises *(© Steven Caras)*

then lets us go, to see how we move. About twelve years later she
added the diaphanous leg panels. No one will see them—no one will
know—but the effect will be magnificent: ambiguous, suggestive.
Mr. B loved legginess.

They sip their tea and discuss the bodice—how many panels,
how low the neckline, shiny or matte satin. Cut on the bias, of
course, so the dancer can still breathe while wrapped tight. The skirt
will be offset on a diagonal around the hips, not the waist as with
the classic tutu but slanted, higher on the right, lower on the left,
making it even more flattering, verging on sexy as it reveals the trim
hips of svelte young bodies. There can be no limit to how beautiful a
dancer for Balanchine can be. Will be. Was.

At 8:04, everything is secure, in place. It's all I've got, all I can control. Once the ballet begins, who knows? The variables are endless—

the tempos, the new girl, a blown light in the fourth wing, a slip. A slip that could end in tearful embarrassment, or end your career completely with a torn Achilles tendon, or a chipped hip bone. We were dancing on the edge before we knew what it was. But we knew where it was. And so I learned early on that everything, anything, that is beautiful is perched on a precipice. Mr. B just placed us there, and it was trust in him that gave us balance.

"Places, please, ladies!" In rehearsals we're "girls," but onstage we're "ladies." Rarely "women." Modern dancers are women: they don't dance on their toe tips, and they have been to college. We haven't. We have barely finished high school. Some outsiders like to highlight the backstage use of "girls" to illustrate how ballet dancers are infantilized, belittled. But they miss the point entirely. We are classical ballet dancers, which is vocation not gender, novices in Balanchine's ministry. We are unconcerned with words, much less semantics—physical manifestation is our sole interest. Besides, we *are* girls. I am not yet twenty.

This is it. I am alone onstage. With sixteen others. Each so alone. Together. Seventeen pairs of parallel, silky peach toe shoes (we wear Freeds, which are English; Capezios are American and pale pink, rather bourgeois—except the divine Allegra Kent, who preferred Capezios, but then she proved the exception to every rule) lined up side by side, so sweet, as in a dance shop window. This is so unusual for a ballet dancer: we are always turned out, heels together, toes at opposing ends, a flat line. But for *Serenade,* in the beginning—as in Eden—we are parallel, like ordinary mortals. It is harder to balance, really, and there is such an urge for the feet to pivot, for the toes to pop apart. So strong is our training that parallel feels positively pigeon-toed.

I grab the crisp tulle and pull it up flat against my tighted legs, look down and line up my feet, inside ankles locked together, and then let loose the tulle, refluffing it to remove any finger indents or creases while not budging my feet. My head is turned ever so slightly to the right and the cheek barely tilted, ear toward the shoulder. Mr. B always told us to turn the cheek as if waiting for a kiss. The kiss of fate, the kiss he might bestow. Being so young, we didn't know we had already been kissed, being there with him and all.

The left arm hangs down soft and loose. Right arm up, to the side but a little to the front, palm upward and facing away, fingers soft and separated, middle one heading toward the thumb but not touching. A salute. A protection.

Head and eyes follow the arm, looking toward the uplifted hand. But everything is only hinted at. This arm has been here, there, for nearly ninety years now since Balanchine made this ballet—girl after girl after girl after girl holding her arm in that place. Mine is there now, holding that invisible torch like the Olympic flame. Holding it there until the curtain rises and still after that. Inextinguishable.

I feel so isolated out here, supported only by air. What a profession to have chosen! No wonder my parents thought college was a good idea. Fifteen years of daily training, 22,000 hours at the barre, and I feel like I might just keel over. Squeeze the pelvis tight, grounding, torso up, lifted, reaching. I think of Muriel Stuart, one of my teachers at the School of American Ballet, who had studied with Anna Pavlova in England, saying in class in her crisp British accent, "Lift up, and softly drop down." While she said this, she would place two very firm and pointed fingers right under one buttock and dig in mightily, the "lift up" part (that grounds), while placing her other hand firmly on the shoulder, the "drop down" part (that lifts). Ballet is based on physical opposition—turnout of the hips being its central contradiction—and this defiance is one route to the ethereal.

Mr. B appears now, in his dark gray sports jacket and yellow silk cravat, in the first wing on stage right.* This is where he stands night after night. It is his wing, right next to the stage manager's giant, black, flashing computer motherboard. No one else stands there, though there is no rule, no sign. He bends his right elbow, leaning it along the two-inch-wide horizontal wood plank that braces the back of the wing. He props his face on his knuckles, his hand a curl. If he were only one inch more to his right, he would be visible to the audience, the profile of his nose passing from backstage to onstage. But they don't know he is there; he is visible only to us, onstage with us.

---

* Stage directions are named from the performer's viewpoint, thus "stage left" is to the right for the audience, "stage right" is to the left for the audience, "upstage" is the back of the stage, and "downstage" is the front of the stage, before the orchestra pit.

Not only does everyone notice his quiet appearance, but every muscle in every body onstage receives a mad rush of adrenaline as we stand in our places. The only one we care about is here now. As young girls, we are all scared of him—he has the love we want, the only love we want. He is ready for the show.

After twenty-three seconds of Tschaikovsky's* violins, the heavy gold curtain lifts swiftly upward and a cool breeze blows across the stage as the cavernous space of the audience enters our private world. Squeeze harder; pull up. Don't breathe. This is not a moment to be mortal. I am a Balanchine dancer.

---

* This spelling, instead of Tchaikovsky, was the spelling Balanchine preferred, and was used by New York City Ballet during his life, during my own years there. It continues to be used to this day.

INTRODUCTION

Serenade is a slant shadow on my heart. She bifurcates my being, my life. Though I have had far more life with her than without her. Three-fourths, to be precise. She—like countries, ships, and chandeliers, she is feminine—lies at the near shore of Balanchine's kingdom, beckoning, luring, yet so exacting as to not be exactly welcoming. Her countless diagonals, ever ascending, both begin and end the ballet, pointing everywhere, though always to here, here, here. Her shapes and lines and waves rise above the ocean ledge like a ghostly cathedral, suspended, the misty blue there but not there, hardly here either. This is the shoreline of my past, and of my present too; they are the same. One cannot, you see, leave the kingdom once there, despite its apparent loss. Unknowing is not possible, though the balance is precarious. There never was a time before I danced. Or after either.

And so we went, us fortunate few who happened to be in the right place at the right time, with the right physical and psychic makeup. We who wanted it enough, whose yearning, even when so young, translated into grinding, relentless, hard work despite failure's daily visits, hour upon hour, day upon day, month upon month, year upon year. The standards were indeed impossibly high: I know of no other way to achieve beauty beyond beauty. The endless competition was one of our greatest aides, a fact we all acknowledged in a paradoxical comradery of unshakable, lifelong commitment to one another. Our individual ambitions subsumed in our far larger common goal: to dance Balanchine's ballets as he wanted them. It was his vision for ourselves, individually and together, to which we were devoted. Devoutly devoted. It was work that rendered any idealism, romanticism, or dreams of fluffy tutus and sparkling tiaras as decorative distractions. There was never enough, only more, always more. Through this endless physical work, through an improbable, arduous technique that enabled, occasionally, the submission of ego, Balanchine made us luminous, spiritual creatures for a few moments now and then.

None of us have ever been more incandescent than when dancing *Serenade*, a ritual that purifies the sublunary. Yes, we look lovely in our elegant costumes, our faces pale with black eyes, in the low blue lighting and flickering shadows, the gold proscenium framing our proceedings, but internally is where the chemistry happens, what the audience is really seeing.

Dancing *Serenade*, Balanchine is rushing through our bodies. But we didn't, you see, just dance it for him, his steps, his moves. We inhabited him in those steps, those moves—we him, he us. His spirit was inside our bodies, propelling every movement, every stillness. Virgins all, until we loved him and gained eternal innocence.

Our love, my love, for him was not an adolescent infatuation— that intoxicating trifle was for the rare, though occasional, boyfriend— that soars, dims, then dies in time. This was lifelong devotion found young. What a very particular offering Balanchine provided, waking in us, in me, a wide-open, unstoppable, unquestioned desire to give one's self, one's best self, one's better-than-one's-best self, to something, something deeply physically and morally beautiful.

I am all too aware that my love, my respect, for George Balanchine might appear unchanged, undiminished from that of my youth when I was dancing for him. Hasn't time done its wising up, I am asked? Or at least provided a flattening of wonder? I have never had to ask myself these questions, the answer so intrinsically known. Though indeed youthful adorations of a beloved artist do often recede, or at least fall to their rightful level on the scale as one grows older, learns more, lives more, sees and hears more. How many teenage idols fall to a lower rung as time marches forward? I will always love Henry Miller for having opened my eyes, but no, he is no longer the same god to me as when I read him at age seventeen.

But what if, unlikely as it is, one chances upon a truly great artist at that impressionable age, one such as Shakespeare, Mozart, Blake, Bach, or Balanchine? I will tell you what happens. As time adds wisdom and experience—a test of genius—these artists not only keep apace but remain ever so far ahead in their mysteries, in their teachings, that one's love, not only increases with age but deepens too, for their potency contains such multitudes, such layers—such distilled truth and beauty. And so, random fortunate that I am, I fell into the world of Balanchine and his ballets as a child and, yes, I am the same girl now in my love, only now I have loved for longer, far longer, and with ever more open eyes.

Do I know his immutable greatness from knowing him a little in person, through a handful of conversations, many classes and rehearsals, and loads of elevator rides? Or from dancing his ballets, seeing his ballets as you can see them? Both. Though in truth, an elevator ride with him alone, the inescapable privacy for those often silent moments, did show me, as a young dancer, a quality of being he exuded. I dare not call it an aura, but it was one. This was not a display of power but its opposite, a stillness and calm, that he emanated. I can only surmise this to be a mélange of self-respect, confidence, and an ease with himself. Like spirit purified.

Serenade is how a woman's blood rushes. Balanchine listened so closely. It was my career, my life, in thirty-two minutes and forty-nine seconds. "*What* are you waiting for?" he always said to us. "Tonight? Tomorrow?" Tonight and tomorrow don't exist. "Only now, *now!*" It was impossible to get into that world, but once there, I never left. I cannot leave. Bound.

This book started out as something else, a rigorous discourse on a Balanchine ballet called *Serenade*—its precarious alfresco premiere in 1934 at a New York estate under threatening skies as a birthday present to the scion of a rich American family, and its nine-decade evolution, the shifts and changes and additions in steps, in movement, in music, in tempos, in casting, in stage designs of curious complication, and costumes of every length. Even a wacky wig or two. As Balanchine's first American child—she was forty-nine when he died—*Serenade* became the ballet he most frequently revisited and revised in all its aspects, showing a rare lifelong interest in her. This book will be that treatise on *Serenade*—though perhaps the rigor has given way, along the way, under the great force of my love. Here too will be the silk, the ribbons, the mothers, the tears, the slips, the tendus that make the dance exist. Layer upon layer, each cushioned by tulle, fuses to form the scaffolding behind the proscenium, to tell a tale of Lear and his twenty Cordelias.

How do you write about a masterpiece? How do you know it is one in the first place? Who makes that determination? And what gives them the right to do so? What qualifies? How do you learn from one? How do you describe it? How do you speak of it? How do you dance it? What if you are one twenty-sixth of one? How do you live inside it? And later, how do you live outside it? I don't know the answers to these questions, and so this book became my search, though I don't really expect any answers. Whenever people asked Balanchine "Why?"—and they asked him a lot—he replied, looking like a mischievous elf, "Why not?"

On the subject of "masterpieces," Balanchine himself said only, "If you set out to make a masterpiece, how will you ever get it finished?" His own standards were considerably lower. "If a ballet is decent, I am satisfied," he continued, eloquently articulating Susan Sontag's assessment that "his imperial talent allowed for impudent modesty."

In 1986, just after I stopped dancing, Lincoln Kirstein, who founded the New York City Ballet (NYCB) with Balanchine, suggested that I write an "update" to his history of the company, *Thirty Years,* covering the years 1978 through 1988. He didn't want to do it. A suggestion from Kirstein was like an order from a five-star general: there was no saying no. I did a lot of work and research and sent him some early pages—which, along with many facts and dates, included writing about him that was accurate though also exhibiting a certain fondness on my part.

I promptly received a response suggesting that perhaps my "heart [was] too full at the moment," that I lacked the requisite "detachment." He was counseling, I think, that in the war of art that he waged his entire life, that the best way to introduce and seduce the public to ballet—and Balanchine in particular—was to take a measured approach. But my mission was not thus directed then, nor is it now: he had an audience, an entire culture, to educate, and an institution to feed and maintain. I am but a witness to what I lived inside, what he and Balanchine created. What I know now about this reprimand is that he couldn't bear my writing of my great affection for *him:* in my memoir *Winter Season* I had written much about my affection for Mr. B, and Lincoln had praised the book.

But I had no such perspective at this time, only obedience and insecurity, and I promptly put that manuscript about the company in a drawer, where it remains. The decades since have only deepened the loss of Balanchine's world, my world, crystallized it, and despite years and years of trying to find a dispassionate voice, I cannot climb outside the beauty of *Serenade,* a beauty so deep as to have changed the double helix of my DNA, my body and my mind literally reshaped. I have tried to view this "work of art" through the objective eyes of a "critic," safer as it might be, more proper to the cause. But in this I have failed completely: dancing dictates my writing. I remain not only entrenched but, in truth, unwilling to be elsewhere, still standing in parallel waiting for the curtain to rise.

The two great men of my life—George Balanchine and Lincoln Kirstein—are dead. While I have a certain detachment from NYCB now—it is, inevitably, a very different company from the one I danced with and over a hundred other companies around the world now dance Balanchine's ballets—I remain incapable of neutrality toward *Serenade,* or the man who made it. I see Lincoln up there now in his black, double-breasted Savile Row suit, hovering with his eagle's eye on my flagrant, unchecked subjectivity.

As for Mr. B, what would he think of my reflections on his first American ballet? I imagine him saying "Too fancy!" as he did when one critic deciphered one of his ballets. "Why do Americans," he asked, "always have to see meaning in everything?"

I am one of the dancers Balanchine chose for the New York City Ballet between its official founding in 1948 and his death in 1983—we stand at less than five hundred in all, many already gone, others going each year, a few hundred still here, reduced; we are a dying breed. By the turn of the twenty-first century, while his ballets thrived around the world, no dancer he chose remained on a stage still performing. A finite few now, we are his disciples, he the father of us all. I was one of the very last he chose when he was old and legendary. I lived in his world from age ten to age twenty-six—seventeen years. But once you've lived there, you never leave. This, then, will not be a traditional history and analysis of Balanchine's first American ballet but rather the story of its ghosts, my ghosts, the ghosts of a paradise lost that lives inside memory, mine and those of other dancers and audiences who were magnetized by the emanation of what I know to be Balanchine's soul, his practical, on-union-time" ("I don't have creative pangs," he said, "if it doesn't work one time, it will the next"), no-nonsense Sufi-master soul.

Who was this man, this "cloud in trousers," as he called himself after the poet Vladimir Mayakovsky, who captured us in his magic realm and kept us forever enchanted, awakened, immune to any other kiss?

The author, in costume for *Scherzo à la Russe,* with Balanchine backstage during the Stravinsky Centennial Celebration on June 12, 1982 *(© Paul Kolnik)*

. . .

Love, you see, is not blind when it comes to Balanchine and you are one of his dancers. It is utter clarity. History told straight can be found elsewhere. As if one could write a history of spirit made visible.

It has taken me over thirty years to be able, barely, to revisit the man and the ballet that are the story of my life. To feel the shattering of beauty passed, a sadness so spacious as to be a kind of welcome perversity that will never abate. I don't write this now because I've finally found the courage—that beleaguered audacity—to push past the gaze of grief. I do it now because I am simply defiant in the face of my fear. I know I will not do this man, or this ballet, justice, but I have waited too long for the intellectual, the analytical, the diagnostic, the critical negative to assert themselves, and it has not happened: it never will. To separate myself from him and from this ballet, to regard these with a detached and cool eye, is not possible. He is family; this is dynasty. And besides, why would I want what is less? When so few are so fortunate as to have had an actual genius as their live teacher? I can no more remove myself to a dispassionate consideration than I can remove the muscles in my body that he trained or the skin that enfolds them. This is it.

As time passes, the loss, the permanence of transience, only increase. As do the dimensions of comprehension: the view of the vistas he provided acquire superior lenses, and the vast panoply he laid before us, and before his public, only grows more detailed, while more broad. He taught us to live "Now!" not only so we would give him everything then but, I suspect, so that we could survive him. We were so young when he was old, it was inevitable, I suppose.

It is a curiosity, knowing that the deepest experience of one's life is long gone and never coming back. But Lincoln cautioned me once that "nostalgia is pure vanity," so there is little recourse. This, then, will be the story of Balanchine, his masterpiece, and my own experience in the vicinity of both.

Sometimes in class, he talked to us about "Paradise." "There it is!" he would say with delight, pointing upward jauntily with his right forefinger in a soft curve, one of his frequent gestures, ever indicating that a moment, often a conundrum of wisdom, usually laced in humor, was about to be delivered. "You can see the door—but you can't get in!" Unless you're dancing *Serenade*. He never danced it. But I did. Over fifty times.

It remains inconceivable to me who I would be without this man or without this ballet, which more than any other gave us, his girls, a map for our lives. And the competition is fierce: the sublime grandeur of *Concerto Barocco*, to Bach's Double Violin Concerto; the complex depths of romantic love in *Liebeslieder Walzer*, to Brahms's love songs; the loss of romantic love in *Robert Schumann's "Davidsbündlertänze"*; and the distilled merging of the erotic and romantic in *Stravinsky Violin Concerto*—these all without a soupçon of sentimentality. But the truth is that there has never been a more beautiful ballet than *Serenade*, and there has never been a ballet that so brazenly declared the beauty, the power, of women—and the trials that make them so.

Serenade is a blueprint for Balanchine and, I believe, for the entire art form called ballet. And it is a blue ballet in a literal sense as well. Not cerulean, or cobalt, or indigo, or sapphire, but slightly closer to aquamarine, a kind of soft gray blue, not so gray as a gloomy day, but not so bright as sunshine either. And at certain times, a glowing all-but-midnight blue. The color of wraiths caught between the rays flung by the night sky who are but shadows of their shadows.

Balanchine said that *Serenade* had no story. It was, he said, just "a dance in the light of the moon." He made this ballet to Tschaikovsky's music in the early months of 1934, just a few months after landing in America for the first time, arriving, via western Europe, from Russia, where he was born during the reign of Nicholas II, the last tsar of imperial Russia. It was not only the first ballet he made in America but also the first complete American-made classical ballet by anyone.

For the fifty years Balanchine lived after he made this ballet, he kept being asked the same question over and over: "What, Mr. Balanchine, is *Serenade* about?" But he kept saying the same thing about the moon.

It is among the pale blue tulle, the peach satin shoes, the dusty rosin box, and the soaring violins that the ballet lives. It commences with a shielding of the night light, then moves to a closed opening under the moonlight, where rites of love, of freedom, of fettered fate are performed, and finally to a death—or is it?—headed straight into that beam of the moon.

I believe *Serenade* is about the birth of an artist. A woman artist. But, uncannily, though simply, it doesn't tell the story the way a poem or book would: it is the story itself, the woman herself. She is our Rosetta stone. As a dancer dancing it over and over again—meaning you have already had your ten years or more of daily training and reached a sufficient level of accomplishment to be in the position to learn it in a professional ballet company—you might actually become an artist, meaning one who can transcend the quotidian and make beauty, be beauty. Might. This book will be about this transcendence and about what lies behind that luscious maelstrom of movement, poured metaphor, blind yearnings, thwarted longings, and the many losses necessary to attain flight. Never before had a ballet moved like this, like peeling waves of ocean, like rising and falling tides, with eternity always near, not as illusion but as place.

Serenade is about the ascendance of a dancer, a straight shot in just under thirty-three minutes. A dance about dancers? Yes! It is all of Balanchine one needs to know in order to know the man, and if there had been no other ballet after this, if he had died young as was expected, his name would still be legend. Here are the jazzy hips; the fleet of Amazon women; the protean nymphs; the unattainable beloved; the mad running, running, running; the lavish sways; the off-balance turns; the dangerous leaps into destiny; the falls of rebirth; the transient romance; the less transient tragedy; and the terrible solitude of it all.

Serenade bookends my own career on the stage, being the first ballet of Balanchine's that I learned at age sixteen as a student and the last I performed too. Flying by the seat, and absent wings, of my well-worn tutu, I am here to tell you of this dance in the moonlight, of a life under Balanchine's moon. I will give you a glimpse of the ballet from the other side of the orchestra pit, from the stage, from the wings—so much happens in those barely concealed black corridors of space—as seen from one pair of toe shoes: my own. These hard-blocked tips, pointing down so as to rise, are a dancer's eyes.

SERENADE

1. AUDIENCE

went alone. My relationship with Mr. B had involved no more than nine short exchanges: some in private in his office on the fourth floor of the theater or the elevator and a few during class or rehearsal, in front of everyone—but I still knew I had to go. At that time of my life, as one of the youngest members of the New York City Ballet, I was not particularly close to any of my peers, peers I aspired to but would never equal, even though I danced right alongside them. It never occurred to us few girls that Balanchine chose from his School to be in his company that we might be the last he would choose before he never chose again. We knew him at the end when we were so young. Our loss is not greater, but we will live with it longer. It haunts me now.

Balanchine was omnipresent in the theater in those final years before he became ill. His presence has only increased since then: now he is entirely unavoidable. It was in those long, low-lit, winding narrow hallways of the theater that ran their slim course around the great body of the stage, which rose like the apse of a church in our midst, that we first noticed he was occasionally pushing off of a wall, as if stabilizing himself. It was upsetting to see him vulnerable, the man whose entire art can be viewed as a supreme high-wire act of balancing the spiritual inside the physical, seducing each from its entirety, making them merge. Even his name, Balanchine, contains the word "balance." This teetering was just one of the symptoms of what he did die from—diagnosed only after his death as Creutzfeldt-Jakob disease—but it was the one we saw, the one I think he must have hated most. It seemed especially cruel.

Not long after that he never came to the theater again, never taught class again, never took a dancer's foot in his hand and showed it what to do, never walked those halls again. But before this, on those random meetings with him in the theater, I was always too shy to say anything more than a quiet "Hello," said more like a question, so filled was I with uncertainty. He would always give a small bow and a nasal, elongated "Hellooooww" back, as if imitating my American accent. It occurs to me only now that he respected us, me, as much as we did him, though such a notion was entirely unimaginable back then, when we were just out of the School and so in loving thrall to this man, this magician, this maker of ballets that made us far more beautiful than we were.

Mr. B knew, all too well, that we viewed him as God. He neither encouraged this nor liked it; it was simply the way it was, inevitable. "When I pull the toilet chain," he liked to say, in a doomed attempt to make himself human to us, "it is for the same reason that you do." While amusing, this did little to unthrone him in our eyes.

When Mr. B performed his small and ready bow, there was always the nod that went with it, the nod that we all still imitate when we speak of him. How much was conveyed in that small tilt of his head. Mr. B was our very own Fred Astaire, only more distant, more esoteric, more old-world, though equally elegant. That nod— up, then down—carried that amazing face with the chiseled, aquiline nose and that slight exotic inflection gleaned from his Georgian blood. With a small move on an inclined surface, he looked at you as if he were far away, but then his gaze would shoot out like a laser beam and pierce you.

I sometimes thought he was looking at us through a kaleidoscope of time itself, from St. Petersburg, where he was born as a dancer at the tsar's Imperial Theatre School, from that unimaginable extravagance and luxury and velvet-lined carriages to the famine, cholera, and horrors of the Bolshevik Revolution, then to Europe and the convergence of modernism in Diaghilev, to us, the American dancers, the many Ginger Rogerses that he dreamed of after leaving the blue and gold Maryinsky Theatre.

By now I had been in the company for six years, and I still had nothing to say to him. I knew only one thing: the desire to dance for him. But he was in the hospital and he was dying, and I knew I must go despite the fear.

I took him a little loaf of orange-walnut bread that I had baked and then soaked in good brandy. I put a great deal of time and thought into my outfit: bright red overalls with white stitching over a pretty, gauzy white-and-green chiffon top with tiny red flowers on it and great blouson sleeves to the elbow. A wide, black elastic belt with a vertical gold clasp cinched my small waist tightly inside the red overalls.

I wore most of my voluminous dark hair up in a clip, not in a secure top-of-the-head tight Balanchine bun but soft and loose about my face, like a Gibson girl, with a single long dark braid hanging down my left side. I bathed myself in my perfume, Hope by Frances Denney—an American perfume with the old-world tones of a great Guerlain scent and a silly name. We Balanchine dancers drowned ourselves in our various perfumes, perpetuating, American-style, the wafting perfumes of our Russian ballerina teachers.

I remember precisely what I wore so long ago when it was so very, very important. But why I thought this was what to wear for an audience with George Balanchine is now totally beyond me. Today I would wear a long sage silk gown and an even longer dark green velvet duster, with peach roses in my hair, and I would bring him a bottle of Cristal rosé, his favorite champagne, the one designed for the tsar, where the glass of the bottle is so thick that it can have a flat base, unlike other champagnes, which have inverted bottoms to alleviate the pressure of the bubbles. But this was then, and I arrived at the hospital for my last visit with him in red overalls with homemade brandy bread wrapped in tinfoil, a red satin ribbon tied about its center.

I didn't know if there were official visiting hours, and I didn't know if he would be seeing anyone, if he might be sleeping or, most likely, if he had many other visitors already at his bedside. I had heard that he had a heavy stream of them—not just his dancers and balletmasters, but musicians, Russian friends, the occasional gawker, and Father Adrian, a Russian Orthodox monk and priest who looked like Rasputin; he visited Balanchine during his final months and would later bury him. I had even heard that there had been more than one little "party" held at his bedside with food and drink and merriment. But I had never partied with Mr. B, and I couldn't imagine being flip or glib or even light with him. To me he was serious and sacred, and small talk was not an option.

I told no one I was going—I didn't want to be told not to go—so I just went early in the afternoon, after morning company class, on a Tuesday in early February, taking my chances. After asking numerous friendly hospital personnel where to go, I arrived on his floor and went to the nurses' station. "I am looking for Mr. Balanchine," I said, ready to be turned away. I later heard that the nurses had been directed by him to allow dancers in to see him even when their visits were not during the prescribed hours: he wanted to see us. By now they had seen a parade of lean men and women with bulging dance bags coming to visit the man in the room at the end of the hall. Apparently the staff at Roosevelt Hospital had never seen anything like it—the scale of it, the often eccentric beauty of the earnest young people visiting this elderly man. When I appeared in my curious outfit to ask which room was his, the nurses looked me up and down and told me, "Down the hall, last room on the left." It felt surreal that such a vital man would be in a hospital.

I found the room. The door was open and I stood on the threshold. There he was in a large, bright, airy room, under a white sheet, wearing a crisp white hospital gown, sitting up in the narrow bed. He reminded me of Don Quixote, as he had choreographed the Don's death scene in his 1965 ballet; the knight-errant rose higher and higher on a platform in his final exaltation, his long white gown trailing after him. Mr. B was alone—no party, no Russians, no priest, no dancers. I did not cry. I was not going to cry. He beckoned me in.

"Ah, the writer!" he said, with a twinkle in his eye. I was amazed. I was always surprised that he recognized me at all—though he always had—since I had been so well taught at home to appear unseen. But these were the all-seeing eyes, and who was I to think I could hide? A few months earlier, I had published some of my diary as a dancer in his company as a book; he had read it, and I was told via an intermediary that he liked it very much. He had been most amused, I heard, when excerpts had been serialized for a week in the *New York Post* with sensational headlines that hardly matched my modest text. I had been afraid that he would fire me for writing that backstage story, but he hadn't. With great trepidation, I had told him about the publication in his office before he became ill. He listened to my brief speech and then asked one question: "So, dear, is it about *me?*" And in my innocent narcissism I said quickly, "Oh no! It's about *me!*" (Ha! Everything was about Balanchine once you knew him.) So now I was "the writer." Funny that, when all I had ever wanted was to be his dancer.

I pulled up a chair, but he patted the bed next to him and told me to sit there, beside him. I obeyed, of course, and never had I felt such closeness with him: the young girl so in need of the father's love, of his blessing. But had he not blessed me so many times? By choosing me from my large dance class at the School to dance Princess Aurora in the Rose Adagio of *The Sleeping Beauty* for the annual Workshop performance; by choosing me for the Workshop again the following year, to dance the ballerina role in *Allegro Brillante*—a ballet, he said, into which he'd put everything he knew about classical ballet into sixteen ferocious minutes; by making me an apprentice to the New York City Ballet; by making me a company member and all that meant: a contract, a salary, twelve pairs of new satin pointe shoes every week, gorgeous tutus and tiaras and the opportunity to learn and dance so many of his glorious ballets, to inhabit his world. But still, I thought he didn't know me, and felt myself unchosen. The frailties of ego.

No matter; there we were alone in the room, me sitting in the red overalls on the bed. He thanked me for the walnut bread and asked what I had put in it—he was a master chef himself. Then he placed it carefully on his side table, patting it gently, saying, "For later." I wonder if he ever ate it.

"So, you are still with us, dear?" he asked. Yes, I was still with him, I told him, dancing at New York City Ballet. My book had received some recognition, and he must have thought I might have moved on from my position in his corps de ballet to a possibly more prominent position as a writer. Ah, no—this he had wrong. I not only still wanted to dance but also knew one thing: that dancing Balanchine was a harder, deeper, and more beautiful endeavor than writing, and that being a Balanchine dancer was where the real beauty lay. My ambition was not to be recognized by others but to overcome myself, to be a better dancer. All I ever wanted was to be a better dancer than the one I was. All I still want, even now, in a way. To be that curious creature that is so close, so far: the one I could be. Ballet, you see, provides the most fantastic future for every devotee, something far beyond the promise of public acknowledgment or the flicker of fame. It provides the prospect of conquering one's own self to find, possibly, transcendence. If that is not a more interesting pursuit than renown or fortune, then I know nothing.

Mr. B was looking at me closely. He was so very concentrated. His ability to be inside the moment of time that is actual, this one, now, was of such an ease that sitting on his hospital bed, I somehow disembarked right then, right there, from my ever-nervous, buzzing self, and landed in a microsecond in the very place he was in, the only existing one, a place I usually avoided. The effortlessness of his demeanor was as a magnet, and the weight of the armor of my endless worries—including my awe of him—fell right off me, and the resulting lightness was literally transporting. So unprecedented was this strangely happy place to me that I felt it to be magic. It reminds me now of his explaining how he had no past, no future, only "a continuous present": this was that. One more lesson from a master teacher—never giving up—even though he was himself about to relocate from mortal to immortal. But I had no time at all to think of any of this—I understand it only all these years later. Then, it just happened. Total simplicity. It felt like I was in a timeless bubble— the exquisite irony of a real moment.

He reached out and took my left hand in his right, and I felt the warm current of his energy: finally ready, willing, at zero hour. I almost cried feeling the sweetness, the closeness, but stayed quiet, watching him while he watched me. He then let go and moved his hand up to my wrist slowly, feeling my skin, circling his fingers around my small wrist then up to my forearm. It was not the first time he had taken my wrist, touched my hand or arm: ballet is a physical profession, and he had been moving me around—adjusting head, legs, feet, fingers—in class and rehearsals for well over ten years, since I was eleven years old as a child dancing in *The Nutcracker.* Our entire profession is about being in a particular shape in three-dimensional physical space; rearranging bodies, and body parts, was the choreography he did all day long with us in the theater. But the circumstances here were different, more personal, and the unspoken sadness of finality invaded me.

I was with him entirely in a calm accord that I had not had with him before, my resisting fear finally absented itself for this last dance. He moved his hand up to my elbow, feeling the size and shape of my arm and shoulders through my thin blouse, across the bones of my clavicle, my neck, and then traveling sideways to my other shoulder, and then down that arm taking hold of my right hand. A symmetrical surveillance.

Never has anyone touched me with such gentle deliberation as Mr. B did on his deathbed that day. In what was likely only a minute in clock time, he made, in his dying grace, an invisible girl feel visible—one final adjustment.

He touched me as if he were memorizing, as if my body were Braille. He must have known that he was not leaving that bed, that he had little future left. But he had the present. He was like a scientist studying a young dancer's body. His kaleidoscope vision was adding my small parts into its prisms and patterns, as if he were taking me, my shapes—the shapes he had shaped—with him. Not a word was said. The air was still as if a rite had, silently, imperceptibly, arrived and passed. I felt known in a way not known before. I loved him. We all did.

Finally, he took my left hand in his again and I held his hand in return. His grip was so strong, not that of a man ready to go upstairs. So went my brief pas de deux with Mr. B and how he partnered me beyond my scope, beyond my obstinate disbelief in either of us—he too great, me too slight. He looked me straight in the eyes then, still holding my hands, not letting go. Not yet, anyway.

After a long silence, while still holding my gaze, he spoke again.

"Maybe, dear, you will write a story about a man and two women. A man and three women. A man and . . ." He was tired now, and he closed his eyes. I kissed his cheek and left.

The next time I saw him, less than three months later, he was dead, lying in his open casket at his memorial service, where I, like all of us orphans, stood alongside four of his five wives for hours and hours holding a single white burning taper, wax dripping like tears. Once the service was over, we lined up as only dancers can, in the longest chorus line of his life, like Busby Berkeley ballerinas—the line trailed out of the church, down the stairs, and down the block and then curved around onto Park Avenue—each waiting to kiss him one last time. So many of us kissed him. He traveled to that other world carried high on a raft of dancers' kisses. He was the first person I loved who died.

His last words to me have echoed through the decades and become a kind of koan, the last one, from the master. "A story about a man and two women. A man and three women. A man and . . ." For Balanchine, the story was her, always her. Each one, many ones—even, perhaps, one like me. His devotion spawned the greatest body of work by a single choreographer in the history of dance. It will never be surpassed—these portraits of women—not in all future lifetimes.

Five decades earlier, just off the boat from France, in early 1934, Balanchine had declared this single and abiding love in *Serenade:* to Tschaikovsky's soaring, sweet but mournful score, he made the world in a story about a man and two women . . . three women . . .

As *Serenade* begins, the curtain floats up on a sea of maidens, Botticelli's Venus multiplied into a small platoon. We are dressed in pale blue, right arms raised toward a light, against a light, long layered skirts filled with air, legs like vertical pale sea anemones beneath. Though we are seventeen, if you care to count, in the formation we appear as if we are simply an arbitrary slice, a section of a pattern that goes deep and wide, to the right and to the left, and stretches far, far back to an unknowable horizon. As if these girls are just the ones the audience happens to see now, at this very moment, as they stand and pass by on a conveyor belt. The ocean is large in Balanchine's world, the infinite denoted with precision.

Mr. B said that we, his dancers, were like fish, music our water. This image describes exactly the interplay of dancers with gravity— our ally, our enemy—where the lush fullness of any movement is slowed as if by the viscous counterpull of liquid. Dancing in *Serenade*, we are contained inside a giant aquarium where water echoes spirit and our bodies stream into freedom.

There are so many patterns laid out in this opening that after years of watching, you still won't see them all. We are standing in two diamonds, each of nine girls, equidistant from each other in diagonals of three, but viewed from one corner of the square, set on its head. The two diamonds are connected by one girl common to both diamonds, the seventeenth girl. She links us, at center stage. She is also the pivot, the middle girl of two larger diagonals of six girls each who divide the stage in a large cross, four quadrants. A crucifix, tic-tac-toe . . . you choose.

Our parallel feet, seventeen pairs strong, mark the planting of ballet, quite literally, in America. Balanchine even said, years later, that he placed the dancers in the pattern of a California orange grove. What orange grove? In 1934, he hadn't been to California; he was barely past the authorities on Ellis Island. What a trickster. So lies the legend of Balanchine and the orange grove and *Serenade*'s famous opening scene, smoke and mirrors all.

There we stand, ten parallel lines, five of each in opposing diagonals, with five girls forming a straight line that bifurcates the center of the stage both horizontally and from side to side. If you are sitting in the audience to either the far left or the far right of the center of the stage, you may not perceive the two diamonds but will rather see parallel diagonal rows of girls of varying lengths in repetitive succession. Confusing? Ah, but not at all. I have merely described just a few of the many ways in which this opening garden of girls can be viewed if one were studying Balanchinian geometry. He had the rare ability to devise Euclidean formations, and then move those formations all about a stage, fast and slow, and faster still, in endlessly shifting symmetries without a moment of awkward transition. He spoke once of a ballet being like "a string of pearls" held upon "an invisible horizontal line" that "extends unbroken from the point where the dance begins to where it ends."

As dancers, not one of us knew any of this, nor could we see it, nor did we need to, nor, frankly, did we care. We were not only on the ground, looking toward what Lincoln Kirstein called an "intolerable lunar light"—that is, stage light RF961, infused with a light blue gel—which for us was more a midnight sun, but we, each a piece of the plan, were also in the midst of the pattern, of a grand design, a cog in Balanchine's wheel. It is a design so beautiful that to this day there is an audible intake of breath from the audience when the curtain is raised and the pattern is revealed: a gesture to infinity that by the ballet's end will have expanded into eternity.

The opening of *Serenade* shows how Balanchine was somehow able to reach straight to the gut through unexpected divisions of the three spatial dimensions. He was primarily, after all, an architect of spirit, wrangling its evanescence to the stage, into our bodies, and then out again in our movement. If one were overhead, in the nosebleed-section seats that used to be cheap, one would see all these patterns at a heightened angle, adding an aerial view that is perhaps the most encompassing one. But in this tableau, there is no bad angle, no incorrect angle, no angle devoid of a kind of lacerating solace. We danced knowing God was watching us from everywhere. That is just how it was.

In our group—eight and eight, plus one—I always felt like the odd dancer out, the one just outside the symmetry, who doesn't quite fit, what with my not-so-good feet, too-busy mind, and belief that I had been chosen by mistake. We are seventeen because that is how many dancers Balanchine had that first day in rehearsal on March 14, 1934, on the fourth floor at 637 Madison Avenue at 59th Street, where the School of American Ballet first opened its doors a few months after Balanchine got off the boat in New York Harbor. "If I had only sixteen," he explained once, "an even amount, there would be two lines." And just how different it all would have been then is unimaginable—the two-diamond lineup now being known as *Serenade*'s first heraldic device.

Choreographers will more often than not choose even numbers for a corps de ballet—eight, twelve, sixteen—symmetry being such an element of beauty, and so much easier to move around en masse.

But Balanchine began with the girls he had at hand—a jumbled lot with mixed levels of previous training, some of them wearing bathing suits as leotards—not a preconceived idea. He wanted to use them all: How else could he teach them how to dance? And *Serenade*, more than any other of his ballets, was made to teach his new American students how to dance—how to take all those classroom steps and put them together, how to work in cooperation with each other. We learned, all right.

2. INITIATION

"We are worried about her feet," Diana Adams said to my mother a few months after I had been accepted into Balanchine's School of American Ballet. Miss Adams, as we called her, had been a great ballerina for Balanchine, and she was now the director of his School. And so I worried about my feet for the next twenty years. From that very moment, my Achilles' heel became, literally, my feet. Funny about that since my true Waterloo became my right hip. But for a ballet dancer, they are connected. Everything connects to everything else. Every bone and muscle and tendon and sinew and fascia and ligament and nerve is connected to every move, every emotion, every desire, every ambition, everything you love.

I was eleven years old, and after a number of years of not-very-serious once-a-week ballet lessons, I had suddenly been accepted into the elite pool of young girls from which the best dancers in the world were chosen. There was good reason for panic. I learned much later the unwritten rules of the School:

Rule One: There Is No Justice
Rule Two: No Complaints
Rule Three: Shut Up

But none of us needed to read these rules; we just lived them, knew them in our bodies and minds.

Lincoln Kirstein (author of the rules) elaborated: "We don't run a charity. There is no psychotherapy here. We're turning out professionals."

Now, I did not, as easy supposition and common romance might have it, experience a coup de foudre the first time I saw a live ballet, a real ballerina, or a pink tutu. I did not upon seeing this world of sylphs and satin shoes decide that I wanted to be one of them. I knew I couldn't be one of them even as a tiny girl, so I harbored no dream. I really didn't. This kind of specialness was simply out of the question for the little girl in my European family. For one thing, it would be rude to be that beautiful. Unbecoming and not likely to produce what was to me clearly the purpose of my existence: invisibility and silence. And perfection. I have failed at all three to date.

But my mother was alarmed at my absent appetite and skinny little body—I had started the parental war straight out of the womb, it appears, with incredibly fussy food habits (macaroni only). So when I turned four, a doctor was finally consulted. A German, he said two things to my mother: "Mrs. Bentley, she is just 'tin' child." And he suggested that I be given some exercise to encourage my appetite; thus I was carted off to a weekly ballet class, one of the many satellite programs chartered by the Royal Academy of Dance, whose patron was "Her Majesty the Queen," and whose president was "Dame Margot Fonteyn de Arias, DBE, D.Mus."

The only thing I remember liking about this extracurricular activity was the outfit: a white cotton tunic with a lovely wide, flat, red grosgrain belt. The sides of the short tunic were slit to the waist, and we held up the front flap when we danced; I thought this was a very nice thing indeed to wear—and to do. Dainty. We were living in Bristol, England, at the time, and within two years I had completed the "Primary" level syllabus. I still have the report, very official. The preparatory card states in no uncertain terms: "Jewellery must **NOT** be worn." This was serious. This report remains the only written "grading" of my talent, ever.

Toni stood well and exercises well given.
Nice easy spring with soft alighting.

Careful and earnest polka.
Very good expression.
Result: Honours

Such pomp and circumstance, in a royal, majestic manner, for a six-year-old—though I am relieved, even now, to know that my polka was "earnest." Also, of course, the report is perfectly ridiculous. No wonder Balanchine and Kirstein never had the School of American Ballet give any written summation, or "diploma." Words like "nice," "careful," and "good" haunt me still with their proposition of safety as the supreme goal. These attainments of my six-year-old self stand in staunch opposition to the Balanchine ethic—"more!" "bigger!" "now!" "why not?"—that I would attempt, carefully, to embody a few years later at his School. The watchwords of largeness, boldness, and fearlessness so fundamental in Balanchine's house were the very antithesis of those in my parents' house.

Shortly after starting my ballet classes, I was taken by my mother to see Margot Fonteyn dance in *Swan Lake* at Covent Garden. I did not know until then that adults also did ballet, much less in such elaborate tunics with so many stiff layers of white skirt all gathered up. But there was no wide red grosgrain belt in *Swan Lake*. This might actually be where my problems with Balanchine began. The ones in my head. The battle that still rages more than three decades later between him and me, between who I was supposed to be and who I was. Between what he saw and what I saw lies an abyss. One for which he provided a long crossing rope, but I still had to leap. I am still trying to find my way to the other side, to him—and now he really *is* on the other side, or up there, or wherever he went when he left us here.

My family emigrated to North Carolina when I was six, and during our few years there, I attended a ballet class once a week in Chapel Hill—an expedition that ceased before the end of the semester when my mother found out that she was expected to sew me a tutu and headdress for the graduation performance. One look at all those competitive mothers spending hours stitching their yards of pink tulle and she fled with me in tow. I didn't protest. After moving to New York City, my mother looked, yet again, for a local ballet school for her still-very-thin little girl to attend. She heard in the laundry room of our huge apartment complex on East 77th Street that the "local" ballet school in Manhattan was the School of American Ballet at Lincoln Center, directed, like New York City Ballet, by George Balanchine. We did not realize that it was also the greatest—and most competitive—dance academy in America. My mother had never heard of Balanchine or the New York City Ballet—we knew Fonteyn, Nureyev, Antoinette Sibley, Anthony Dowell at the Royal Ballet. Mom had grown up in England and her considerable knowledge resides in her lifelong love of opera, not ballet.

I auditioned for the School late one weekday afternoon with a handful of other girls under the terrifying eyes of a few fast-talking Russian women who lifted my limber little stick legs to the front and side and seemed pleased that they went up high with great ease. I had a nice bouncy jump (that "easy spring"), a small head, and a slim body, and within fifteen minutes they told my mother that I had been accepted into the School. I don't think anyone else at the audition that day was. So it began.

I had not been on pointe yet, so I was instructed to get the color leotard—shocking pink—for Children's Division 5, and to get my first pair of toe shoes. The prospect of those shimmering cylinders of hardened satin did have quite an appeal to me, but it was, like the white tunic and red belt, the appeal of apparel, not the appeal of a dream, of being a ballerina. Thus I acquired, at great expense, to my mother's great consternation, my first pair of pointe shoes, from Capezio's Broadway store. The most expensive shoes I had ever had by more than half. Fifty dollars. My mother was appalled and said, "Well, you'd better make them last!" Not a very likely prospect with toe shoes, which are not worn like a pump, sneaker, or boot as a foot covering for protection and occasional decoration.

Toe shoes are made for work, for dancing about at great speed, with great precision, with enormous force being placed on their seams and most of all on their tips, where all that twirling takes place. Those rock-hard tips are made not with wood or metal but simply layer upon layer of glue and burlap that allow for their ready melting and merging with the wear and warmth of a dancer's feet. While a professional dancer can use up as many as twelve—yes, twelve—pairs of pointe shoes a week, a little girl's first pair might well last for six months or even a year as she first learns how to rise up onto her toes while supporting herself with two hands at the barre for ten minutes each day at the end of class. That first pair became my most adored possession: the shoes of all shoes. Might I dwell in such satin splendor?

Miss Adams phoned my mother at home one evening, several months after I began at the School.

This is when she spoke to my mother the fateful line: "We are worried about her feet."

She said that I had, in fact, been on probation all this time and that they would be watching me in the coming months to see if pointe work might improve my arches—perhaps the stretching and stressing of rolling up onto my toes, over the toes, would increase the curve.

My mother hung up the phone and told me what Miss Adams had said. Neither I nor my mother remembered any mention of probation at my entrance audition, only adulation. They were backtracking: I was no good. Oh God. Oh God. And I went mad. Completely mad. I was born a dancer in that moment. And so the first emergence of burning passion in my life was incited not by a man, by love (though that would appear a few years later), but because someone—and Miss Adams was not just anyone—said I might not be able to dance. Only then did I really want to.

No romance, no tulle, no tiara, no spotlight, no dreams of stardom, just an unwavering surge to survive when I was told I might not. For me, it was about defiance, not love. To not fail, to not be humiliated ever again by my wretched feet. For the first time, the impetus to really dance, to dance classically, took me over, and it never let me go for the next two decades. It is still here now, manifesting on this page in my desire to make Balanchine real for myself and possibly for you. To understand it all, this man and his emanations, his ballets that not only changed my life but also gave me a life I did not have. Rescued from the promise and counsel of decency, I was given a chance at something better than perfection, to learn to love more deeply than unconditionally.

The dream to be onstage in a tutu is far too weak a concept, at least for me, to rouse the internal power to overcome just about everything—pain, competition, fatigue, one's own lazy, parallel body—to become a real flesh-and-blood professional classical ballet dancer. Besides, for me the thought of being on a stage with a spotlight outlining my every imperfection was no dream. It was terror.

I screamed, and promptly went into my bedroom, took that first pair of beloved toe shoes, the long satin ribbons tightly wrapped around them, out of my dance bag, ran out the apartment door and down the long, dim hallway to the garbage-chute room, the ribbons unraveling, and threw those shoes down the incinerator. I put not myself but my most beloved symbol of beauty, that to which I aspired, in the oven. It was the suicide of my eleven-year-old life. Down they went, *bang, bang, bang,* twenty-three floors, landing, no doubt, in a soupy pile of coffee grounds, potato peels, dirty tissues, all that dreck from all those busy New York apartments. Pink ribbons soaked in slime.

My father was not yet home from work to take charge of the situation, so my mother, who assumed little authority in such matters, panicked at her little girl's pain and did the unthinkable: she called the School and asked to speak to Miss Adams. She told her that I had gone mad and thrown my toe shoes down the incinerator and was completely out of control and asked if she would please talk to me. She did. Miss Adams told me to calm down, that everything would be fine, to buy a new pair of toe shoes and come back to class and we would go from there.

I listened to my accuser, the woman who had judged my feet unworthy—her feet were gloriously arched—and obeyed her every word. Lovely, tall, long-limbed, no-nonsense, tough-as-hell, no-excuses, don't-cry, now-gone Diana Adams. One of Balanchine's great loves.

My mother was distraught that she had to once again spend a great deal of money on a pair of toe shoes, but she conceded: she had seen my madness and did not want to see it again. I had earned the upper hand with her—through dread—though I never knew it. She did not tell my father what had happened, nor did she tell him about the extra pair of toe shoes I would need. She didn't want more trouble.

My feet did improve a great deal with pointe work, but never enough for me. I blamed my mother for this. I saw that my father had gorgeously arched feet and my mother, alas, had flat feet with rolling ankles. My feet were a perfect composite of the two, which I viewed not with gratitude—for my father's feet probably saved me from sure death in ballet—but with impotent fury that my mother's feet had tainted the perfection of my father's, leaving me with questionable feet, neither very bad nor very good. But good, in a profession of perfection, was bad.

How I envied the other girls for their voluptuously curved feet. They became, to me, the members of a club I could never join. I was always standing in the portal of that arched cathedral with my half-flat feet looking in at those blessed girls whose parents' genetics had not failed them. That I had a body many coveted was unknown to me at the time, but the possibility of such a consideration was annihilated by my overwhelming need for the arches I did not have, would never have.

Besides, awareness of any adequacy I might have would not have served me nearly as well as my abject inadequacy did. So this was my first step toward Balanchine and *Serenade*. Not a plié or tendu, not a dream of stardom, but one of those powerful, horrendously painful internal battles that any dancer who is serious will inevitably wage. To confront herself. And she must do this when so young that she doesn't even have a self yet. But when it is tested anyway, the devils rise and threaten disarmament; thus self and self-knowledge are born together. In this manner, I was given that rare chance to manifest a heretofore unknown drive, physically, consciously, before my body had even formed its final shape. The work of a young ballet dancer is only superficially, externally, about those endless classes, and tendus, and sweat: those daily repetitions are changing who she is, turning her out, literally, so that her insides are on the outside. It is not an act of words, of verbal expression, but of the body revealing something previously unseen, unknown, nonexistent.

Within five years of this turning point, I rose from being the worst dancer in my class at the School to being one of the best. Along with Carole, Nichol, and Lauren, I was asked to become an apprentice and then to join Balanchine's company. That is how it happened for me. The fire in me never went out after that phone call from Miss Adams. She was, for me, both cause and cure. She was also the woman who found the young Roberta Sue Ficker in

Diana Adams, 1952 *(© Norman Parkinson Archive / Iconic Images)*

Cincinnati in 1959 and told Ficker's mother that if she brought her fourteen-year-old daughter to New York, she could audition for the School. Thus it was that Suzanne Farrell was discovered and Diana Adams gave Balanchine her own replacement—and the greatest dancer he said he ever saw. Thank you, Miss Adams.

3. MR. B

Self-portrait

The first time I ever laid eyes on Mr. Balanchine was only a few weeks after I had incinerated my toe shoes. In October, children from the School audition to be in the Christmas performances of *The Nutcracker,* and I was selected to be a "Hoop" in "Candy Canes," one of six divertissements in Act II, which takes place in the Land of Sweets. This was the most exciting thing that had ever happened to me—and very encouraging, particularly coming shortly after the trauma of Miss Adams's phone call.

I was the shortest Hoop that year, and so I began the whole dance, stepping out alone, in silence, from the back wing on stage left, my large white-, pink-, and green-ribboned hoop held high. I then had to watch the conductor, and when his arm lowered, sig-naling the orchestra to start, I began grand-jetéing as hugely and as high as I could—one jump after another after another in speedy succession. First I aimed straight across the enormous stage of what was then called the New York State Theater, the home of New York City Ballet at Lincoln Center. I was followed by seven other grand-jetéing little girls into a stage-size circle, and for those first few minutes it was just us children onstage, leaping as if our lives depended on it—and they did. It was exhilarating and fantastic.

Once we'd completed our circle, we all landed on one knee facing center, four girls on each side of the stage, and held our hoops straight out in front of ourselves, forming a presentation circle. A single male soloist, dressed precisely like us but with a much larger hoop, entered and took over the proceedings. We accompanied him for the remainder of the dance as he executed some pretty wild pyrotechnics—spinning, turning, bebopping, and executing multiple lightning-fast jumps through his hoop, upstage and downstage. This display usually brings down the house with a great roar of applause.

I found out much later that as a young man of eighteen—only a few years older than us—Georgi Balanchivadze had danced this role at the Maryinsky to considerable attention. "Balanchivadze dances the buffoon with a hoop," wrote the great Russian dance critic Akim Volynsky in 1922, "with an energetically expressed and folksy rhythm."

> He stands in the hoop slantwise, in profile to the audience, and totally sparkles in the silvery design of his costume. His face is deathly pale from agitation. The youth is tall and full of wild intensity. He waves the hoop and tosses it under his feet. Then he encircles himself with it and rushes downward like a hurricane. In his day Romanov won fame for this number, but now Balanchivadze has gained the upper hand with his young, lively and superbly disciplined talent.

We Hoops were dressed alike in skullcaps and stretchy jackets and pants of white, green, and pink spiral stripes—pastel candy canes. Both the hat and costume were covered with little silver bells, all sewn on by hand at the costume shop. We tinkled when we moved.

My first year as a Hoop—I would go on to be one for three more years, by which time I was the tallest—we were getting new costumes. This required being called for fittings and having my name, "Bentley," written in black felt pen on the famous black-and-white "Karinska" label in all three parts of the costume: cap, jacket, and pants. Wow! I cannot describe the thrill to a young girl to be standing in Karinska's magic workshop with numerous Russian ladies, some large, some minuscule, and a few in between, fussing about, talking nonstop in Russian while sticking in pins to adjust a costume to fit your very own pre-nubile, muddled little body. The notion that one was important enough to need a new costume contoured to one's every inch with one's own name in it was overwhelming for an eleven-year-old with bad feet. I didn't believe any of it was happening—the costume, the endless afternoon rehearsals, and then the final "stage rehearsal" the afternoon of opening night. That was when I first saw him.

The dress rehearsal for *The Nutcracker* was a yearly tradition: a three-hour call on the afternoon of opening night in the early days of December. Until then, our rehearsal call sheet would always include the time and studio and the name "Richardson." David Richardson was the company member who auditioned, taught, and rehearsed all the children's roles in *Nutcracker*. But this time the sheet said:

Dress rehearsal. All children. In costume.
12–3 p.m.
Stage Level
Richardson, Balanchine.

He was called to rehearsal, just as we were. The hierarchy that defined Balanchine's world was clearly outlined: a democracy ruled entirely by one man. I didn't sleep much the night before. Adrenaline racing. The rehearsal was onstage with orchestra, costumes, hair, photographers—and parents were allowed in the audience, dotting the red velvet seats. Oh no! My mother was there, but, to my lasting resentment, she was not a fierce stage mother, just a quiet, unassuming European woman. Some of those other mothers, my God, the force of their presence in wanting Balanchine to take their child, bless their little girl, anoint their progeny, would have made Mama Rose proud. My mother—who had escaped Hitler with her family at age five—was appalled by their competitiveness and brashness and loud chitter-chatter. She sat alone and took no photographs, didn't even bring a camera. They were snapping all over the place. But I wanted one of them to fight for me, so I didn't have to fight all alone. I have always wondered how things might have been different with a mother who pushed me, who believed in my dancing, whether I was worth believing in or not—my mother was not sure if I had any real talent, and I believe she was right to not know. Reality and rationality prevailed in my household, for better and for worse. My parents' concern was never, ever, would their daughter be a ballerina (inconceivable), but rather, was I getting a proper education at school. I didn't, of course, but I ended up with an entirely different kind of education, far more valuable and rare, in Balanchine's world.

So there we were, all assembled, me in my skullcap and stretchy costume with bells. On our cheeks, we wore precise circles of red blush—applied by a makeup lady after we put our costumes on. No makeup on the costumes, please! Backstage there was an endless bustle of kids—Hoops like me, Polichinelles who would emerge from Mother Ginger's enormous skirt, and the tiny Angel girls who glided about the stage at the opening of Act II, each holding in front of her a minute Christmas tree, mirroring the big one in Act I that grew right out of the theater roof. These were really the sweetest little angels you ever saw, not treacly cherubs but tiny tiptoeing eight-year-old girls wearing soft white ballet slippers and white-and-gold A-line dresses with metal hoops at the ankles to keep the circle wide and clean. At their shoulders rose large vertical gold wings, and a gold halo framed their little round faces. I so wish now that I had gone to the School when young enough, short enough, to have been one of these creatures. How Balanchine loved children . . . and angels. They are everywhere in his work, wings always pointing skyward.

I had never before met a man who loved children the way Balanchine did: with both respect and kindness, like we were actually people, just short. Certainly a novel idea to me, whose father said children were small "animals" who needed civilizing. And so it was here that the love for Balanchine began. Just how much a little girl wants to please that man of authority can never be measured. Looking at the devotion, sacrifice, time—their entire youth—and beauty Balanchine's dancers gave him is one way to see the depth. But what is even harder to grasp is the breadth of what he gave us. So much more than just a benign father, he offered life itself, a life not a single one of us would have had otherwise. Standing onstage at the New York State Theater in a dress rehearsal for *The Nutcracker* with Balanchine on the edge of the apron of the stage, almost in the orchestra pit, half perching occasionally on a stool, I got my first view of the wizard at work.

Every eye of every child, every grown dancer, every stagehand, every wardrobe lady standing in the wings, pin cushion in hand, was on him. He spoke quietly, always very quietly, and for much of the rehearsal said nothing, just watching, head held high, with the occasional sniff, and then, *bam!* He would stop everything. Fast off the stool, he would walk up to a dancer—usually not a lead dancer but perhaps a Flower dancing in the Waltz of the Flowers—and he would laser in and spend five minutes focused on her. And we all focused on them.

"Do you have somewhere else to be, dear?"

"Oh no!"

"Are you tired?"

"Oh no!"

"Then what are you saving it for?"

Bang! His philosophy—"There is no future; it is the present forever"—was as simple as it was irrefutable. We all felt it as if he had addressed this to us personally. There was never a good answer to this question from Mr. B. And, as I saw over the years, he asked it often. The pretty pink Flower wouldn't even try to answer but would just blink back her embarrassment as all other eyes in the theater watched, looking from her to him, him to her, listening to the exchange. Then he would clap his hands briskly, and the rehearsal would continue—with everyone dancing with extra verve, precision, energy, speed, commitment. All his lessons, I would learn, were about moral choices, and our bodies were the chariots displaying the results.

Mr. B would often stop at a *Nutcracker* rehearsal and spend quite a lot of time on the young Prince's extended solo at the start of Act II in the Land of Sweets, where the Sugar Plum Fairy presides over all things light and beautiful after the dark Hoffmannesque turmoil of Act I.

Dressed in his crystalline pink silk suit with knee britches, and white slippers, the Prince, in his pantomime, tells the story of his army of child soldiers fighting a multitude of oversized gray Mice and how he killed, despite terrible odds, the multiheaded Mouse King, anointed Marie with the rodent's gold crown, and saved the world. Or Marie, anyway. It is a rare piece of Balanchine choreography composed entirely of gesture that tells a specific story, and it always receives great applause at its crescendo, when the Prince illustrates his well-earned victory. The triumph of the good and the young over the hilarious, bouncing-bodied, cheese-obsessed Mice and their massive overbites.

Now, with the little boy, Balanchine was amazing—none of that grown-up stuff he gave his older dancers. Often he would demonstrate sections of the pantomime for the boy to see what he wanted. He was a sight to behold in his late sixties performing the Prince's solo. He was the boy, and the boy was him. The young Prince was always strangely self-possessed as Balanchine demonstrated for him, and when he did as he was told, Balanchine looked very pleased, turning to his company dancers and saying, "See! He understands everything!" Many of those Princes went on to dance in the company for Balanchine as adults, just as I would.

It was always a contradictory experience to be in rehearsal with Balanchine: having his focus and attention was one's great dream, and yet when it happened, it was usually to receive one of those big lessons where shame could wash over you like a tidal wave. The embarrassment was beyond bearable. He almost never stopped to focus on a dancer because they were doing something wonderful. Only if they weren't. Everyone was available to be this example. And laziness was often the root cause. "The body is lazy," he would say, holding up his forefinger to alert us to a revelation. "That is why I am here!"

Once performances started, many nights we would see Balanchine in the right front wing, watching. Occasionally one had an entrance or an exit from his wing. A few years later when I became a new company member, I was dancing in the snow section of *Nutcracker* at the end of Act I where endless waves of cutout paper snow were dropped on the stage from great rolling sleeves, high above the stage. As if toe shoes weren't precarious enough, the snow made dancing very hazardous, very slippery. One evening I was making a grand jeté exit just as high and exuberant as I could straight into Balanchine's wing. Crash! I landed down on my rear, slipping upon landing, still onstage but only inches from his feet in the front wing. Disaster. He didn't flinch though I could have hit him. I scrambled up in record time and ran offstage past him. But on my way I heard that sniff of approval. At least I think I did, though it was a sniff in the midst of the orchestra playing Tschaikovsky so I'll never really know. As I noted in my journal at the time, he approved when you slipped from overextending—it meant you weren't being careful, weren't "saving" it. And he didn't give one hoot that the audience might see a dancer, an ineffable being, skidding to her derrière. Perfection was of less than no interest to him and besides, he knew no single dancer could mess up his work, built, as his ballets were, like medieval cathedrals in the air: a single sin unable to dent the edifice.

As children who danced in *Nutcracker*, we earned $6.95 a performance, for twenty performances a year (there were two casts for a total of forty performances). This was the first, and most thrilling, money I ever earned. We were required to get a Social Security number, and then we received official payroll checks each week—totaling $139 for the season—with "New York City Ballet" written on them. Was I dreaming? I saved every precious penny.

Over the next couple of years in the School, while in the more advanced Divisions B and C, I almost never saw Balanchine. He came to the School very rarely in the mid-1970s except for a visit in the early part of each New Year when the end-of-the-school-year Workshop, to be performed in early June, was being cast. I remember the day he came for the first time to my C-1 class. We had been given warning that he was expected at Madame Danilova's early-afternoon Variations class. But sometimes this announcement proved a false alarm. It was simply the most nervous I had ever been in my life.

Halfway through the class, the heavy black door at the front end of the studio by the mirrored wall opened and he walked in alone. No sidekicks, no posse, no secretary, just him. He had on slacks, a jacket, and a silk cravat, as he often did. Very elegant. Very simple. He walked over to Madame Danilova and they greeted each other, extravagantly, in Russian. Though they were never legally married, she is included in the list of his five wives as number two. They were together during their years in France with Diaghilev's Ballets Russes and just after, when he looked like a young Chopin with glossed hair and dark, smoky eyes and she was a dewy young diva—Danilova was the Dietrich of ballet. They were just starting out, yet both fully formed.

Five decades later, each well into their seventies, neither was any less glamorous, but now their glamour had gravitas. Together, so loaded with the history of ballet in the twentieth century, it is surprising how upright they both were. But none of this occurred to us then: we were worried about how we looked, how we looked to them—but especially him. There was great cordiality between them as she flirted with him shamelessly, leaning in close to discuss us while he surveyed a sea of nervous young dancers.

She was a perfect picture, dressed as always in a scoop-neck leotard with short sleeves and a dyed-to-match chiffon skirt, long to her calves in the back and swerving up the sides to nothing in the front so that her still-amazing, world-famous legs showed all the way to their summit. She wore a matching kerchief around her head, and another, neither large nor small and with no discernible purpose, was tucked for safekeeping into one of the lower front edges of her leotard or at her still-wasp-slim waist. It resided there, waiting for her to use it as a prop for any number of effects, including dropping it on the floor so that she could pick it up with a grand gesture—sometimes to teach us a lesson, sometimes for fun, sometimes because it was simply time for a flourish of beauty among her straining, perspiring young students.

Madame Danilova had this multipiece costume in every color: yellow, blue, red, orange, green, lavender, all dyed to order. But I never saw her in white or black—the colors we, as the School's advanced students, wore. And that face! Beneath the halo of her always perfectly coiffed hair, she wore makeup just a notch beneath full-on stage makeup, with silvery blue eye shadow setting off her sparkling blue eyes that resided in deep, shadowed sockets, framed by great swooping black false eyelashes, the whole topped off by high arched brows—all so effective at registering in the cheap seats of a theater, not to mention a classroom. It was surprising that her lids could hold up those lashes, but then she was of Athenian resolve. Unapologetic to the core, she was a creature for a young dancer to behold—and all this before she opened her mouth. Between lips of pale pink lipstick came witticisms in French (some of us understood), slighting sarcasms in English (we all understood), and outright cutting comments in Russian (none of us understood, only her pianist). Madame always counted—as did all our Russian teachers—in Russian: "*Raz-dva-tri . . .*" So we counted in Russian too, the only Russian we knew. The steps were in French, so why not count in Russian?

Before teaching class, Madame Danilova could be found, well into her eighth decade, in an empty studio, standing at the barre in one corner doing an entire set of exercises for at least thirty minutes. Once warm, she would try out combinations she would then give us in class later, but mostly she did this because it is what a dancer does: takes class every day, no matter what. Like brushing your teeth.

Of her many bons mots, the one I remember best was this: "Za men zay vill come and zay vill go, but you vill always have your vork." We were then rather too young and uninterested in "men" to understand, but how this has reverberated through my life since. She, being a famously sexy, impossibly sophisticated, mightily charming woman—she was inviting young men to lunch with her well into her seventies—knew of what she spoke, with several husbands and many lovers in her wake.

Madame Danilova, an orphan as a child, was the very embodiment of self-respect. She showed me, and all of us, far, far more than how to dance. Her dignity, her pride, her authority, her confidence, her relentless discipline, her wit, but most of all her courage—courage as grace—showed me, as a young girl, what could be. What could maybe be. And how best to navigate time.

Madame Danilova and Mr. Balanchine stood at the front of the class together, chatting away in Russian as we continued dancing. It was like being on the executioner's block, hoping for a stay. She started pointing out various girls to him in concealed collusion, even asking certain girls to step forward, come to the front of the class. For this Variations class, we wore white leotards and short white

Madame Alexandra Danilova *(Jack Mitchell/ Archive Photos/Getty Images)*

skirts with our usual pink tights and toe shoes. So exposed. Though we wore little stretchy cupless bras underneath the leotards to preserve our modesty.

I saw her point to me. He looked my way. Then she pointed to someone else and he looked at her. Then he left as swiftly as he had arrived. Only just before exiting, he turned to face us all directly for the first time since his arrival and performed a small, almost military bow. Until then, he had clearly stood with Madame as her accomplice, and her lesser one at that: she was formidable. He allowed for this; he was not yet our teacher. But in that moment, he separated from her. And in his bow to us, he let us know not only that he respected us but also that he knew who he was for us. We all looked on mute, sweat dripping down our brows, hair pulled tight in perfect buns, faces tense, eager, like baby hummingbirds, vibrating with the intensity of the short yet epic encounter.

This was the first year I was chosen to be in the Workshop. Madame Danilova was to stage the Petipa-Minkus ballet *Paquita*, and she placed me in the corps de ballet. But she also had me learn, as an understudy, one of the solo dances. Very exciting and very scary, and then at the last minute, I performed this solo, once, in the final of three performances. I wore a red rose at my waist on the white tutu (we wore *Symphony in C* tutus on loan from the New York City Ballet) and another red rose in my hair, with black lace hanging down like a small Spanish mantilla.

Madame had a particular fondness for me, though I never understood quite why. A few years later she gave me a sleek pair of black silk capri pants she had had designed for herself while on tour in Japan with the Ballets Russes—they fit me perfectly. High waistband, side zipper, front pleats, lined, a tailor's label inside, totally elegant. I still wear them occasionally—despite being almost eighty years old they remain in perfect condition. Like Madame.

This same year of my first Workshop was also the first year that Suki Schorer, who had been a principal dancer for Balanchine in the company during the 1960s and '70s and had recently begun to teach at the School under his guidance, would stage a ballet as well for the year-end performance. It would be a Balanchine ballet. It was called *Serenade*. I was cast as one of the seventeen girls in the corps. I had just turned sixteen.

4. SIXTEEN

*S*erenade was the first Balanchine ballet I learned. It was also the first entire ballet by anyone that I learned. I had never seen it in performance, so I came to it from inside, by learning the steps, the formations, the music. By then I had been a student at the School for nearly six years. Not only had I never seen *Serenade*, the truth is I had seen very little Balanchine at all at that time. I had been so busy studying at the School, and despite the close affiliation—Balanchine was the head of both institutions—they did not give us free tickets to see the company perform. By 1974 Balanchine was already being called a "living legend," so there was no need to paper the house with students as they had in 1948 when the company began. The house was always sold out, full of faithful longtime subscribers heavily peppered with cultural celebrities—Edward Gorey in his full-length fur coat and sneakers, Susan Sontag sporting her signature white-striped hair.

Until this time, I had only seen the classic ballets performed by the Royal Ballet—*The Sleeping Beauty, Swan Lake,* and *Giselle.* I loved *Giselle* best: the mad scene with Giselle's hair flailing about as her love turns to insanity. This was high romance to my young self.

It was mid-January 1974, and it was the first rehearsal for *Serenade.* We were all gathered in one of the big, bright studios at the School, which was at that time located in the imposing white Juilliard Building at Lincoln Center. Leaning on the barres stretching, we all waited, as dancers do, for direction. Suki, petite, pert, pretty, and quick in her navy leotard and navy chiffon skirt, started leading girls to places around the studio and told them to just wait there. She started with the tallest ones, putting them in various spots toward the back of the studio. Thus an empty open place, a dancer's canvas, becomes defined, carved, by bodies in space. From blankness and nothing, complexity is soon created.

I was not very tall, so I waited with the other small girls with considerable trepidation: Still uncalled, unplaced, where would we go? Maybe we would be only understudies? One by one, Suki took each girl and put her in what seemed like an arbitrary spot. Then she took the next girl and placed her at some distance to that one's side. And then another like that. And another. The formation was not apparent.

Then Suki started adding girls in front of those girls—not, as expected, directly in front of them but rather centered in the space between the two girls behind her. It looked quite strange, but Suki seemed to know what she was doing, and we were all impatient obedience. She kept adding girl after girl in row after row, working her way forward while we smaller girls watched and worried. And stretched. Stretching for a dancer is her great pastime, her way of waiting, staying warm and useful, improving her dancing while not dancing.

Finally, Suki placed me and one other short girl in what amounted to a very small front row of only two—again, with each of us, quite far apart, in the spaces formed by the girls behind us. Being young dancers in serious training, none of us had budged from our assigned spots during this process, which took quite a while. After placing us last two, Suki backed up to the front of the studio, with her back to the mirror, and surveyed the scene. She then walked from side to side, squinting her eyes to home in on the lines—there were many horizontal, vertical, and diagonal lines in the formation she had made with our bodies. As she moved back and forth in front of us, she nudged a couple of girls a little to the left or right, so that they were perfectly centered between the girls behind them or two rows in front of them.

"Okay," she said finally. "Good."

Dancers love to hear this word. They are, after all, on a moral course.

"Now everyone stand with your feet tight together, parallel."

We did as we were told. But never, never before in all our many years of training (most of us, like me, had already been dancing for over a decade) had a teacher asked us to stand in parallel. Ballet is turned out. Always. Turnout—the rotation of both legs from the hip sockets in opposite, outward directions, simultaneously—was everything, the core of ballet itself. It was what we practiced in class all day, and then in our beds all night. I often went to sleep with my feet together and both knees bent and pointed to the far sides like a little frog to be even more turned out in the morning. But now we were told "parallel." No one knows the meaning of the natural human stance of parallel quite like a ballet dancer, who lives her whole life in opposition to it.

"Look!" said Suki.

To a dancer in a studio this means "look in the mirror," that vast watery upright screen that was our daily companion, that brought us close to ourselves, but in reverse. So we looked, and there we were, seventeen girls—very odd. Choreography by Marius Petipa was always in even numbers, two girls and two boys, or six girls, or sixteen girls and eight boys. But here with Balanchine in *Serenade* we were seventeen. There were many things to notice about this unusual yet unexpectedly symmetrical formation we were in. But none of us knew—or needed to know—what I see so clearly now, without the mirror's deflecting reflection. At that very moment when Suki said "Look!" and we stood together in the opening position of *Serenade,* we were each of us born to Balanchine. As if just christened, slightly perplexed at the formation, very perplexed at the parallel position, but so delighted to be there, in the very midst of him. He was no less than a world, one we now entered and hoped to never leave. I have never left.

Little Alices all, we had, in taking our places in *Serenade,* each gone through the looking glass of the ballet studio and become a ballerina, that magical creature who lies on the other side of a young student's mirror. And there was Balanchine, this compact, graceful, exotic Russian man waiting for us. Waiting, not to sweep us off our feet—how very useless that would be for a dancer—but to show us how to dance, how to navigate, alone. Except for him, of course, the ghostly lover of each of us.

There was, I think, not one of us who did not have a full-blown romance—conscious or not—with this man, the kind only young girls can have: unconsummated, consuming, life-changing, and one-sided. Perhaps it's an unknown blessing that this all happened back then, when such young passions could still retain a purity hard to imagine today. It is the kind of hungry desire that conjures a young girl's energy to levels unexplained by science and that, among other things, literally took us up upon our toe tips. Like Princess Aurora in *The Sleeping Beauty*, we compressed that hundred-year sleep of hers into a decade of training, hoping to be kissed by the Prince who could break the spell, to be taken into the company of what he called, with no irony, his "beautiful girl dancers."

The Sleeping Beauty, Petipa's great work, a cornerstone in the classical ballet tradition, gave birth to little Georgi Balanchivadze on the stage in Russia, and he always wanted to stage it at New York City Ballet but never did. He said the theater was simply not equipped for what he envisioned: real fountains and multiple over-lapping, rising, and descending stages. But there it was, the time-less story of first love awakened, being lived over and over and over backstage, onstage, in the studio, on the other side of the mirror, once we passed through. The theater was big enough for this: all these many private romances—many Beauties, a single Prince.

This man gave us more than any other man could ever offer: he showed us how to become our highest selves. Should we be up for the challenge. All this and we hadn't even met him up close yet. That would soon change. But in his poses, his positions, in the endless repetition of his steps, we became his dancers, his children, his bal-lerinas, his lovers. Lovers of this man's intense inner beauty, which he externalized for the world to see. This is, is it not, what an artist does: turns his or her inner landscape outward? This is why turnout, upon which classical ballet is based, is such a profound stance—a "dancer's being, body and soul," wrote Russian critic André Levin-son, "is dilated"—dictating a physical practice that, in its outward manifestation, delineates the divine.

Serenade is, for me, a map of Balanchine's soul. The cartography within its music, its steps, and its dances of loss, of love, of blindness, of destiny, of fortitude, of a beauty that defines beauty. In its portraits of women—its glorious, untethered women who display such tenderness, such vulnerability, and yet are propelled by a ferocious independence—lie a vision so clear as to render *Serenade* his autobiography, a story carved in three dimensions, when he was just thirty but already fully born.

My being introduced to Balanchine through *Serenade* was a chance landing. I was in class C-1—the youngest girls culled for the Workshop—the year when Suki first staged the ballet for the School. Other years she staged other ballets. But because *Serenade* was the first ballet Mr. B had made with American dancers exactly forty years before, the poetry of the eternal return, while lost on me then, is well found in me now. It makes for a symmetry of initiation: every girl who has stood in one of those two aerial diamonds of the opening formation has stood where many have stood before her in apostolic succession.

5. 1934

Feet parallel, right arm raised, palm up, we begin. *(© Paul Kolnik)*

As instructed by Suki, we all took a good look around ourselves. Dancers need to know where they are not only in three dimensions but also in the unmeasured space that lies outside geometry. So we looked, in front, behind, to the side, to the far side, and to the in-between angles, while still holding a tight parallel with the feet. This involved constantly looking down to make sure our feet remained perfectly lined up—toe to toe, arch to arch, heel to heel—and that the two were suctioned together as one.

Once this position was established, there was a good deal of fidgeting, as we wobbled on that flat-footed pedestal. Frequent giggles erupted as each girl's verticality was threatened by her alien parallel perch.

Suki offered a suggestion: "Pull in your stomach tight"—this direction applies to everything we do all the time, every time, forever and ever till death do us part—"reach down into the floor, and then reach up." This apparently contradictory direction, echoing Miss Stuart, is not in the least foreign to a dancer but a well-understood paradox in a life lived so literally in the balance where opposition—up and down, right and left, in and out—reigns. Young dancers learn irony in their bodies, a literal, muscular irony, long before they might know its conceptual meaning.

Our survey over, we were ready for the next step. But it was not a step. It was an arm position. We need to talk about this arm. It is mainly the right arm in question, though, naturally, what one arm does for a dancer by definition involves a symmetry or, often, an asymmetry, but one that still retains a kind of balance, even if an illogical one. The arms connect as one across a dancer's upper back, and across her torso, always making a single line, though sometimes a broken line. But always a line.

Suki directs us to the opening position: left arm natural to the side, right arm up in a softened diagonal, palm out, fingers apart. What Suki does not tell us is how this arm position came about at that first rehearsal in a dingy dance studio on Madison Avenue one evening in early 1934.

This slanted extended arm and its gentle hand tracing an ascending trajectory has come to symbolize so much to dancers and audiences alike. It is the single most famous image in this ballet—except for the other ones—and as such, all but a trademark of Balanchine himself. It is the identifying arm, literally, of his body of work, so truly, with him, a body. This position repeats the raised arm of the Statue of Liberty holding her torch, before whom Balanchine had passed just five months earlier in New York Harbor when he immigrated, a refugee of sorts, to the United States. What a kind of poetry it would be if Lady Liberty had indeed been the reference for Balanchine, who had escaped the Bolsheviks, illness, and starvation and landed in the Land of the Free. This, however, was never mentioned as an influence, its patriotic poetry too sentimental;

something far darker was suggested. Lincoln Kirstein, the wealthy American from Boston who had brought Balanchine to America only a few months earlier, alluded to something more obscure, writing in his diary, "Hands are curved to shield their eyes, as if facing some intolerable lunar light."

"Intolerable lunar light"? Is it blinding, thus "intolerable"? Or, rather, is there a darkness behind the moonlight? On one occasion over the years, Balanchine, uncharacteristically, told a dancer that it was "the light of God, too bright for human eyes." Compounding the mystery, Kirstein recorded what Balanchine told him at that first rehearsal: "He said his head was a blank and asked me to pray for him." A rather inauspicious start for Kirstein's dream of a flotilla of pointe dancers pirouetting into American culture: a choreographer with a blank head asking for prayer. Perfect.

"He lined everyone up according to their heights," wrote Kirstein in his diary of that first rehearsal on Wednesday, March 14, "& commenced slowly to compose a hymn to ward off sin." Or was it "a hymn to ward off the sun"? Kirstein's original, handwritten diary entry appears to read "the sun," although there are three baffling dots about the word: one above the "u," another squiggle above the "n," and yet a third dot above the period. Kirstein was not a particularly messy writer, and random dots do not abound elsewhere: Is the first the dot above the "i" of "sin"? His own later transcriptions into type clearly read "sin." Both evocative, though differently so. Did he, with a writer's prerogative, choose to change "sun" to "sin"? And if so, why? Did he think his own original writing said "sin" when transcribing it later? Or did he know, as an actual observer in the studio, that it was "sin" and what he wrote in his diary was incorrect? And larger still: Is the concept of a "hymn" Balanchine's indication or Kirstein's interpretation, attributed to Balanchine? Or something else yet again?

"Sin" or "sun"—we will never know precisely and this conundrum is emblematic of the history, the myth, of all that is *Serenade:* the endless dig for clues by dance scholars, as if the ballet itself were an archaeological site, and they are seeking its origins, its meanings, its making, its changes, its shallows, its depths. Even its pronunciation has been debated: "SerenAHde" or "SeranAde." (We say the former, Balanchine over the years apparently said both though I only heard him say in his later years, "SerenAHde.") The search will never end, the Gordian knot that is *Serenade* will remain forever tied, forever alive.

Kirstein continues: "He tried two dancers breaking the composition, first in toe shoes, then without. Without won." Soon enough it lost.

While Kirstein recalled that this first rehearsal transpired on a rainy evening, Ruthanna Boris, a fifteen-year-old dancer, one of the original seventeen, remembered it was a "nice sunny day." But then Lincoln was a rainy-day man even when the sun was blazing. And for his part, Balanchine refers to the "first night" of rehearsals.

March 14, 1934, was three days before Boris's sixteenth birthday, but she had already been dancing at the Metropolitan Opera for some time and would go on to a long career as a lead dancer and choreographer herself. Before she died in 1988, she left her testimony of that time. Her witness is unique.

One Sunday I was reading John Martin's dance column in the *Times* and I saw a notice that Mr. Lincoln Kirstein, the editor of a magazine called *Hound and Horn,* and Mr. Edward Warburg were founding a school and a company and were bringing in Mr. George Balanchine as the artistic director. I went for the audition wearing what we wore at the Metropolitan—pink dresses below the knees, pink tights, pink ballet shoes, and little bows tied so our brassiere straps wouldn't show. In a room at the School on Fifty-ninth and Madison there were two men. . . . [Balanchine] was young and handsome. Gorgeous. The other man was very austere . . . I could jump like a flea. Balanchine said, "You are Italian. Italiansky." His English was charming. Then he said, "Do a double pirouette." But we weren't allowed to do that at the Met, and I told him I could only do single turns. "No," he said, "you will do it. You will see." So I tried . . . I went around twice and fell down. I looked at him and knew this guy was making jokes. And I loved it. I wanted to be taken in.

Boris was indeed "taken in." And began that journey every dancer Balanchine chose took: of falling in love with him and dancing, a triangulated affair where body, heart, and spirit were woven together with his presence, bonded by beautiful music. "But," said Boris, "I didn't look at Balanchine the way a woman looks at a man. I looked at him more as an inevitable force—like I would at lightning, at Niagara Falls, at Mount St. Helens, at cosmic events."

A few months later she remembers Balanchine saying, "Today, I think I'll make a little something." Thus he began *Serenade*, placing the girls for the first time in two diamonds, as Suki placed us forty years later.

> He excused the gentlemen and started putting girls in place and standing back to see what it looked like. Annabelle Lyon and I were the two smallest, and we already knew he liked tall ballerinas. He took forever to arrange everyone; he wanted all his girls to show. He placed Kathryn Mullowny, Heidi Vosseler, Holly Howard, until finally Annabelle and I were the only two left, standing across from each other. Her face told me what I felt: "Oh, God, we're too small; we're going to be the understudies." But then he jumped up on the bench and summoned us: "Ruthanna, Bella." We came running and he put her in front on stage left and me on stage right.

Boris and Lyon were the front points of the two symmetrical diamonds, across the stage from each other side to side. All those decades later I stood where "Bella" stood, "front on stage left." There is the legacy, and the honor, of knowing who the girl was who stood there first, whose place I and so many before—and after—have taken, will take. Annabelle Lyon was eighteen years old that sunny rainy day (night) in 1934. She died at age ninety-five in 2011.

When the girls stood in parallel before him as we later stood before Suki, Balanchine stopped to chat a bit, something he did, though not often, with us too, in class or rehearsal, and how our ears were pricked and eyes glued to him as we gathered closer to listen in church-like silence. Gathered like family but alert as to a priest.

"He was looking for a way to begin," Boris said. "He started talking about Germany."

> I was there with Diaghilev. There was an awful man there [Hitler]. He looks like me but he has mustache. The people know him, they love him. When they see him all people do like that for him. [Balanchine put his arm up in the Heil, Hitler salute.] . . . I am not such an awful man, and I don't have mustache. So maybe for me you put together this. Your hand is high.

If one believes Boris—why fabricate such a strange story?—Balanchine derived the signifying opening arm in *Serenade* from having seen the Hitler salute when still in Europe the year before. What to make of this? Was Balanchine simply doing as he always did, taking things from life to use in his ballets? He said that he found the open-shut, open-shut hand motion of Apollo in *Apollo* in the flashing lights of Piccadilly Circus in London.

While the extermination camps were still years away in March 1934, Hitler was already making inroads toward his final solution. On the first of January that year, all Jewish holidays were removed from the German calendar; the next day, "non-Aryans" were barred from adopting "Aryan" children. During the next few months, Jews were arrested with increasing frequency for a variety of reasons, the Nazis published a new version of the Psalms of David excising all references to Jews, and the film *Catherine the Great*—starring Douglas Fairbanks, Jr., and Elisabeth Bergner, a Jewish actress—was banned in Germany only four days before Balanchine began making *Serenade*.

We will never know about this exactly, and it becomes just one more Serenadian obscurity, though, in the light of history, one of the more intriguing ones. Balanchine's ballets were never political, always classical, and he never made any direct references to politics in his dances. When he became an American citizen in 1939, he was thrilled and proud. He was conservative, Republican, and dancers during the 1960s recall him telling them all not only to vote but whom to vote for. But only rarely did he assert his patriotism publicly. When the Iranian hostages were released in January 1981, he arranged a special performance of *Stars and Stripes*. I was in it, and it was a fantastic night, with Mr. B in his front wing looking quite pleased.

After the Hitler speech, which, Boris reports, both confused and bored most of the young girls—"I still didn't know who 'Mr. Hitler' was"—Balanchine asked the girls to put that right arm up there, palm facing out.

There was a second young man besides Kirstein at that rehearsal. Edward Warburg, a son of the Jewish financier and philanthropist Felix Warburg, had been convinced by his Harvard classmate, the brooding Kirstein, to pay for Balanchine's passage to America from Europe. Eddie didn't know much of anything about ballet at the time, but he knew something about world politics, and he was concerned when he saw Balanchine put the girls' arms up at this rather alarming angle. After considerable whispering between the two young men, Mr. Kirstein, a mammoth figure, lumbered over to Mr. Balanchine, a wisp of a man, and told him that Mr. Warburg thought the girls looked as if they were hailing Hitler. Not perhaps a good way to begin an American ballet, like a Third Reich rally.

Did Balanchine, in fact, intend to appropriate Hitler's choreography of fascism and hate and reshape it, convert it, into one of beauty and freedom? Was he seeking, in part, to make a ballet to counter that "awful man"? Was this the "sin"? Balanchine told the girls to "soften" the arm, to bend the elbow ever so slightly and move the arm a little more to the right, fingers apart. And there it remains today.

Fifteen days later, on March 29, Balanchine invited "an enormous crowd of people," according to Kirstein's diary, to a rehearsal, a good indication that in two weeks a significant section of the ballet was polished enough that even Balanchine welcomed viewers. By April 7 it appears that three movements were completed, "very ragged," wrote Kirstein, "because abt. 10 [dancers] were missing." It would be unheard of now to have more than half the cast of a ballet missing from rehearsal, but these were the scattershot early days.

On April 24, some "dark blue uniform practice costumes" arrived at the rehearsal studio. "They didn't fit very well," Kirstein reported, "because Bal. as usual had wanted them cut low over the breasts and they were cut too low and consequently they had to be worn backwards." Oops. Thus began the ensuing twenty-year saga of *Serenade*'s search for her appropriate apparel.

At the request of their son Eddie, for his twenty-sixth birthday, the Warburgs had agreed to present the new School of American Ballet's debut performance (in reality, a recital) of three ballets by Balanchine—*Mozartiana, Serenade,* and *Dreams*—outdoors, on a small erected stage, at their estate called Woodlands in Hartsdale, in the town of Greenburgh, New York, near White Plains, twenty miles north of New York City. The date was set for Saturday, June 9, and 250 guests were invited. It took two performances for the three ballets to finally make it onstage.

As the date was fast approaching, the costume quest continued: "Hunted for bathing suits for the boys in *Serenade*," wrote Kirstein on June 5, and the following day: "Hours spent more or less fruitlessly with Bal. at Bloomingdale's . . . while he tried to make up his mind abt. costumes for the Boys in *Serenade*. He has a spoiled boy's vanity which makes him at once refuse any given suggestion. One must approach him always from behind. Even this no cinch as there are always more than two alternatives. . . ." The day before the performance suitable shirts for the men were found "at last at Abercrombies."

That same day, at 3:00 p.m., the unlikely troupe set out for Hartsdale to set up the stage and rehearse for the premiere, but, as Kirstein recorded in his boots-on-the-ground unpublished diary, things were touch and go every step of the way. "The Warburg mansion, when we arrived," he wrote, "had the air of a castle deserted before the onslaught of invaders. No one was around. . . . Frances Mann, one of the important 2nd line dancers, hurt her foot. Caccialanza tripped and fell. Another girl wept and was suspected to have female ills . . . The students looked peaked and were cold and hungry and I feared a revolution . . . Vladimirov [Dimitriev, Balanchine's volatile Russian manager] was in all his states: Voila vôtre Ballet Americain. ["There's your American Ballet."] I said 'Nôtre Ballet Americain.'" ["*Our* American Ballet."]

---

* Both *Mozartiana* and *Dreams* (formerly called *Les Songes,* and with different music) had been choreographed by Balanchine the previous year for Les Ballets 1933 in Paris.

Serenade rehearsal, Balanchine right of center, on outdoor stage at the Warburg estate, June 1934 *(Source:* The New York City Ballet *by Anatole Chujoy)*

The following day the plein air premiere was all but entirely subject to the weather forecast while recalcitrant dancers and difficult costumes added to the tension. There was much prayer all around, not so much for success or recognition of the arrival of a new art form on American soil but for the rain to not moisten that soil—or the makeshift stage perched precipitously upon it. Or the piano that was hidden in the nearby bushes for the music.

"I made myself as boring as possible," wrote Kirstein, "by asking & praying & wondering abt. the weather." The pianos were covered and uncovered with tarps repeatedly and the stage dismantled and reassembled three times under the threat of a downpour. "Balanchine wholly indifferent," wrote Kirstein, "went off in his car into White Plains to get some decent food. Fair weather came & Dimitriew searched in vain for him to rehearse." By evening: "more rain: Bal. said calmly God's will be done. Around 8.40 . . . I got nervous & screamed at two of the boys to hurry & Dim. came in & roared at me. General apologies afterwards. *Mozartiana* looked lovely: went off well. Ridiculously stupid audience . . . *Serenade* was prepared. But then the rain set in, in earnest."

"With the music of Tchaikovsky, the lights went up," wrote Eddie Warburg, picking up the story of this now legendary non-premiere, "on the assembled group of dancers, each one standing with an arm outstretched, looking up towards the heavens. It was a moving moment. I can never look back at that scene now without remembering the White Plains performance. No sooner had the dancers become visible when, as if in answer to their raised arms, the heavens opened up, and it poured!"

The show was shut down, the audience ran for cover, and *Serenade*'s world premiere did not happen. "A more agonizing and inauspicious occasion," said Kirstein, "could scarcely have been planned by the Devil himself." The audience agreed to return the next day, a Sunday, for a redo.

Kirstein's jottings the next morning continue the weather surveillance:

> A little sun when I woke up—but considerable heat and the threat of rain increasing as time went on ... at 5 o'clock in spite of threats we again completely embarked for White Plains with an added cargo of husbands, mothers, friends, etc.... Rehearsal of "Serenade" on the sticky stage. The weather seemed to clear. Blue skies with holes in dense cloud. I looked for every slight change of wind. It seems to split 2 ways over the house. Nelson Rockefeller called up from Pocantico [Pocantico Hills, the Rockefeller estate] to say there'd been a cloudburst on the Hudson but it had passed ... it started a light rain just as they were going up for "Serenade." I'm glad to say however it was pushed through— with little enough confusion—although the piano keys were so wet that Mikeshina and Kopeikin [*sic*] cd hardly play ... "Serenade" looked very lovely, the boys OK in red pants and brownish polo shirts. Laskey's make-up left something to be desired ... Conditions were very difficult & everybody behaved extremely well.

Less than two years later the "red pants" were dropped while "red wigs" were added, and the curiosities of *Serenade*'s clothing continued.

The mishmash of costumes remained, understandably, uncredited, though Kirstein did provide an interesting program note for

the audience, something of an artifact not least because for the ensuing decades there has been no program note at all, in keeping with
Balanchine's edict to explain nothing. Notably, Kirstein deemed the
ballet a "tragedy," a female one.

> Without an implicit subject, the music and its thematic
> development indicate the tragic form of this primarily
> feminine ballet. Its lyricism is the large, fluent sentiment of
> Tschaikovsky shifting from the fresh swiftness of Sonatina,
> the buoyant accumulating passage of the Waltz, through the
> sustained adagio of the Elegy. The classic dance has been
> used here in conjunction with free gesture, developed logi-
> cally for the whole body's use. The corps de ballet, as such,
> scarcely exists. Each member is inseparable from the sche-
> matic design in personal individual meaning. The soloists
> crown the action alone, their tragedy prepared by the frame
> of the previous dances.

The audience at this, the actual premiere, comprised not only
more people than the previous evening but many of note, including Nelson Rockefeller and Alfred Barr, the young director of the
newly founded Museum of Modern Art—and money was pledged
toward the struggling venture. "Alan Blackburn [assistant treasurer
of MoMA] looked at me," wrote Kirstein, "as [if] I had deflected
the Warburg millions from the Mus. of Mod. Art. A group of fifty
repaired to a banquet at a New York restaurant [Chestney's] where
"toasts of all were drunk including the weather, the City of Philadelphia etc. . . . Bal. read a little speech sober and comic ending with
'we only have one Dollar . . . but soon we hope to have many dollars.'" And soon they did—at least enough to push through to 1935,
when, on August 19, Kirstein recorded the uncertain progress of the
fledgling enterprise: "The Ballet had a great success in Philadelphia
though Helen Leitch fell into the cymbals."

6. TURNOUT

After one minute and five seconds* of Tschaikovsky's strings, we are still palms up to the lunar light, and then gravity wins a round and wrists release, lifting imperceptibly as upheld palms drop down. "Maybe the hand is tired," said Balanchine to one dancer. It is the first actual movement of our stilled bodies since the curtain rose. Just this: seventeen wrists bending, both rising and falling, the first breath. Seventeen statues come alive. Ah!

The broken wrist pulls to the forehead, palm still down, but now flipped away from the head as the head turns away and slightly down from this hand. This stance is repeated later in what we have long called the "Aspirin" dance, as in, "I have a headache and need some Bayer." Dancer humor—and Mr. B always joined us in these inside jokes; he made many of them himself. They were a quick, simple way to identify exactly where we were in the ballet, much faster than saying "four full phrases and sixty-four counts after the second high note." Navigating within a ballet during rehearsals is not a science but a name game.

Our heads then turn to the other side—our right, your left—

---

* The timings in *Serenade* referenced in the text are based on the 1990 film (available on YouTube), but the seconds noted would vary slightly in any live performance depending on the conductor's tempos.

forehead lowered and eyes too as the hand pivots and drops to a cradling, a crescent moon around our hearts, not a flat palm as in allegiance to a cause but more a cause of heart. But so briefly that the sentiment does not settle—just registers, perhaps, and passes.

All this time the left arm has been still, but now it moves into action as the heart hand drops down to the center of the lower body and joins, both palms curved inward, which now is also upward. Our heads, too, are now bowed before you. Our feet in their tight sheaths, tense and ready, are still pressed in parallel. Still.

The chord we are waiting for arrives at one minute thirty-three seconds, and with it—not after it; we anticipate it—my 10 toes and 160 others flip out 180 degrees. It is sudden. Boom. Seventeen flat lines land facing the audience, infinity sideways. Parallel provides forward and backward direction, perhaps with a pivot to a different forward and backward, and up and down, but boxed. Turnout offers all directions, any direction, every direction. When parallel splits open, the world splits too. A spherical realm appears. Possibilities explode.

The unexpected sudden parting of those thirty-four parallel pointe shoes in Balanchine's first American ballet was the implantation, albeit a shaky one, of all that followed, not just in *Serenade* for

A crescent moon around our hearts *(© Steven Caras)*

the next thirty-one and a half minutes, but for the next fifty years, during which he established the highly improbable: America as the "home of classical ballet." A most unlikely arrival in the land of dancing bears, Calamity Jane, Walt Whitman, Mae West, the Ziegfeld Follies, and that curiosity, the "right to pursue happiness." Lincoln Kirstein liked to ask in a rather wild manner, "Happy? Happy? What is that? Who's happy?" Ballet dancers do not pursue the vagaries of happiness; we pursue excellence—though happiness can be a random result. Classical ballet, in its essential evanescence, presents a larger panorama than a cursory feeling or hinted-at pleasure: on occasion, it offers grace—via actual corporeal grace—an action of salvation where physical beauty in motion denotes a celestial domain.

When our toes rip apart, heels locked, turnout is instantly asserted, and each dancer connects to herself like a plug to a socket, her spine the motherboard, head to toes, mind to soles, moral to amoral, and she is born alive. This unnatural swiveling of the hips, legs and feet out, simultaneously, signifies the source from which ballet originates, and Balanchine showed it here to the audience as the very first motion of the legs and feet after the curtain has risen. But it had never been shown before as an end, a place unto itself: first position! Ta-da!

Rarely seen onstage at all and even then as a transient place, as its name indicates, first position is, and remains, the very foundation from whence all—all—ballet movements emanate. Its openness, aroundness, announces in no uncertain terms that turnout is ballet's most fundamental, defining, and distinguishing characteristic. One might say, in truth, that turnout is the very core, the uncontested essence, of the art form. While first position is seemingly the simplest and most basic, and perhaps the most famous, of ballet positions, even to a layperson—who hasn't on some occasion wiggled themselves into it, often for a laugh—any professional dancer knows that its perfect achievement requires not just the feet, legs, and hips rotating in unison but also symmetrical alignment of the entire body, both horizontally and vertically. First's open declaration was, is, revolutionary: this is an art founded on a subversion of Mother Nature herself. Human hip sockets are not skeletally designed to rotate externally, away from each other.

When we split open to first position at the start of *Serenade,* we connect to our deeper selves, selves before unknown. To understand anything about ballet in general, or about *Serenade* in particular, one must understand the tension, the insanity that is turnout.

This flip open of the feet converts the body, in an instant, into a quiet, defiant new definition of oneself. This, I believe, is why little girls everywhere, unknowingly, have always and will always want to study ballet. Verticality, from first position on, endows us with a dignity, a singularity, a pride, a grace, even a nobility that life so rarely otherwise proffers.

But the focus on turnout is always in training, behind the scenes, in class, in rehearsals, with teachers and balletmasters, a backstage obsession. Never before *Serenade* had such intimacy—the rotation of a woman's legs outward from their centered summit—been presented to the audience so explicitly, so sweetly. No other form of dance—modern, hip-hop, jazz, tap, jig, ballroom, striptease, flamenco, whirling dervish—is sourced in the remarkable notion of turnout. Though each inevitably employs its effect with passing frequency, none worship as completely, devotedly, and dependently at the great altar of turnout as does classical ballet. She is our mother goddess, Terpsichore wound out.

This physical requirement is why we begin training at age four, or five, or eight, when the body and mind are both still pliable. Otherwise it is too late in a child's development for them to function well, much less naturally, in this other dimension. Too late for the brain to conceive that it is possible, or for the body to master it without cheating (which involves swiveling the feet alone outward while ankles, knees, and hips remain parallel).

Positions in ballet are fixed in space—a dancer's mind's eye knows perfection—and steps are the links, consecutive movements that connect them. But here, in the very first minutes of *Serenade*, Balanchine made the first position of ballet's lexicon, upon which the entire pyramid of the language is firmly perched, into a step, a movement: a place. He shows both his dancers and audience where it all came from, where it all began, where it still begins, where it will always begin for every little girl and every great ballerina. It was an announcement of great import—and elemental beyond imagining.

Ballet is the unique language that ensues from that extra, unlikely dimension of legs revolving away from each other. It is a lone new world, a crazy, unnatural invention that gives the human body extra space, longer lines, and extraordinary beauty—the erotic beauty of irrational rotation.

Martha Graham, the great queen of modern dance, wept the first time she saw *Serenade* and those seventeen pairs of feet swung open. "It was simplicity itself," she said, "but the simplicity of a very great master." Graham, leader of the barefoot underworld, was as Persephone looking up at a Tiepolo cupola as she descends. Like an atheist seeing heaven, as it was for me.

A quick historical dip here suggests itself in order to see, really see, the tiered beauty of Balanchine's explicit use of first position to begin *Serenade*—and its absolute assertion of turnout as a dimension unto itself. It was a radical, undeniable statement, an unmistakable restart in his new country. The birth of turnout—wretched, sexy, unnatural, exquisite turnout—is inseparable from the birth of ballet itself.

First position, "première position"—followed by second, third, fourth, and fifth—was formally identified and named by a French balletmaster during the second half of the seventeenth century. Once clearly defined, thus reliably repeatable, the art form came into possible permanency through re-creation and repetition. Following the five numbered foot positions, the French terms of the discipline take over the language, codifying more complex movements—glissade, pas de basque, tour jeté, révérence. Easily forgotten but worth recalling is that the word "ballet" itself is an entirely French word, but, as with "cabaret," "champagne," and "parasol," reaccented and so entirely absorbed into English that we forget its Gallic (and Italian and Latin) origins.

The language of classical ballet, an entirely new language indicating very precise—*very* precise—positions, movements, and modes of execution, was thus conjured, distinguishing ballet from the myriad other kinds of swaying and jumping and stepping that human beings have so joyously, so naturally, done since Adam and Eve sashayed about, one assumes, in the Garden of Eden. More specifically, codification extracted and refined ballet, as we understand it, from the popular and prolific French Renaissance court dancing of the sixteenth century, during which approximately two hundred new dances were performed within a span of six decades.

"There is a great difference between ordinary dancing and ballet," wrote a French Jesuit dance scholar in 1658; "the first is only a movement of the body, which consists in the rightness of the steps, and is merely an amusement, taken with no other rule than those of cadence and harmony; whereas the other [ballet] must represent the passions of the Soul and its movements." Ballet thus not only became about "Soul" but reached further to cosmic cause: "the Author of the Universe," wrote another scholar, "is the great master of the Ballet which all creatures dance with well-regulated steps and movements." Codification converted manners into art: an art of etiquette.

Ballet's movements have endured few sweeping changes over time, but they have been subjected to ever-higher standards of what constitutes beauty, perfect execution. Our many specific steps are like musical notes, the Lego bricks of our language. Mr. B did not like being called a "creator," saying, "God creates. I assemble."

It was a king—and not just any old king, but a king who danced—who presided over the birth of ballet as a classical art form, forever endowing the art with its inherent, fundamental nobility, no matter the politics of the state under which it has since thrived: ballet's origins are tenaciously, ineradicably hierarchical. Louis XIV, the longest-reigning monarch in recorded history, ruled France for over seventy-two years, ascending the throne in 1643, just shy of his fifth birthday. He began his private, daily dance lessons the following year.

Dancing was, at the time, deemed a necessity "for a young nobleman to be polished," wrote Saint Hubert in 1641. "He must learn how to ride, to fence, and to dance. The first skill increases his dexterity, the second his courage, and last his grace and disposition." The art's enduring kinship with military regimens is not by chance.

Dubois de Lestourmière, Louis's valet de chambre, reported on the child king's morning routine:

After having said his prayer, he sat in his chair and combed his hair, and was handed a little outfit, a pair of woolen breeches and a shirt from Holland. He then entered a large room behind his antechamber where he did his exercises. He vaulted . . . fenced, jousted and went back to his alcove room where he danced. Back in his great chamber, he changed and breakfasted.

The king continued his daily lessons for more than two decades, and was by all accounts a very good dancer of professional quality: Louis loved to dance! This passion of the king's might well be said to have been the driving force behind the conception of ballet, a new and distinct art, under his rule.

Louis's designation as the Sun King derived from his debut, at age fourteen (having reached his majority a year earlier), in Paris, as the god of the sun in *Ballet Royal de la Nuict* (now referred to as *Ballet de la Nuit*). This massive spectacle began at dusk on Feb-

Louis XIV at age ten, the young dance student with his impeccably turned-out legs and feet beneath the royal sword and ermine cape of his coronation robes. As these most famous legs in history turn in their royal sockets, their position uncannily presages the stance—even the slight right knee bend—of the sculpture *La Petite Danseuse*, made almost 250 years later by Edgar Degas, another Frenchman obsessed with ballet. *(Henri Testelin)*

ruary 23, 1653, and came to its close at dawn the following day, thirteen hours later. It took place in the Grande Salle du Petit-Bourbon, an enormous hall by the Seine, near the Louvre Palace, just north of the Tuileries. Along with *ballets de cour*, it was the site of plays by Corneille and Molière. In a long rectangular hall with a rounded apse at the end, the audience sat on two raised tiers around three sides, and the venue held as many as three thousand spectators.

For the piece, commissioned less than six months earlier, teenage Louis rehearsed for just two weeks prior to the premiere. The production was divided into four sections of three hours each, called "Watches," and consisted of no less than forty-three "entrées," featuring 266 roles played by eleven children, twenty-nine courtiers (including two exiled British nobles), and fifty-nine professional dancers—all men, some *en travestie*.

This multimedia spectacle included flying figures and chariots drawn by owls and was set in caves, beaches, towns, and forests. There were sea demons, sorcerers, magicians, amputees, gypsies, shepherds, pilgrims, and soldiers; even gods and the moon herself, each with identifying props. And, of course, a young king. The content included myth, allegory, comedy, satire, burlesque, and tragedy, plays within plays, and ballets within dances, all told in verse, song, mime, and dance, accompanied by music barely audible above the noisy moving scenery. It was the greatest story ballet ever told—all stories; every story.

Writer Jean Loret reported in the *Gazette Burlesque:*

You'd never seen the like of it before . . . the heavens, sea and earth, games, mirth, peace and war . . . now an attack, now rough combat; witches attending a sabbath, wolf men, dragons and monsters; gallants, gossips, goddesses, blacksmiths, Christians and Turks, thieves; monkeys, cats, a coach, a fire; a fair, a ball, a ballet, a play; one saw such enchantments.

The end of the Fourth Watch, as dawn approached the next day, showcased Louis's younger brother, Philippe, Duke of Orléans, age twelve, announcing his brother's entrance in verse by Isaac de Benserade:

The company of the stars flees away
As soon as this great star advances;
The dim glimmers of Night,
That triumphed in his absence
Dare not withstand his presence;
All these fleeting fires vanish:
The Sun that follows me is the young LOUIS.

Quite the introduction by one's kid brother—and hence ensued a lifetime of Philippe's being sidelined so as never to threaten his sibling's sovereignty. The sun appeared, and it was the king himself, radiating light as he descended through clouds from the heavens. The entrée was titled "Glorie," a literal staging of royal authority akin to God.

"The king's costume was covered with a rich gold embroidery with a great many rubies," reported *La Gazette de France*. "The sun-rays which appeared around his head were of diamonds, and the crown around his head as of rubies and pearls with a great many plumes, red and white." Louis exuded light from every royal region: from his shoulders, wrists, and delicately splayed fingers to his belly, hips, knees, and, yes, even the monarch's ankles glowed.

It was an outsized political declaration, propaganda on a royal scale, a sumptuous illustration in three dimensions of the reestablishment of order and centralized power following the years of the civil wars, the Fronde, that prevailed in France before, and just after, he inherited the throne. This was Louis XIV as Apollo, the god of light, poetry, and music, bringing harmony and illumination to the theater, to the monarchy, to France. To the universe. It was an entrance that entered history.

I sometimes look, with pleasure and considerable astonishment, through a keyhole of time, shooting swiftly back a mere 281 years and 107 days to that grand evening of February 23, 1653, when *Ballet de la Nuit* clocked in at 780 minutes with its hundreds of performers showcased in the grandest reception venue in Paris with an audience of thousands. I peer at all this from behind a tree near the rickety stage of that first unlikely performance of *Serenade* on June 10, 1934, where a scattering of students dodged raindrops before a couple of hundred guests at a private home in a New York suburb. I see an oscillating but clear through line, from the story of stories, the tale of all the world, the gods on high, the underworld below, and every machination of man in between, to no tale at all, just some moonlight; from political positioning to beauty for beauty's sake; from autocracy to democracy; from pointed shoes with heels to heelless pointe shoes. Curiously, both ballets premiered on a Sunday—the day of worship—though *Serenade,* with her usual historical whimsy, was intended for a Saturday, but the weather decided otherwise.

And, writ large, I see, with equal delight, in the substantial reduction on every level—duration, performers, intrigues, tales, scenery, costumes, jewels, kings, goddesses, and plumes—the ironic progression from an endless extravaganza, an act staged to ascertain a monarch's inherited power, nobility, and superiority to Balanchine's thirty-three-minute distillation: an uncorrupted aristocratic art form no longer defined by birth, a difficult but attainable democratic nobility.

Ballet de la Nuit introduced, in a blazing light, Louis's long reign, during which culture, art, and classicism not only flourished but played a defining role by both occupying his court and keeping them from inciting trouble in matters of state, and furthering, as the king wrote in his memoirs, his "desire for glory." When Cardinal Jules Mazarin, the powerful Italian minister who had ruled the French government during Louis's minority, died, the young Louis did not appoint a successor. From age twenty-three on, he would rule himself: his *pouvoir absolu* was absolute. Within weeks, in one of his first acts as head of state, Louis XIV established, by royal decree, the first academic national ballet school in the world.

The Lettres Patentes du Roy for l'Académie Royale de Danse were drawn up, signed by the king, and ratified by parliament into law the following year. It was the first of five royal academies that the king would establish over the next decade, consolidating the arts under his control.*

---

* Prior to Louis's ascension to the throne, the Académie Française was founded in 1635 and the Académie Royale de Peinture et de Sculpture in 1648.

The royal decree issued by Louis XIV, establishing the first national ballet school in history

The charter stated that the academy would comprise thirteen dancing masters and scholars, appointed by the king, and put forth twelve statutes aimed at defining, regulating, and raising the standards of dancing technique. The legislation went so far as to require a review of all existing and new dances, licensing them or imposing financial penalties for "each violation," upon the "infinite number of ignorant persons [who] have disfigured and corrupted the Dance," with their "abuses" in order to "reestablish this Art in its initial perfection." The king was going to clean up the rampant practice of jumping about any old which way! This was a unique attempt in dance history to censor, monopolize, centralize, and control dance through political legislation—though evidence of any actual success in the prosecution of flagrant frolicking is scant.

From this royal decree arose the parameters—the idea of a training academy, parallel to the French Royal Army—that would give birth to what we now call classical ballet, dancing that required military precision. Louis's concerted efforts over many years in the name of dance would, in time, raise the form from comic and burlesque amusement, however elaborate, to something serious, a civilizing act.

Would ballet as we know it have even been born without Louis XIV's passion and ambition—both personal and political—for a systemized new art? Though the steps and positions are now deemed irrefutable, abiding, without Louis's insistence spurring their codification, we cannot know if it would now exist.

"The Art of Dance," begins the king's introduction to the decree, "is one of the most advantageous and useful to our Nobility, as well as to others who have the honor of approaching Us, not only in time of War for our Armies, but even in Peacetime while we enjoy the diversion of our court Ballets."

But, alas, while the significance of Louis's Académie Royale de Danse is historically unique, astonishingly, no actual documentation by its distinguished members exists. Jean-Georges Noverre, a great dancer, choreographer, and scholar of dance, proclaimed a hundred years later, "This Academy, the most sprightly of all the Academies, lightly hops on its glorious name and devotes itself to the most profound silence. No instructive memoires, no speeches, no reception, no eulogy . . . the meetings took place in the 'Epée de bois,' a favorite bar." The royal decree itself remains, ironically, its first, last, and only record.*

A decade or so later the king went further, asking for the invention of a system to write down dance, a way to establish both its standardization and its stature, and to put it on equal footing with the arts of poetry and painting by giving it an existence in a permanent visible form. As such, it was rationally posited, the liquid three

---

* Within eight years, in 1669, the academy was folded into the Académie Royale de Musique and became what is now the oldest ballet company and school in the world, the Paris Opera Ballet.

dimensions of dance movement could be rendered both conveyable and enduring, and dance could meet its sister arts as their equal. Dance documentation needed to exist, if only to raise the art form's prestige, outside of fungible, unreliable human beings.* Until now, with one notable exception, as one English writer put it, dance had been "destitute of all Pens."†

It was to a Monsieur Pierre Beauchamps—literally "beautiful fields"—that the king turned to execute his idea, and it is to him that we owe the first five positions of ballet's lexicon, the earthly platforms from where the art blasts off, and up.

Born in Paris a few years prior to Louis, into a large family dynasty of musician-dancers, Beauchamps was a man of gargantuan accomplishment—a virtuoso dancer, prolific choreographer and composer, conductor, and inventor of the first widely known dance notation—yet he remains little celebrated, even in dance history. His life span ran parallel to the king's. The eldest of fourteen children—"all who played danced, all who danced played"—whose father was a court musician to Louis's father, Louis XIII, Beauchamps debuted, rather inauspiciously, at age sixteen as both a statue and a nymph. He was soon recognized for the "fire and vigor" of his dancing, and his spectacular tourbillon: one can but imagine. At age nineteen, Beauchamps became the twelve-year-old king's unofficial private dance teacher and proceeded to teach Louis daily for decades. He was so deft as to become one of the very few dancers who performed alongside the young king, as in *Ballet de la Nuit*, breaking the tradition of presenting nobility onstage apart from their subjects.

By the 1660s Beauchamps was a busy man: choreographing, composing, and conducting music for numerous court ballets; pro-

---

* History, however, has shown that such a transmutation of liveness to paper, of animate to inanimate, of three dimensions to two, is a battle rarely won in ballet. Unlike the absolute precision of a musical score to reproduce music accurately, dance notations are not easily reconstituted to living bodies.

† A century earlier, a French Jesuit cleric, Thoinot Arbeau, produced a curious treatise titled *Orchésographie*, a handbook as much a dating manual as a dancing one. Dance, he opined from his priestly perch, was to be perfected to attract and please the "damsels," so as to "not be reproached for having the heart of a pig and head of an ass."

ducing dances and music for the Jesuit colleges of Paris; and engaged in a twelve-year collaboration with Molière, choreographing the dances, and often composing the music, for his new *comédies-ballets*, including the premiere of *Le Bourgeois gentilhomme* in 1670.

While several other forms of dance notation were developed in the latter half of the century, it was only Beauchamps's that had widespread influence. Delivered to the king in five volumes, the work was never published by Beauchamps himself; in 1700, Raoul-Auger Feuillet published *Chorégraphie*, wherein he set Beauchamps's invention. Beauchamps sued Feuillet in 1704, and despite the evidence of twenty-five scholars, he lost his case; but history vindicated him, and the system has since become known as the Beauchamps-Feuillet notation.

Pierre Rameau, dance master and author, explained in 1725 the importance of Beauchamps's codification:

> What is termed a position is nothing more than a separation or bringing together of the feet according to a fixed distance, while the body is maintained upright and in equilibrium without any appearance of constraint, whether one walks, dances, or comes to a stop. These positions were discovered through the application of the late Monsieur Beauchamps, who wished to give a definite foundation to the art. Before his time these positions were unknown, which proves his deep knowledge of this art. They must be regarded as indispensable and unbreakable rules.

They remain "indispensable and unbreakable" to this day.

The English poet Soame Jenyns prophesied far-reaching historical significance for dance notation's effect in his 1729 poem "The Art of Dancing."

> *Hence o'er the world this pleasing art shall spread,*
> *And every dance in ev'ry clime be read.*
> *By distant masters shall each step be seen,*
> *Tho' mountains rife, and oceans roar between*
> *Hence, with her sister arts shall dancing claim*

An equal right to universal fame,
And Isaac's rigadoon shall live as long,
As Raphael's painting, or as Virgil's song.

The ambition to write down dance so as to tether its inherent flight to some terrestrial form is now well over three hundred years old and has had many brave adventurers along the way. But, in truth, none have accomplished the permanence Jenyns predicted—a quality not only antithetical to the form but directly opposed to its very purpose. Dance, like desire itself, evaporates even as it conquers—

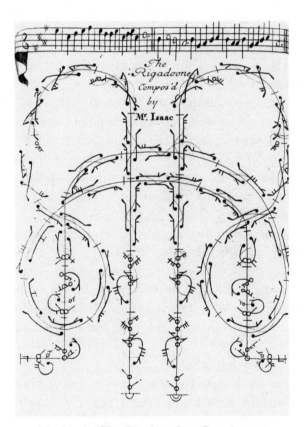

Mr. Isaac's "The Rigadoone" in Beauchamps-Feuillet notation, 1721 *(*Dancing by the Book : A Catalogue of Books, 1531–1804, *in the collection of Mary Ann O'Brian Malkin)*

like Mr. Isaac's noble rigadoon,* whose exquisitely drawn notation now resides only in dusty dance archives, hardly the fate or fame of Raphael's Madonnas or Virgil's *Aeneid*.

The Beauchamps-Feuillet system named and illustrated in broad, moral terms "the good/true positions" ("les bonnes positions": toes out) and, curiously, "the false positions" ("les fausses positions": toes in; i.e., pigeon-toed), while also outlining with intense specificity no less than ninety-four forms of pas de bourrées—a virtual periodic *table de bourrées*.

"When I came to France," wrote the king's sister-in-law, the Duchess of Orléans, in her memoirs, "I saw there a gathering of men of talent such as will not be found again for many centuries. It was Lully for music; Beauchamps for ballets; Corneille and Racine for tragedy; Molière for comedy."

And of these immortals, only Beauchamps, ballet maker, remains all but unknown, having endured centuries of vagaries, not least the uncertain date of his death. Though it is often stated as 1705, there exists public record of his living more than ten years longer, and an obituary has yet to be found. He has no dedicated biography, and none of his many ballets survive—a particularly ironic footnote for the man who invented a way of "writing dance." He left no wife or children, only some notable paintings by French and Italian masters (Poussin, Raphael, Giorgione, Veronese) that now hang in the Prado, the Hermitage, the Louvre, and the Metropolitan Museum. The single lithograph bearing his likeness is an imagined concoction devised a hundred years after he lived, and even his very name continues to be spelled two ways, with and without the final "s." Though it appears that in this last alone, Beauchamps left us written evidence: a signature so round, clear, and musical as to echo his profession.

While history has lobbied against this balletmaster, he nevertheless labors on daily, in righteous anonymity but evident visibility, in perhaps the most fitting inheritance of all. Thousands upon thousands of ballet dancers over the centuries have stood in his first position—the beautiful field of Beauchamps's circumscription—to

---

* The celebrated Mr. Isaac was the British queen Anne's dancing master, and he composed his rigadoon, in 1711, to celebrate her forty-sixth birthday.

Premiere Pofition.

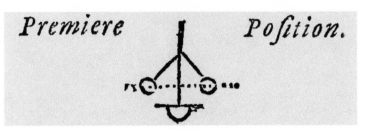

Premiere *Pofition.*

TOP "Good" first position—toes turned outward 90 degrees—in Beauchamps-Feuillet notation, 1700. The two adjacent circles indicate the heels, and their two diagonal offshoot lines indicate the direction of the feet. BOTTOM "Bad" first position—toes turned inward (pigeon-toed).

begin their daily morning class. Surely more first positions have been taken, will be taken, and are being taken as you read this than there are stars in the universe. Always first in first. As we stand now in *Serenade* at minute 1:33, in our shamelessly open first position, each of seventeen dancers doubles Beauchamps's prescribed 90-degree angle to a saucy 180 degrees: the finished line of progress. Firmly planted inside the legacy of the love of a king and his loyal ballet-master for dancing, we stand, truly, with history rushing underfoot.

7. POINTE

I t is now a minute and thirty-five seconds into the ballet, and while our feet have spun wide, our legs have still not moved. From this first position, we lift our arms softly sideways and extend the right leg to the side in battement tendu. This is one of ballet's most basic steps, and Balanchine liked to say—and he said it often, taunting us—that if you could do a tendu well, you could dance "anything." This kind of statement kept things very clear for us, in our tunneled vision. It conveyed an impossible order of deceptive simplicity, one that will keep any ballet dancer at the barre all her life.

While appearing to be just an extension of the foot on the ground of no more than twenty inches with a straight and turned-out leg to the front, side, or back—or anywhere between those three—this move, in fact, takes years and years to master and, being a perfect step, is never perfected. A tendu, a small and short movement, is the great physical metaphor for the pursuit of virtue that is a ballet dancer's vocation: it requires the entire body, head to toes, in a state of unwavering fortitude and precise one-pointedness, to execute with the kind of beauty and conviction that will register as an event in the farthest rows of a theater.

And there, at the tips of those seventeen taut right legs in tendu, is a pointed foot, its toes sheathed in peach satin, ankles bound in ribbon. It is now one minute and forty-one seconds into the ballet, and so much already has passed, yet only now do we point our toes. Here is ballet.

There they are, an upward breath, those feet, those shoes, these shimmering crescents of improbability; upon their silhouetted soles begins our art. These great arcs of light upon which many a poet and photographer have settled their sentimental lens, require, in truth, arches of iron, and minds more so. It is here, on the ground, at our farthermost reaches, where flesh crashes into the spirit of Terpsichore most definitively, for inside those pastel tubes of tight uniformity lie our feet, our ten toes, and the wounds and scars from our crusade against gravity. An unlikely wager is won inside these satin cylinders, Newton's apple upended, cored, and spun into a vertical liquid of unlikeliness.

Not only is pointe dancing, unique to female ballet dancers as a serious endeavor, as a way of life, ballet's most recognizable attribute, but its mastery also defines a world, sending a dancer into yet another dimension—a higher plane—and also into the realm of blisters and calluses, even as it raises her inner being to far greater heights than the six inches that it raises her body. To be up there with ease, where the act is no longer a gravitational gamble but a war won, changes a girl forever. She has landed on Olympus, and the cliff's edge is now her home.

And as she stands there, she rests upon the toes, as it were, of Mlle Marie Taglioni, the first wayfaring sylph who dared this absurdity and who now resides in immortality on her impossibly tiny pointy pointes in lithographs as if in actual memory. This young ballerina—called "the most famous dancer that ever moved on a stage" by one critic—learned to dance on her toe tips with, as history has it, no visible effort at all, and in slippers, without the hard, supportive blocks of today's pointe shoes. But her will was very great.

With Taglioni's rise, ballet had turned east from its French epicenter to Italy for its next great injection of innovation and energy. With pointe dancing, all movement literally leaned frontward, as ballet dancers moved their balance from Louis XIV's heels to Taglioni's toes. But it also lifted the ballerina up from flat-footed life, so that gravity now bends around a tilted orbit. This is indeed a forward move—of opening, of offering, of availability—and yet the increased agility also aids speedy escape. Pointe dancing provided an erotic repositioning of the entire body.

The great ballerina, in her vast fame as an early-nineteenth-century superstar, also established the supremacy of female dancers, of the ballerina, over the male-dominated dancing of Louis XIV's court, two hundred years earlier. Taglioni became the muse to the French poets of her day—Théophile Gautier, Victor Hugo, Dumas père, Chateaubriand—as the epitome not only of femininity and grace but of a freedom of spirit that rendered her "both saintly and a force of anarchy and dissolution."

"She swims in your eye like a curl of smoke, or a flake of down," wrote one American male admirer. And you "find with surprise that a dancing girl, who is exposed night after night to a profaning gaze of the world, has crept into one of the most sacred niches of your memory."

But, more notably, Taglioni captivated women. Countess Dash explained how she presented to them an alternative to their ever-understated, proper behavior, suggesting they might "abandon their soft and calm existence" for "storms of passion" and "dangerous emotions."

Marie Taglioni was a formidable Italian-Swedish woman, born in 1804 in Stockholm, whose entire career unfolded under the strict guidance of her equally formidable Italian father, Filippo Taglioni, a member of a dancing family of Taglionis. Until then, dancing on the toes was only an amusing stunt, a grotesquery, used on occasion by the Italian Grotteschi dancers, but Taglioni's refinement transformed a trick into a language all its own, lifting ballet's proposition of grace, from the pointed shoes of Louis XIV's court to pointed feet. And there it has remained, albeit with many a mishap, ever since.

Taglioni describes in her *Souvenirs* the kind of work she did in the endless hours of daily training with her father in the six months prior to her debut, at age eighteen, on June 10, 1822. This study took place in a room in their apartment in Vienna that Filippo had out-

Marie Taglioni in *La Sylphide* *(Jerome Robbins Dance Division, The New York Public Library)*

fitted with a steeply raked floor to mimic the theatrical stages of the time, which required negotiating verticality differently than on dry land.

> During these six hours, at least two were devoted only to exercises, thousands for each foot. It was extremely painful, arid and boring, and yet it is the only means to soften the nerves, to fortify them, and to arrive at a certain perfection ... Then two more hours were devoted to what I will call aplombs, or adagio. Thus I would take poses held on a single foot ... and I counted up to a hundred before leaving it ... These poses must be done by standing on demi-pointe

on one foot—that is, by raising the heel so that it does not touch the floor.

The final two hours of training, just before bed, were devoted to jumps. She would begin "by loosening the instep and the tendons (the most delicate part of our person)."

> We do thousands of these exercises before we attain a certain degree of perfection, and then we start to jump . . . Finally I will say by dint of jumping, one ends up finding the spring of a doe. For me I know I could launch myself across the stage in one or two leaps . . . One did not hear me land, because it was always the tip of my foot that landed first and my heel would come down gently . . . I actually vibrated in the air.

Taglioni was famously unbeautiful, rendering her mythic status as a creature of magical beauty all the more moving, an example of self-creation through discipline and devotion under the tutelage of morality. "Ill-made," wrote one who saw her, "almost deformed, quite without beauty and without any of those conspicuous exterior advantages that generally command success." Her brutal self-assessment is an example of that required of any ballet dancer of real merit:

> When one has to appear before the public, one naturally exposes oneself to its criticisms; that is why we must make a general study of one's whole person—see one's defects and seek as much as possible to make qualities out of them. Thus, I was not pretty: The top of my body left much to be desired. I was slim without being thin; my legs were very well made—a little elongated, but well proportioned; my foot, remarkably small and graceful. I knew how to walk on the stage like nobody. Finally, what I am going to say will seem ridiculous: I had spiritual feet and hands.

One does not doubt her. That she sought to perform on her toes with such weightless poise was a truly radical undertaking. Is not standing, not to mention residing, on the tips of one's toes impossible? In channeling her integrity and desire and no small ambition into her feet, Taglioni literally raised an entire art, encoding it with the language it still speaks today. She could not have known the repercussions. This was not innovation but revolution: Taglioni guillotined human flat feet and honed her pointes into blades that would pierce memory, slashing her craft open to longevity and lifting ballet to an art form that could depict spirit and purity. Thus it began to depart from its long, though ever-lingering, association with women of pliable bodies and easy virtue. A ballerina's pointe shoe became the upright motif of a woman worthy of respect, despite the tulle and pretty legs above—unveiling what Akim Volynsky called a "vertical culture" where "everything will ascend upward . . . the conscious spirit in its highest moral and individual soaring." And this instruction was the brilliant, conscious intent of Taglioni's father for his daughter from the start.

Louis Véron, the director of the Paris Opera during the time of Taglioni's reign, wrote of the ruling French balletmaster Auguste Vestris demanding "provocative smiles," "postures without decency," while counseling his students, "Be charming, coquettish; display in all your movements the most stirring freedom; you must, during and after your pas, inspire love, [to the extent that] the audience and the orchestra would wish to sleep with you." In contrast, Véron explains that "Mr. Taglioni père said quite the opposite":

> He demanded a graceful ease of movement, lightness, above all elevation, ballon; but he did not allow his daughter a gesture, a posture that lacked decency and modesty. He would say to her: "Women and girls must be able to see you dance without blushing; let your dance be full of austerity, delicacy and taste." . . . Mr. Taglioni demanded an almost mystical and religious naivety in dancing. While one taught pagan dance, we can say that the other professed dance as a Catholic. Mademoiselle Taglioni danced better and differently from the others who had danced before her . . . among her admirers she had all the women and men of good society.

This embrace by "good society" enabled Taglioni to marry an aristocrat: Count Alfred Gilbert de Voisins. But here, her offstage life, absent from her memoirs—"all the past would be too painful" to recollect, she wrote, while she was "very happy in all that was related to my art; I do not think there was a woman more beloved and more spoiled by the public"—renders this sylph a breathing flesh-and-blood woman offstage.

She left the count within three years—though retained the title of countess all her life—and, while still performing, proceeded to have two illegitimate children by two different lovers, culminating in the father of her son, Prince Alexander Troubetzkoy, marrying her daughter (by her previous lover) when the girl was sixteen. The prince bought his lover—and future mother-in-law—the Venetian palazzo the Ca' d'Oro, the first of four she would own, all on the Grand Canal. In addition to her Paris, London, and Lake Como homes, Taglioni's real estate holdings today would render her, in a profession known for the poverty of its remuneration, the wealthiest female dancer in ballet history. All this from those much-darned little pointe shoes and the soles of steel inside them.

Each time any dancer rises on pointe around the world for all time to come, though she likely will not know it, she stands upon Marie Taglioni's delicate daggers of defiance. Just look inside any

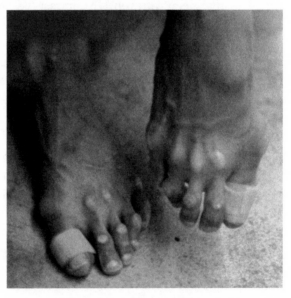

A dancer's feet *(Courtesy of the author)*

well-anointed pointe shoe and see the bleeding beauty that connects us all to her.

Our toe shoes are not like Taglioni's. They are expensive, not least because so many are required, a pair often not lasting longer than a single performance of a single ballet—many hundreds of pairs a year. I have a pair of Suzanne Farrell's used pointe shoes from the early 1980s beside me now. I can see her feet inside them and all that this very great ballerina wrought. They are dirty on the sides and bottom from the stage, but the tops still shine.

Toe shoes have no right or left: they are all identical tubes, and we each decide which foot goes in which tube, thus we also mix and match from different pairs. There are shapely slim shanks both inside and outside, the inside made of layered board, the outside of pale beige leather. The hardness of what dancers call the "box" of the shoe, where the toes live, is not made of anything hard at all, just layers of glue and burlap that, when dried, become fixed, like rock. New, they are hard, dangerously hard, a weapon if you needed one. It is this hardness—*tap, tap, tap*—that you often hear on the stage as a dancer runs about. Balanchine did not want any noise on the stage, so we spent a great deal of time and ingenuity softening the box to the point where it no longer made any noise upon hitting the stage but still remained hard enough to support the foot up there on Olympus. We aimed for the finest possible line between soft and hard, knowing, of course, that in performance the shoes would get quickly softer with every move.

What a totally off-the-floor invention is the toe shoe, surely the craziest footwear ever conceived that has actual purpose. Like in Chinese foot-binding, they must be fitted so closely on the foot as to be like a second skin; they must never, ever fall off despite all the action they see. The foot inside the shoe is squeezed so tightly from side to side, with the toes rounded under, that the same foot outside its shoe could be, literally, twice as wide. This binding helps make it strong, able to stand upright like a column of stone. The shoe is slim and round like a Pillsbury biscuit canister before you pop it open to unfurl the dough.

Pointe shoes are handmade, and a professional dancer gets her own particular maker, someone she will likely never meet but with whom she has an intimate connection. Every element of her shoe will be made to her precise specifications—the heel, sides, vamp, box, everything measured to within an eighth of an inch of her desire. Until she changes her order. She knows her maker only by their mark, stamped on the outside shank of each shoe. Mine was "AAA" until he died, and then I had "XX." Farrell, I see, had "S." This pair of hers is stamped on its sole with a date: "8 SEP 1983." They were made for her four months after Balanchine's death.

They have the satin cut out at the toe tips in a neat little circle. We all did this—the satin is too slippery to dance upon directly and if not removed, will inevitably tear during a performance from the friction with the stage, especially during pirouettes. The underneath outside shank has deep, gouged scratch marks as if it had been attacked by a lion cub. We bought heavy, metal, clawed scrapers from the hardware store for this vital operation, to gain traction with the stage. We would then place the shoes flat on the floor and stand with one heel on the round hard box with our full body weight to crush its roundness, or else close the front of the shoe in a door jamb, to make it flatter, more fitting to a foot.

So strange how a clean, smooth, shiny pair of new pointe shoes must be immediately attacked, scraped, cut, and butchered right out of their plastic bags before even being worn once. Then we hit the underside of the tip on the cement walls of the stairwell near the dressing room—*Bang! Bang! Bang!* They are loud, and we hit them until they are not so loud. Mr. B told us that our feet needed to be flexible and delicate like an elephant trunk, with the soft landing of a pussycat's paw, so our toe shoes needed the utmost flexibility and silence within their support.

The ribbons and elastic are sewn on by hand by the dancer who wears the shoe. They are not pre-sewn. We all had a slightly different method for securing the ribbons and ankle elastics upon which our lives depended onstage. Farrell's ribbons are sewn inside out, the shiny satin side against her ankle—most of us did this—the matte, wrong side, facing out so as to blend the ribbons into her ankles and pink tights. Farrell's ribbons are very secure: multiple strong stitches around the three lower sides of the ribbon and several big long stitches along the top edge. But she, like all of us, was careful to not stitch through the inner drawstring that circles the entire inner edge of the shoe. The drawstring is tied in a tight knot, the long ends trimmed short and tucked into the shoe's upper inside—but it must run freely so it can be adjusted.

We sew the ribbons on the inside of the shoe, about halfway between front and back, leaving the two ribbons very long. The first time we wear the shoes, after we wrap the two lengths of ribbon across each other and then around our lower ankle, the ribbons meet on the inside of our ankle, the most invisible place for a small very tight knot. This knot must never loosen, else we are lost. Just lost. If your pointe shoe comes untied onstage, it is humiliation, total failure. Once the knot is tied, we take scissors and cut the ribbons' two loose ends very, very short, perhaps one inch long or less, so as to neatly tuck and hide the ends invisibly, securely underneath the ribbons already tightly wrapped in layers around the ankles. After cutting but before tucking, one final step: we light a match and singe the cut ends of the ribbons so they will not fray.

The elastic loop, unlike the ribbons, is sewn onto the outside of the heel of the shoe, through the satin. If sewn inside the heel, it would be too bulky and counterproductive to the purpose: the short, tight-but-not-too-tight ring of pink elastic—Farrell's are now faded, the decades-old elastic warped—is a loop whose sole purpose is to help hold the ankle of the shoe onto the foot. This is vital. It is not such a sure thing since the heel of the shoe is so shallow, rising around the heel so minimally, less than an inch. The whole purpose of the shoe, the tightness, the scraping, the cutting of the ribbons and elastic, is to make the shoe all but permeate the dancer's foot, not a shoe at all but an invisible casing for the weighty work that the foot has to do not only to live, literally, pointedly, but to dance up on pointe.

At close to two minutes into *Serenade*, we are still not yet up there. Still down here, with you, though not quite. Those extended right legs close in unison from tendu to fifth position. Fifth is our launching pad: both feet suctioned together, heel to toe, toe to heel, turn-out tightly tucked underneath our core. From here, we can explode anywhere. But we don't. Instead, we lift both arms forward, rounded, fingers all but touching, elbows softly curved to the sides forming a circle at heart level. We open them wide to the sides in a classic port de bras, with a twist: from the classical stance of forward direction to you in the audience, we drop our elbows slightly and rotate our curved palms upward while bending back and tilting our faces up, to the rafters of the stage. Here we pause, seventeen strong, young girls in a unified offering. It is a simple, harmonious image and an early harbinger too: the ballet's first allusion to sacrifice, a surrender to the above. Minute 1:46.

We don't move for six seconds, a long time for a dancer, time for the image to register not as transition but as end point, not as movement but as statement. For us, it is a public reckoning: we transform ourselves before your eyes from human to dancer, from parallel to turned out—ten years of work concealed in that single six-inch pivot that changes the world—in just over ninety seconds, so honed, so condensed is Balanchine's mastery of time.

From the moment the curtain was raised until now, we have each remained an island, not moving from our assigned ground. Now we are ready: a battalion of female cadets.

Look. Look out.

8. THE GREAT RUN

Pow!

At minute 1:52, seventeen left legs shoot up onto pointe, rapiers to the ground, as seventeen right legs swoop fast, sharp, and high, straight side. Everything was not all with Balanchine. But it might be a start.

In class, Mr. B explained to us that when we moved any part of our body—a leg, an arm, a finger—it must be "placed" where it was going, and not simply land somewhere by chance. Total consciousness, total control. With our flexible bodies, our legs, after all, would fly up all too easily to great heights around our ears—but this kind of unaimed showiness was not what he wanted. It was not sufficient for a leg to rise and amaze with its athletic, gymnastic force. "It must be *your* leg," he said, "from *your* body." Without this self-knowledge and conviction in this knowledge, that high-swinging leg will be of little interest once it has arrived at its summit, however impressive. The limbs of a dancer's anatomy contain the vocabulary, the alphabet, for communication, and just as the mind shapes consecutive words into meaning, the mind must shape our limbs, our movements. A leg must say, he said, This is *my* leg. *Look* at *my* leg—*see* my wonderful leg! It was a tall order to ask a still very young dancer to understand this concept, for it is, in fact, a quest of character, manifested physically.

Seventeen legs up and we are off, never unintertwined again. Quickly a kind of asymmetrical chaos ensues—"In order to make order," Balanchine liked to say, "you make a mess." Some mess. The right leg comes down, and we lunge onto it in a deep arabesque, body low, back leg high, we bend right, left, swooping around ourselves, arms trailing like half-moon comets. Suddenly two girls break rank and run in speedy circles around the rest of us before returning to their places as if they had never left. Anarchy sprung, the convent opened, our covenant sealed.

We plié, we lunge, we développé our legs, not high but with hips jutting forward, extending the leg farther forward, breaking, through literal extension, with all nineteenth-century classicism in a single, sexy move. We then roll up via bent knees onto parallel toe tips, hips leading the thrust forward yet again, in case you missed it before. It's 1934, it's swing, it's jazz, and it had been five months since Balanchine had sailed into New York Harbor; nine years since he'd fled the Bolsheviks; five years since *Apollo*, his first masterpiece. He was on the move.

We quickly convene upstage left, our backs to you, while one girl, imperceptibly, runs offstage, though few if any of you see her leave. It is said in *Serenade* apocrypha—which is divergent and plentiful; it's fitting to have so many unsolvable mysteries in a work about mystery—that this seventeenth girl "had to leave because she had a date with a man!" Man or no man, she is gone, and the pattern is changed.

Now a neat sixteen, we separate into four groups of four, bodies aligned directly behind one another, torsos and arms reaching, at graded angles, some sideways, some up, some in between. We are four eight-armed Shivas making consecutively higher circles, ring upon ring overlapping like the looped edges of a Hindu doily. Minute 2:27.

Separating again, we pace out but curl wrist around wrist until we are all hooked in a daisy chain, some girls sitting on the stage leaning, others standing in an arabesque par terre, four jagged, oppositely symmetrical, diagonal lines, everyone reaching, always reaching, never not reaching. Never quite here: purity resides in the reach.

Then she enters. Alone. Minute 2:39.

She is another girl, an eighteenth in total thus far, if you're still

Rings of overlapping arms (from left: the author, Bonita Borne, and Barbara Seibert) *(© Steven Caras)*

counting—though one of us has already departed, so with her we are seventeen again—but it is hard to tell if she is us or other, since she is dressed exactly like us, no differentiating costume or tiara or hairdo as is traditionally the case with solo dancers. This girl will become the center of *Serenade,* if there is a center, and I think there is—the heart-and-soul girl, the virgin, the love interest, lost, broken, and then leading, whole. But we just call her the Waltz Girl—since she later dances the Waltz section of the music. Just now she has no history but is happily jumping around with big sautés and high grand jetés, an exemplar of what Edwin Denby, the great poet of dance, wrote: "Ballet is a lot of young people hopping about to music in a peculiarly exhilarating way." And of *Serenade* in particular: "The thrill of *Serenade* depends on the sweetness of the bond between all the young dancers."

When she enters, this dancer cuts a path through us, from upstage left and then across the front of the stage and off again in a grand jeté into the first wing. You get only a brief glimpse of her, but she will be back. Oh yes, she will be back.

After she leaves we take off all over the place, bourréeing (tiny steps in rapid succession on pointe), chaînéing (tiny steps in rapid succession while turning in succession on pointe), soutenuing (two tiny steps while turning once on pointe) on the run, always on the run. We congregate again upstage left, backs to you, but in a different formation this time: a giant, diagonally situated triangle, each girl touching the shoulders of two girls in front of her, in five rows of descending numbers: six, four, three, two, ending in a single girl who is the triangle's apex—and also its base.

But Balanchine has not finished his origami and takes this upright set of sixteen, interconnected girls and melts their verticality from above, so that the farthermost girls remain standing but each row behind them is lower, with the next lower still, until the last girl is lunging so low that her back leg is draping its length diagonally along the stage floor, an upside-down toe shoe tip extending out from her tulle. We are thus in multiple diagonals horizontally and vertically, at all angles. We bend as one, our torsos backward, heads vaulted up and then back, faces to you upside down. We are a pyramid on its head, melted by Dalí, imperialism razed to surrealism.

This off-center centerpiece that I have always thought of as a

We bend as one. *(© Steven Caras)*

kind of balletic barracks marks one of the few moments in the ballet where we, en masse, gather tightly before taking off again in our constant pursuit.

The story of *Serenade* is told through running more than through any other single move—it is the great run. We run here, run there, run upstage, run downstage, run offstage, run onstage, run to each other, occasionally run into each other, run from each other, run around each other, run forward, and run backward to our fate, eventually knowing that, like sand pouring through an hourglass, running is the place itself, time itself, running.

How strange that this is a dance of the young, by the young, many still virgins—I certainly was one—when they take that opening stance. Innocents dancing a wisdom they do not have. But it is in our bodies, our limbs, our fleet feet, and the way we run and run and run through this ballet. The way we run to a destiny we do not yet know, but will.

Serenade is like a labyrinth that Balanchine has constructed to guide us, gently, but with no recourse but to proceed. To where? To our lives? To love? To beauty? To joy? Perhaps—but existentials have no place, no expression, onstage. We are simply back to that first pose. The beginning of the labyrinth is the end, back to parallel to start again, the eternal return. For a dancer to dance *Serenade* really is, you see, everything, not as metaphor but as fact. Not art imitating life. Art is life. Minute 3:15.

9. JOHN'S GEOMETRY

John Taras was one of a small, unchanging group of people who helped Balanchine do his work, live his life. This group was very much not an entourage; each was devoted, quiet, in service—Balanchine had no time for ego indulgences, his own or others'. There was Betty Cage (general administrator), Eddie Bigelow (manager), Barbara Horgan (Balanchine's personal assistant), Leslie "Ducky" Copeland (who oversaw men's wardrobe), Mme Sophie Pourmel (who oversaw women's wardrobe), all the Russians who ran and taught at the School, and various balletmasters over the years, of whom John Taras was one of the longest lasting. He first came to work for Balanchine as an assistant balletmaster in 1959 and he remained until Balanchine's death twenty-five years later. Despite his British accent, John was born in New York in 1919 of Ukrainian heritage and by age nine was dancing for a Ukrainian troupe. His busy résumé is indicative not only of his extensive experience but of the itinerant nature of the dance world. John trained with Michel Fokine and Anatole Vilzak and at the School of American Ballet, and he worked variously over the next decades as a performer, stager, regisseur, and choreographer with eighteen different companies, including the Monte Carlo Opera, de Basil's Ballets Russes, the Paris Opera Ballet, La Scala, the Royal Ballet, Dance Theatre of Harlem, and the Bolshoi Ballet, and, after Balanchine's death, as a balletmaster at American Ballet Theatre. His long and winding career exemplifies the art form itself—dancers ever in search of the elusive, and expensive, stage, in the struggle to establish the art of the ephemeral.

In 1963, John choreographed Stravinsky's *Arcade*, which showcased the young Suzanne Farrell in her first solo role—likely at Balanchine's suggestion, and certainly with his approval. It premiered just months before *Meditation*, Balanchine's first public declaration not only of his love for the eighteen-year-old Farrell but of her future in his oeuvre: the yearning of an older man for a mystical young beauty who blesses him only to leave him, as in a dream: his muse.

John staged Balanchine ballets for both NYCB and other com-

John Taras and Balanchine *(© Paul Kolnik)*

panies around the world, and *Serenade* was one of the ballets he staged numerous times, its being then, as now, the piece most in demand. John taught company class frequently during my own years in the company.

For the wildly complex comings and goings of the dancers in certain places in the ballet, John created a fascinating series of diagrams for his own reference. One of these sequences charts a few minutes in the first movement, including the aforementioned pyramid. Twenty-two drawings—two per page, each in a sharply drawn rectangle denoting the stage—cover one hundred bars of music totaling 2:35 minutes of the 33-minute ballet—from minute 2:14 to minute 4:49. Each detailed image denotes a mere 10 seconds of the ballet and the individual placement of the dancers, providing a unique hard-copy, aerial view of the three-dimensional density of Balanchine's imagination.

The drawings are done in pencil on graph paper using a ruler whenever a line was fortuitously straight, though the majority of movements are never straight, only for seconds during transitions: it is all curves leaning into spirals, merging into diagonals that split into squares that lead into circles that shift into another diagonal— on it goes and goes. These graphs show only the movement in space on the stage of the dancers' bodies; each dancer is given an alphabetical letter, and is illustrated by the symbol of a small circle, her head, with a short line denoting the direction of her body. There is no indication whatsoever of what each dancer is actually doing with her legs, feet, body, arms, or head—that part is easy for any dancer or balletmaster to remember once learned. But Balanchine's patterns of moving bodies about the stage can be staggering in their often simultaneous complexity and simplicity, and re-creating them precisely is difficult, thus John's notes.

Despite dancing the ballet over fifty times and knowing it as a part of my own body, I only ever knew in detail my own place— designated in John's graphs by the letter "K."

In the next minute and forty-three seconds—as depicted in the graphs—the following activity ensues:

1. A new girl, a solo role, enters for the first time—we call her the Russian Girl because she later leads the Russian

Dance, though, of course, in NYCB she was never Russian (she is also sometimes called the Jump Girl)—with backward-moving plunging jumps and arabesques, then fast chaîné turns offstage right.

2. We dismantle from the pyramid barracks. The back two rows of dancers run out and forward, rushing about each other, between one another, splitting ourselves in ordered chaos, then run some more here and there, though never entirely randomly.

3. One dancer, at the back center of the barracks, turns, inhales, runs, and does a huge grand jeté and exits stage right.

4. Now reduced to fifteen, we divide into groups of nine and six, but the six soon run offstage left, and the nine—in three rows of three—face the wings of stage right and step backward six times in arabesque piqué, arms moving together in opposition in front of us, then run back to the starting place and do the same thing again. But this time we do only two piqués before changing course again.

5. We form in the middle of the stage a circle of eight girls with one, the ninth, as our center point, and she alone does a particularly difficult double pirouette, the fast spins on a single pointe so well loved by audiences—though less so by their instigators. While Volynsky called the pirouette the "apotheosis of verticality . . . a genuine miracle of beauty and morality," he admitted that it can be "a lamentable fiasco on the stage." The "pirouette requires a monolithic character, the exultation of the infinite," he explains, "all ascent and heroic exertion."

In this moment, the dancer's last thought is of heroism: she is pure concentration on the mechanics, with perhaps an icing of prayer. Instead of wrapping her arms closely about her body at waist level to minimize the interference

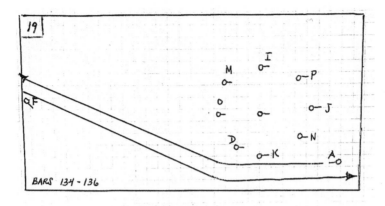

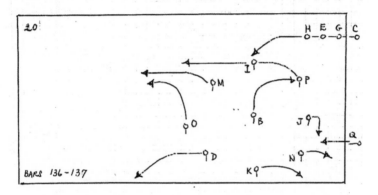

John Taras's diagrams of *Serenade*, first movement, bars 134–137 (*NYCB Archives, Taras Collection*)

of physics, as is typical with pirouettes, she lifts both arms high above her head while whipping around twice, drastically changing the dynamics of the turns—the upward trajectory of the arms working in opposition to the circular movement of the body, thus requiring even greater "faithfulness to the guiding center."

Here, as before, and often again in this ballet—over thirteen times—Balanchine uses a corps dancer to do something alone, singling her out before she merges back into the group again. This is an unusual break of protocol

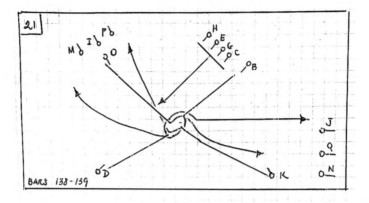

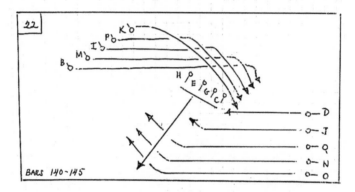

John Taras's diagrams of *Serenade*, first movement, bars 138–145
(NYCB Archives, Taras Collection)

in classical balletic hierarchy, and presents to the various dancers a moment to shine alone. A moment in the sun, as the sun. How we each obsessed over our moment!

6. We execute from our circle more rather extravagant hip-jutting movements while shooting our right legs forward, very not classical ballet—but a hint of Balanchine to come. Two more girls run in and grand jeté from opposite wings and exit off again. They are on and gone. There is more running, chaînéing to one knee, and yet another lone girl runs in to grand jeté. And then with the invis-

ible addition of one more dancer—now we are sixteen again—we run all about and converge into the largest single diagonal yet, splicing the entire stage from upstage right to downstage left on a slant. But getting there was a challenge of time and pathways: Mr. B wanted the arrival to be such that they "couldn't get there," as one dancer explained. "But they got there!" Timing according to Balanchine.

7. From this barely arrived-at long diagonal, we do the great "peel." Starting with the girl farthest toward you, downstage, one by one by one like a windmill, each girl in turn swings her arms up and around and, with a deep lean left and breath up, runs wingward to the right, your left (Balanchine ever employing opposition), straight offstage as the girls after her each do the same one by one by one by one until the last girl far upstage is alone and quickly does her arm-rotation swing and runs off. Like a great east wind blew us, in our pale sea of chiffon, west. Busby Berkeley by Balanchine, ordered undulation. And a not-so-distant echo of Balanchine's 1931 variety show at the London Coliseum for music hall impresario Sir Oswald Stoll—just three years before he made *Serenade*—featuring "16 Delightful Balanchine Girls 16." With this last dancer's exit, the stage is emptied entirely for the first time since curtain up. Blank slate.

Here John's series ends. Like da Vinci's Vitruvian Man, his drawings in their mathematical precision provide the geometrics of a few minutes of *Serenade,* converting spirit to physics and then, onstage, back again. Minute 5:00.

10. STONEHENGE

||||||||||||||||||||||||||||||||||||||||||||||||||||||||||||||||||||||||||||||||||||||||||||||||||||||

The first movement of *Serenade,* the longest of the four, is still only half over. But we are absent. Backstage we are catching our breath, re-rosining our toe tips, grabbing sips from the water fountain in the hallway by the elevator, all the while expertly dabbing—always dabbing, never wiping—beads of sweat with tissues, without messing up our elaborate stage makeup. We have only a few of minutes until we are on again.

During this exit at one Saturday matinee, I had stuffed several tissues into my costume's bodice top to use just before making my next entrance. But, suddenly due onstage, I ran out with a tissue bouquet in full flounce about my neck like an oversized white carnation. The utter dismay. And I had to keep dancing as if nothing was amiss until my next exit. You want to die, just die. A different clock started running simultaneously with that of the music, and it became the longest entrance of my career. Onstage my peers saw my voluminous décolleté decoration and were biting their lips to not laugh. Oh, please, please don't laugh: this is not Chaplin; this is church. Suppressed tight grins abounded. Mr. B, thank God, was not in the wings that day, so my great shame, while known by all, was not known by the one who counted most.

Though he wouldn't have cared. Or not much. As he said to a friend who fell onstage and rushed to him after in tears apologizing for "*ruining* your ballet," "You can't mess up the ballet, dear," at once calling out her ego and his own.

Until now, we seventeen have dominated the proceedings, creating mass movements and patterns of flying blue tulle. Two additional dancers have made such dashing entrances—for twelve seconds and seventeen seconds respectively—wearing exactly the same costumes as us, so that they will not have registered with the audience as new girls, different girls, or even extra girls, though they are. This is about to change. It begins now, with yet one more girl, the twentieth. After her, there will be no more; our troupe of women is complete.

This final dancer makes her entrance alone, on the emptied stage, also dressed identically to us. Focus immediately changes as specificity is telescoped from the swirling, leaning, running urgency of us all en masse that marked the opening minutes of the ballet. No dancer has been alone onstage until now, until her. She begins to represent. To symbolize. To tell a story, perhaps. But if there is a story, it is quite unclear.

We call this dancer the Dark Angel, but she is not dark yet, and your programs will say no such thing. This dancer and the two other soloists—the one we call the Waltz Girl, and the Russian Girl—are simply listed, without nomenclature, above our names, which are in alphabetical order, as was Balanchine's way in my years, his later years.

But as with all things *Serenade,* even the program texts shifted over time: a program from 1957 lists the cast as the "Waltz Ballerina," "Russian Ballerina," and "Dark Angel," not only differentiating their roles but using that much-encumbered word "ballerina," with all its connotations of romance, beauty, artistry—and ranking. While the company always had a known hierarchy of principals, soloists, and corps, both backstage and publicly, over time Mr. B wanted to defuse any notions of personal stardom and its attendant cult of celebrity— something very much present in eighteenth-, nineteenth-, and mid-twentieth-century ballet—by alphabetizing the roster. The message to us and audience alike: choreography was king. "A ballerina is a personality and personality means improvisation," he said, "so she adds things, thus the choreography becomes merely atmosphere." In time, *Serenade's* three lead names morphed from "Ballerina" to the less laden "Girl," where they have stayed.

Over the years of *Serenade*'s history, the choreography of these three solo girls has, depending on the circumstances and Balanchine's choice, been performed variously by as few as one to as many as five dancers. These three roles have come to have signature demands that affect their casting: the Dark Angel requires authority and a particularly resonant arabesque, the Russian Girl must be a jumper and turner, and the Waltz Girl must be vulnerable, innocent, soft, must possess a more internal quality, a quality Balanchine needs in order to render her, by ballet's end, the One.

The Dark Angel enters the bare stage from upstage left, with two sets of big sauté jumps in arabesque followed by a great high-flinging swing of her right leg from side to front, her left foot flat on the stage, her body pulled in, then away, from the impetus of her powerful leg. Once on center stage, she executes three even higher, wide-open développé kicks of her alternating legs to the side, though slightly back, her hips now leaning in the direction of her leg, pulling her torso entirely off-center so that her whole body is écarté—a diagonal that opens out, away.

With the solo dancer and all eyes focused on her, Balanchine blatantly ejects the properness, the squareness, the vertical/horizontal laws of ballet etiquette, where being off-center with the body, or having a leg kicking sky high, was unthinkable, possibly indecent. There was no influence that Balanchine would not use if he liked it, always calling himself a craftsman—"I assemble and I steal everywhere to do it"—and here he pulled the loosened hips of the Jazz Age into his 1934 ballet, plunging the sacrosanct nineteenth-century European art into modernity, into America, while he would still dress it in the crisp gauze of the Romantic ballet. How exciting. How beautiful. And so Balanchine's ever-present, often subtle, eroticism makes one of its wittiest displays while being so fitting to Tschaikovsky's music, ordained.

The soloist performs a little jump followed by a large piqué into a great arabesque, left leg extended high, high behind her, all the while moving her arms in fast cycling circles above her head. She does this twice, each arabesque being held for a few seconds, imprinting for the audience this most recognizable of all classical ballet positions. For a dancer, her arabesque is a vital, particularly unique, mark of her identity. "The leg thrown back into an arabesque is, of course," wrote Volynsky, "nothing but a symbol of consciousness in its forward rush." The position is used constantly, everywhere, in every way, posing, jumping, balancing; sometimes the leg is low behind, sometimes high. Having the upper body upright while one leg is placed high behind you—and turned out from the hip socket so the audience sees the front line of the leg while you are facing entirely sideways—requires a deep bend in the mid and lower back while the shoulders, neck, and head remain entirely vertical, carrying that present but invisible crown.

Like most physical demands of classical ballet, like turnout, this is not a natural bend of the body: the back is happy to lean forward, but to bend backward is counter to the spine's desire. But the language of ballet is based on paradox, on flipping the expected and the known, and the tension created by the opposition of torso and leg reaching creates an image of extraordinary power.

My own rather average arabesque was, one day in company class, the occasion for Mr. B's attention. The enormous fifth-floor studio full of eighty or ninety company members screeched into utter silence while everyone focused on him and me, his prey. Being so ultra-aware of my many inadequacies, I felt an ever-tense juxtaposition between wanting attention and my even stronger fear of getting it. As a child, receiving attention more often than not signaled parental displeasure. On this particular day, we were already toward the end of the one-hour company class, Balanchine's laboratory, when he came over to me as I was holding an arabesque, left foot on the floor, right leg extended as high as possible behind me, on a diagonal.

He stood exactly in front of me, looking at my lines from absolute center. He was very close to me, and my heart was pounding. And everyone—Suzanne Farrell, Patricia McBride, Jacques d'Amboise, Helgi Tomasson, Adam Lüders, and all my peers in the corps de ballet—gathered around closer to hear what he would say. The focus on me was just horrific. Like a war already lost. He gently put a few fingers under my chin and guided it up. Balanchine loved, required, his dancers to not look straight ahead but to tilt the head upward, just so, looking toward that upper horizon. It gives a beautiful line to the neck and completes all the other lines in the body, expressing the art's upward intentions, the physical reaching toward the unseen.

I, of course, knew this—but found it extremely difficult to do. This relatively small physical adjustment took enormous confidence, pride in oneself as a dancer, and belief in one's right of being. And I just didn't have it in me at that time. Placing my head up like a queen, like a goddess, like I merited attention, like I was beautiful, was so psychologically difficult for me I simply had to fake it. This Sisyphean struggle lasted for years. My chin's up now, finally, as I write.

Once he'd hauled my jaw up, Mr. B lined himself up with my forehead, and, like a scientist doing research, he narrowed his eyes in a slight squint and assessed my various lines of head, shoulders, arms, hips, and legs. Without a word, he put his right hand up vertically in front of my nose and moved it to his left, directing me to move my body an inch or so to my right. I moved accordingly, but the already precarious balance on one leg was shaken and I wobbled. Oh God.

Then he said to me that I should do "Pee-LAH-tees"—the now ubiquitous but then still obscure series of strengthening and lengthening exercises, invented by the German Joseph Pilates, that was the only form of study outside our theater that Mr. B advocated—to straighten out the asymmetry he'd just diagnosed in my shoulder and torso lineup. What was astonishing is that he could see this truly minuscule unevenness at all. Everyone has some; mine stems from a very small drop and forward rotation of my right shoulder in relation to the left that even I, at the time, was unaware of. But he was right. In fact, this weakness, five years later, became part of the physical chain reaction down the right side of my body that would cause the damage that would prematurely end my career onstage. I feel the discomfort there now as I write this. No teacher at the School had seen it, and even I, who had already been working on and examining my own body inside out daily for fourteen years in class, was not aware of it. This brief interaction, one of many like it that he had with dancers every day, was for me momentous and not good, not good at all. Having any flaw pointed out to me, particularly by the all-important boss, was more than my fragile ego could take, and I felt such shame. We all wanted to be good and beautiful and perfect for him, and his X-ray vision had exposed an imperfection.

He finished this brief one-on-one by asking, "Are you Italian, dear?" Mr. B was always interested in the heritage of his dancers. With my pale skin and almost black hair, I certainly could have been Italian. But, alas, I had to disappoint yet again: "No, I am Australian." (Though I spent four years of my early childhood in England, I was born in Australia to an Australian father.) So unexotic, so unromantic, so prosaic. He had no comment, and class proceeded. Later, once alone, I cried, obsessed, cried some more, experienced utter failure and humiliation. And called a Pilates studio for an appointment the next day.

The Dark Angel is joined by two of us who enter from one side, and we each get close to her, encasing her with our bodies by lunging on flat feet alongside her outstretched arms and legs. She flips her backbend to the other side and two more of us rush in, surrounding her similarly: we are now four about her. And then, so unexpectedly, the Russian Girl flies in from backstage and does six enormous flying jetés around this close-knit group. The five—the Dark Angel and four of us—shuffle out of our folding formation and open up into a diagonal together, holding close, each left arm encircling her friend's waist. We are as one, stepping forward on pointe, right arms opening down, palms up, and then pulling the wrist back to our foreheads as in the opening of the ballet: the Aspirin dance.

Along with his graphs, John Taras wrote out notes for this complex grouping, illustrating how difficult it is to convey dance accurately in words: this will have any meaning only to someone who already knows the ballet well, providing a few essential details only.

Serenade 1st movement

After Jillana's [Dark Angel's] entrance soloist finishes soutenu & back bend facing S.R. as 1st 2 Girls enter change with large port de bras to face S. L.
First 2 Girls hold soloist in small of back lunging forward on outside legs arms forward.

Soloist goes under arms to face S. R. again as 2nd Girls enter inside arms joined pass over soloist's head to hold small of back as well—first lean forward on inside legs in 4th & then outside legs lean back ...
As 2nd Girls go over head 1st Girls under on inside legs outside arms back & into Aspirin.

Maintaining our Bennet sisters closeness, each girl extends her free right hand outward, a low palm opened up to the audience, and then in unison we lift our arms up, wrist to forehead, head turned left. It is an exact echo of the opening of the ballet, but we are now five, not seventeen, and we have pivoted from facing front. And we all have a headache. The same headache. And, yes, we do this sweet sequence on a diagonal. A few repeats and we split up again. This is the closest, most intimate sign so far of sisterhood in a ballet about sisterhood. There will be more. Minute 5:55.

Soon fifteen of us are back onstage entering entirely on parallel pointes with jaunty toe stabs into the stage, like Goldwyn chorus

The Dark Angel (Heléne Alexopoulos) in a backbend and the Russian Girl (Melinda Roy) in a flying leap, with Carole Divet kneeling and Julie Michael to left *(© Steven Caras)*

girls, and we assemble in a formation that I have always thought of as *Serenade*'s Stonehenge—a timeless place, an outdoor temple of secret ceremony, worship, death, resurrection, and astronomy that exists inside Tschaikovsky's acoustics. Complicit (you have been all along), the audience forms the final section that encloses the circle where we, like druid priestesses, are performing a ceremonial rite. Divided into five sets of three girls, we position ourselves in a wide semicircle around the center of the stage. Each grouping of three dancers is vertically staggered: the front girl sitting low down on her folded knees, the middle girl behind her upright on her knees, and the back girl standing. We each are seen, but as one body.

The Russian Girl now does an astonishing thing: after an effusive aria of mighty runs, jumps, hops, turns, pivots, leans, runs, shuffles, and grand jetés all about the stage, she bourrées to center stage, pulls her right wrist to her brow, palm facing out, echoing the gesture of emotion, of "Oh no," as in the Aspirin dance—and at the ballet's opening with all in attendance. And suddenly this power-house woman, as if overcome by a sudden wave of neurasthenia, like a Victorian waif about to collapse onto a fainting couch, goes down, down, to the stage floor, crumpled, but beautifully, in the center of our half circle. She lies there on her right side, still, draped across the stage, her face turned downward. Has she passed out? Is she taking a sudden rest after her exertion? Did she have a sudden shock? A bad memory? Is she in some unknown despair? Under a spell? Or perhaps dead? A 1940 film clip shows her lying faceup with her hands across her chest, like a corpse in a coffin, but somewhere along the way, Balanchine turned her to her side, as she lies now, elongated, not so dead.

According to witnesses, in the first rehearsals in 1934, this dancer actually tripped and fell by mistake and began to cry. Balanchine told her to stay there and kept her misstep in the ballet in what Kirstein called "a climactic collapse." So goes *Serenade*'s mercurial founding filament.

In the useless, but ever-present, fascination about how genius works, this moment provides ideal instruction on the simplicity, almost practicality, of it all, at least for Balanchine. A fall is a bad enough shock to any dancer whose worth is predicated on her grace, but to fall down right in front of Balanchine, I know from personal experience, was a singular blow. It is unlikely that her tears were due to physical pain, so inured to physical pain are we.

Balanchine looked at her on the floor, and whatever he may have had in mind before she fell—and he may well have had nothing in mind yet—he liked what he saw, and told her to stay there. And so by chance, this became a remarkable moment in the ballet, and quite possibly changed the entire trajectory of the piece as we now know it—later he has another dancer fall to the stage floor twice more, to even greater effect. How quickly Balanchine was able to pirouette on a dime, and use what he saw. "I am made only to see movement and hear sounds," he said. "What I have, really, is that I see better than anybody else—and I hear better . . . God said to me, 'That's all you're going to have.' . . . I said, 'Fine.'"

This downing of a dancer purposefully (via mistake) was another break in the classical dance tradition of the nineteenth century, where a dancer's function was to fly, to be airborne with an unearthly grace that did not acknowledge gravity, much less the actual stage floor. This fall had more in common with the vocabulary of the newer terra firma of modern dance, where gravity pulled inward and downward; an impulse emerging in the 1920s and '30s as Martha Graham took the mantle from the recently deceased Isadora Duncan.

If drama was barely hinted at before, this fall is overt. Here, as in all that's to come, the ballet's inexplicable dramas appear out of nowhere and remain unresolved, as if adhering to the admonition by the Roman general Pompey the Great, *"Navigare necesse est, vivere non est necesse."* ("It is necessary to navigate, not to live.")

While the Russian Girl lies there, we remain at our stations and perform very precise arm and head movements, sometimes in unison, sometimes in consecutive motions that create a sequential ripple, a sequence we called the "Egyptian Arms." The effect of each group of three—each identical—is like a Russian Shiva with three heads and six arms. It is a supplication surrounding the fallen one. She rises up, up, up, all the way to the tips of her pointes as if robustly resurrected by our incantation, and immediately begins jumping with renewed force even higher and more widely and wildly than ever before. And she flies off the stage. She was down for just twelve seconds. Minute 7:46.

Balanchine disperses us sixteen (an extra girl has slipped back onstage unnoticed) into a stage-wide circle and we execute a very simple, and yet cumulatively bravura, series of consecutive piqué turns—stepping far out onto our right leg, all but jumping onto pointe, pulling the left leg high up to our knee while turning. Our circle navigates the entire stage in width and depth in hundreds of yards of turning tulle, and the implied centrifugal force becomes the world ever expanding, as we are each individually carried to the opposite side of the stage from where we began. It is for audience and dancers alike the most thrilling moment of the ballet so far— such an enormous display of reckless order.

After fourteen turns, we sauté jump and run quickly, discreetly, directly to our original places at curtain's rise. We suction our flat feet into parallel and place our right arm up to the side but slightly forward, palm outward to that ever-present lunar light. The space transitions instantly from the lively frenzy of fast movement to utter stillness. But one of us is missing.

She enters quietly, slowly, almost imperceptibly from way upstage left, alone, walking, looking, turning back on herself, looking again, weaving her way through us while we stay still, unmoving, oblivious, while she searches among us: "Is there a place for me?" Finally, she finds an empty spot at the front downstage right point of one of our two diamonds. Opposite to where I now stand. "I felt I was searching for something I knew I could never find," says Allegra Kent, a particularly mystical Waltz Girl during Balanchine's later years. Like an honored new student, she carefully places her feet in parallel like ours, and then she raises her right arm up to the light and becomes one with us. And so the first movement of *Serenade* draws to a close as it began. Though not quite.

The music repeats identically as at the opening curtain; though she starts as one of us, one of many sisters, this new girl, the Waltz Girl, by ballet's end will be our leader, our essence distilled. She flips her right wrist and begins the beautiful opening arm sequence. But we do not. On the same note of music, we all turn to our left and slowly walk with quiet gravitas together off into the wings, our right arm trailing behind us, but the hand turned upward as if passing through water, not air. Immediately, she is alone, again, but the few seconds she had in unison with us sealed an unbreakable bond. Though our backs are now to her, this is no mutiny: it is her destiny, which is ours.

So much meaning and yet, as Balanchine told it, this lone girl's entrance came about, like others in the ballet, entirely by chance. On the particular day he was making this section, one girl was late to rehearsal and came into the studio looking to find her place. He kept her search, transforming a quotidian moment into one of not only nuanced beauty and asymmetric ambiguity but also of far-reaching consequence, one might even say of profound definition.

A woman separate longs for her place with us, to join. Is it possible? Here, in his first American dance, this son of Russian imperial heritage, and several hundred years of ballet tradition, flipped the core of classicism on its head in the ordered anarchy of *Serenade*. Yet he neither destroyed nor negated its aristocratic heritage but, rather, gathered up that grand perpendicular hierarchy and flooded it with a great wave of equality, raising the art higher still in a single surge: the imperial pyramid spreads horizontally while the democratic expanse rises vertically. Spiritual paradox embodied in actual bodies.

This was a revolution that reached beyond mere innovation within the form—like cubism or surrealism in modern painting. Balanchine did not so much change an aspect of the art itself or create a new trajectory as push it, in its lush entirety, onto entirely new ground, higher, wider ground. And yet somehow, he simultaneously equalized its players, releasing soloists from their rigid pedestals and the corps de ballet from its decorative function, thus freeing both.

Never had democracy been brought so explicitly to the aristocratic art of ballet before, and never had it appeared so lofty. From the diamond tiaras of queens and the gold crowns of kings, he molded a live conundrum: an aristocracy of equals, an aristocratic democracy, a democracy of aristocrats. This was Balanchine's America.

As we exit the stage, a lone man appears in the ballet, entering from upstage left, dressed in blue tights and a blue top. He walks slowly, elegantly, diagonally toward the solitary woman while she continues her arm movement, oblivious of his approach. As the closing notes of the first movement play, he gently touches her shoulder with his right hand. "When he walks in through this group of people, almost as if through a forest," explained the dancer Joseph Duell, "he's only aware of the woman. Balanchine told me not to tap her on the shoulder; I rest my hand for a minute—a very gentle touch to bring her to life." She reacts instantly, as if a spell is broken and, swooning, falls away from her independence, from her alliance with us. He catches her waist and she leans in to his arm but looks away as he looks on. Is he a suitor? A lover? A protector? An aide—or an equal? A mirage or a man?

The Sonatina is over. Minute 9:18.

11. WALTZ

||||||||||||||||||||||||||||||||||||||||||||||||||||||||||||||||||||||||||||||||||||||||||||||||||||

Now, at the start of the second movement, for the first time in *Serenade* a woman is partnered by a man. It is an alliance that extends her reach, supports her risks, and allows for her aerial life to rise. And expands the scope of her beauty.

It has often been said that Balanchine didn't care as much about his male dancers as he did about his female dancers, yet what greater need could they have answered for him than in serving his ballerinas? In Balanchine's world, men and women, whatever their story together—and it is often deep, often deeply erotic—inevitably part again, so despite whatever pain she suffers from love, she survives: this is predetermined. Balanchine's women are queens, and when they break, they make beauty. Their triumph ordained.

The men fare less well and often remain in their yearning, left alone after a brief encounter with a woman, real or imagined. Balanchine's beloved is forever just out of reach. He was no sentimentalist—more Brothers Grimm than Disney—and knew that "happily ever after" was but wishful whimsy. For Balanchine's woman, men were stops along the way, rarely destinations, and this is never more clearly stated than in *Serenade*—made just after he turned thirty years old. How did he know so much already?

From the Waltz Girl's soft release into this new man's embrace, he lifts her high in various grand jetés and arabesques, then pivots those arabesques in midair; he spins her, lifts her in arcs and circles; thus she floats. Then, staying earthbound, he puts his right hand about her waist and she places her right hand on his left shoulder while they face each other, but side by side. And they waltz, side to side across the stage. But it is not any waltz you have seen before.

Balanchine liked to say to us that the problem with waltzing was that the music was in three-quarter time—1-2-3, 1-2-3, 1-2-3—but that humans have only two legs: "It would be easier," he said, "if we had three legs." Here he eliminates the two-leg problem entirely. Intertwined with his partner, the man swoops his body and legs around in a deep semicircle while she keeps up with the swirling force of his movement by bourréeing on both her toe tips in tiny, tiny very fast steps, maybe one inch between each. But in parallel. They do this relay six times. She never comes off pointe. With her innocence and joy denoted by her delicate toe tipping, it is just about the sweetest dance between a man and a young woman you have ever seen.

During my years dancing *Serenade,* Joseph Duell was one of the few lead male dancers, along with the incomparable Adam Lüders, whom Balanchine trusted with this consummate job—the man who partners the Waltz Girl. The role is all about presence, elegance, line, and authoritative deference. Joe was particularly tall, lean, and handsome, and a strong, attentive partner, attaining a rare nobility onstage.

In the last decade of Balanchine's life, most of his lead male dancers were still not American trained but imported from Europe, most often from Denmark, where the detailed, fast, and pure technique of Bournonville training (unlike Russian or British training) rendered these dancers not only more able to dance Balanchine's speeds and precision but also more mentally prepared for his de-egotized aesthetic. Peter Martins, Adam Lüders, Ib Andersen, and Helgi Tomasson (from Iceland) all had the fantastic technique and self-effacing elegance that were hard to come by in American dancers. It was as if their being part of a tradition from such old and historied countries imbued them with the manners of aristocracy, without the Cagneyesque "Made it, Ma! Top of the world!" eagerness of young Americans.*

But Joe was as American as it gets—from Dayton, Ohio, one of five children, his father a former Baptist minister. Both he and his brother, Daniel, also a lead dancer in the company, somehow managed through their natural predilection, intelligence, and drive to become, well, almost European, to become American Balanchine dancers.

I knew Joe. We went through the School together, and we both attended a short-lived ethics class instigated by Lincoln Kirstein where Joe was pretty much a one-man participant: we girls sat on the floor, stretching, massaging sore muscles, sewing toe shoes, and trying out new updos while Joe held court on the meaning of a morality and duty that we all practiced but were uninterested in verbalizing. Except him. He once made the largest salad I had ever seen, mixed in his kitchen sink and transported in a cauldron to a rare Central Park picnic. In 1976, during a particularly energized and exciting time in the company when Balanchine was choreographing *Union Jack* with a cast of fifty, Joe played the drums with incredible exuberance for rehearsals, working with Mr. B musician to musician. As a dancer, he worked perhaps even harder than everyone else—no easy achievement. Joe worked morning, noon, and night, his focus on his apparent inadequacies was relentless.

He entered the company in 1975 but shortly was absent: he had some sort of breakdown. But he returned a few months later, and quickly rose through the ranks to soloist, then principal dancer. He was also very involved in extracurricular activities to educate about ballet and Balanchine: he gave lectures, hosted Ballet Guild luncheons, and began choreographing. He showed his first piece to Balanchine, who liked the invention but was not interested in the Elton John music. Later he choreographed for the company itself, at Balanchine's behest, to considerable success.

With his acumen and authority, Joe was considered by Lincoln

* However, Balanchine also loved this keen, open quality—most excitingly exemplified in the Americans Jacques d'Amboise and Edward Villella—and used it elsewhere.

Kirstein to be a likely successor to run the company after Balanchine. I was present at a meeting in 1985 at Kirstein's house, when, during a leadership crisis in the company, two years after Balanchine's death, he proposed the Duell brothers take over directing the company together: Danny the day-to-day, and Joe the artistic and choreographic. "Lincoln, I won't do it, I just won't do it," Joe said in a rare refusal of a Kirstein request. I remember him pacing back and forth as he said this, while we all stayed seated in the back room of Kirstein's Gramercy Park town house. Joe stood up to Lincoln in a way that was unimaginable to most of us.

On February 16, 1986, a sunny Sunday morning, at ten o'clock, Joe jumped out of the window of his Upper West Side brownstone apartment to his death. He had danced the lead in the second movement of *Symphony in C* at the matinee the day before. That evening he had rehearsed his role in Balanchine's ballet *Who Cares?* and when he finished his solo asked an onlooker: "Was that better?"

We were told just before the matinee performance. Stunned, devastated, dancers were weeping on every wall of the theater, stage makeup leaking down every face, but as when Balanchine died, we

Karin von Aroldingen and Joseph Duell, in a rare moment when a man is welcomed into the female world of *Serenade* (© *Paul Kolnik)*

danced as scheduled. It is the tribute we offer. Joe gave all he had; he was done. Born on April 30—the same date that Balanchine departed—Joe was twenty-nine years old.

While Joe clearly had his demons to battle, I continue to wonder if Balanchine had still been alive whether Joe would have jumped. Probably not then, anyway. The state of grace that had magnetically enveloped the New York City Ballet during Balanchine's late years began an inevitable fading in his absence, and signs, both small and large, backstage and onstage, physical and moral, appeared. Within six years of his death, the retirement of our most beloved remaining ballerinas, Patricia McBride and Suzanne Farrell (each had grown up with Balanchine since the early 1960s), removed from our midst two last, vital, irreplaceable pillars. (Violette Verdy, Melissa Hayden, and the translucent Allegra Kent had all retired before Balanchine's death.) These dancers were our examples, our solace, our reminders, our standards, each a source of radiance: their loss marked the end of the Balanchine era. For me, though, during those years of dancing Balanchine while still mourning him, Joe's suicide was the deepest cut of all.

Shortly after the Waltz Girl and her partner complete their duet, he does a large, quiet grand jeté off the stage, leaving her alone again: their communion has lasted just over one minute. Facing the audience, she kneels on stage right where he left her, arms outstretched to the side. As if called, eight of us, facing front, joined by our arms waist to waist, bourrée in from the far wing on her latitude and as we reach her, we kneel down beside her; an arm circles her waist, and she becomes one of us again, part of our lineup. Her interlude with a partner was beautiful, brief. There will be less brief ones to come. Especially when several other women join their affair.

We back up to form a stage-wide three-sided rectangle (the audience is the fourth side)—three dancers on each side, eight across the back of the stage for the long side—and while we hold hands for extra support, we each step forward into deep lunging penché arabesques, our back legs reaching high to the theater rafters, and then step back again, heads turned to our right. We do this sequence six times, and the effect is of a massive yet circumscribed field filled with high-kicking chorus girls. In the space inside the space we have created, various other dancers enter and exit and, sometimes together, sometimes alone, perform spins and spirals, pivot about each other, jump, hop, and lunge, leaning in and leaning out in an orderly maelstrom of activity. Minute 11:25.

We congregate in two horizontal lines of eight dancers each, and the Waltz Girl takes her place in front of us, in a classic lead dancer position. The man makes another brief entrance, arriving at her side just in time to join in the steps we all do, but when we all jump alone, he lifts her way up high as she performs our same steps. The ballet is rising.

We assemble in yet another formation: two diagonals of eight dancers each. The two lines meet on center upstage and fan outward to opposing sides, forming a stage-wide upside-down V to the audience. We each begin a simple three-part sequence in unison: soutenu turn, arms up above our heads, then down to one knee, head down, arms swooped behind us. Upon quickly standing we lean backward on one foot, the other extended in a tendu in front of us, and with both arms do a pliable push movement in front of ourselves. Each opposing diagonal does this sequence five times, but in alternating timing.

When one side kneels, the other side is pushing. When that side pushes, the other kneels. When they turn, the other pushes. For the other side, the juxtaposition is different: when they kneel, the other is pushing; when they push, the other is turning; and when they turn, the other is kneeling. These are what we call traveling steps, and as we proceed, each side of the V travels toward the other, crossing the stage, weaving between each other at the center. When we are halfway through five repeats, we form a perfect cross before moving forward.

While we do all this, the Russian Girl has taken center stage, the summit of our reversed V; as we cross the stage, she performs a series of turns and arabesques that lead her straight down the center of the stage toward the orchestra. By the time we finish, our V is perfectly re-created in reverse, its peak downstage, and there she meets us as our center, yet again. All this in words sounds complicated, intricate, even difficult, and when broken down in this way, it is. But each dancer has to know only her own steps and movement, and with Balanchine guiding us, the appearance is of an ultimate order. It is thrilling. Inevitable. Minute 13:42.

We bourrée into four lines and walk about to do elaborate bows to each other several times over. It is unusual for dancers to show reverence directly to their onstage peers. But then Balanchine goes one further. The Russian Girl walks forward and does a low bow to you, the audience, delivering her right leg to you and folding her body forward, over it. A curious breaking of the fourth wall, like a character in a film turning away from the action and speaking directly into the camera.

12. LITTLE GEORGI

Georgi Balanchivadze, age five
(*R. Charles, St. Petersburg*)

incoln Kirstein once told me that Mr. B was fond of the story of Amelia Arbunckle: The headmistress of a school announces in assembly that Amelia will sing the "Bell Song" from *Lakmé*. A voice from the back yells, "Amelia Arbunckle sucks!" The headmistress responds, "Nevertheless ..." Given the many naysayers over the decades, Balanchine said that "Nevertheless . . ." ought to be the motto of the company.

So who was George Balanchine? A poet of the body. But who was he really? I cannot tell you this; no one can. Nevertheless . . . a bit of history is in order. It won't, however, solve the mystery of how and why a very great artist comes to exist. And, like the history of *Serenade* itself, the story of Balanchine's early life in Russia is similarly apocryphal, dramatic, romantic, and tragic; and, as to hard facts, all but impossible to verify on many counts given the paucity of surviving records from before the Bolshevik Revolution. When Balanchine fled the land of his birth at age twenty, a door closed.

Over the decades, his biographers have told similar stories with slightly differing details about his childhood, and, to further confuse matters, Balanchine himself told varying versions—he was not above embellishing a good story. And he had no interest in writing his memoirs. When asked about his life, his loves, he said simply: "It's all in the programs." And there much of it remains, laid bare inside the storyless ballets and the ballerinas he cast in them.

What is clear is that the dramas of his young life were so extreme as to merit a tale by E. T. A. Hoffmann. From riches to rags: from playing four-handed piano with his mother and being a student dancer in the lavish court of Nicholas II, the last tsar of Russia, to, overnight, all-but-orphaned, enduring hunger, illness, and brutal cold. While his health was forever marked, his spirit, his purpose, emerged seemingly unbroken, if not fortified. Through it all, the theater—its allure, its dreams, its glory—remained the boy's cathedral of worship, the pageantry of reverence his beau ideal.

Georgi Melitonovich Balanchivadze's favorite game as a little boy was not to play a fireman or policeman or soldier or spy. It was to play a bishop. He would close the door to his room, enrobe himself, and stack a few chairs on top of one another to create an altar, and he would bless objects and conduct High Mass before his phantom flock.* He chose his profession early and never wavered. Signposts of a decided destiny abound in Balanchine's life. An acrostic he wrote as a child suggests his own perception:

* Another child who pretended to be a priest was Tsar Nicholas II.

Fate smiles on me.
I am Ba
My destiny in life is fixed.
I am Lan.
I see the keys to success.
I am Chi.
I will not turn back now.
I am Vad.
In spite of storm or tempest.
I am Ze.

When a talent for a certain profession is apparent in one so young and then manifests vastly, as it did with Mozart, it is clear that it was, somehow, ordained from birth. The fecundity of the artists' outpourings—in depth, generosity, variety, radiance—requires this explanation. It is as if these supernaturally great artists learned the mechanics of their craft like their peers, but their output incontestably dwarfs other able, even excellent, practitioners—as if they were conduits, born prefilled with their visions of as yet unknown beauty, and in their human form deliver them to the world during their short time here, allowing us to wake up, to hear, to see.

Balanchine was still conducting his services six decades later, with the theater, in our secular times, as his church, us dancers as his disciples, and you, the audience, as his congregation. His favorite subjects at school were arithmetic, religion, and music—the very three interests for a man destined to physicalize spirit into three dimensions through rhythm and harmonic composition. "The music passes through him," said Martha Graham, "and in the same natural yet marvelous way that a prism refracts light, he refracts music into dance."

Balanchine was born on January 22, 1904,* in the beautiful city founded by Tsar Peter the Great in 1703 on the shores of the Neva

---

* I will use, throughout, for consistency, our New Style calendar dates instead of the Old Style Russian dates from before 1918, which run thirteen days earlier.

River in northern Russia, not far from what is now Finland. St. Petersburg is that rare city that rose almost at once and under the direction of a single architect appointed by the tsar in 1716. Jean-Baptiste Alexandre le Blond was French and given the title of "Architect-General" of the Romanov dynasty. The northernmost large city in the world, St. Petersburg was the capital of Russia for almost two hundred years, from 1732 to 1918. Balanchine was born near its close, making him a lively relic of the imperial tsarist regime, an absolute monarchy that flaunted fairy-tale extravagance, opulence, and spectacle.

"I am often asked," said Balanchine later in life, "'What is your nationality, Russian or Georgian?' and I sometimes think, by blood I am Georgian, by culture Russian, but by nationality Petersburgian."

Meliton Balanchivadze, Balanchine's father, was a Georgian composer who had studied with Rimsky-Korsakov at the prestigious St. Petersburg Conservatory. He was a singer of Georgian folk songs and a composer of operas—called the "Georgian Glinka." He was also a committed bon vivant, benign rascal, and ready wit.

Balanchine's mother, Maria Nikolaevna, eleven years younger than his father, was Russian born, but little more is known of her origins. She was most likely illegitimate, of unclear parentage. It has been suggested that her father may have been German, from a distinguished family—the von Almedingens—and that her mother may have been Jewish. It has been said that she met Balanchivadze as his housekeeper, as his landlady's daughter, or perhaps as his bank teller. But none of this conjecture has been verified, though one hopes a future biographer can settle the matter. Balanchine's mother remains barely more than a vision, as seen in one photograph, dressed in white, serene, elegant, and beautiful. Her aristocratic profile is not unlike Balanchine's, though softer, less articulated.

Balanchine was the most reserved of her three children—his younger brother, Andrei, described him as "closed in, and dry." "Everyone wants to be the favorite child in a family," Balanchine said of himself, "but not everyone has the luck." Due to the early loss of his mother—he never saw her again after age fourteen, though there was intermittent correspondence in the years after—she, unavoidably, emerges as the original archetype for the most persistent, central, and beloved of Balanchine muses: the woman ever unknown, ever out of reach, and therefore most desired. Even if one is not charmed by Freud, Balanchine's mostly missing mother inevitably obtains an almost mythical place when considering her son's ensuing love of woman, and the towering body of work, the great gallery of portraits—the most significant in all dance history—that resulted from his profound, searching-for-but-never-possessed love.

What is known is that Maria was not very well educated, was religious—Russian Orthodox—played the piano, loved music and theater, and was not married to Meliton Balanchivadze when her four children (Nina, a girl born in 1900, died) were born during the first six years of the new century. There are three existing christening documents that record each of her surviving babies—Tamara, Georgi, and Andrei—as a child of "the unmarried Maria Nikolaevna Vasilieva." Balanchine, like his mother, appears to have been illegitimate—though it also appears that he never knew this.

Balanchivadze had a wife and two children he had left—perhaps abandoned—at age twenty-seven, in 1889 in Georgia, in order to study music at the famed conservatory in St. Petersburg. His Georgian son, Balanchine's older half brother, was, curiously, named Apollon, the name of Balanchine's first masterpiece in 1928. There are many such prophetic connections in Balanchine's life.

Sometime after 1905, Meliton and Maria seem to have married—but was he divorced? a bigamist?—and in 1906, when Georgi was two, Balanchivadze legally recognized his three children with her. Along the way, various certificates—as those from the Imperial Theatre School—were likely forged to record their children as legitimately born.

A key event determining Balanchine's childhood came in the unlikely form of a lottery ticket. In 1901, three years before his birth, his mother held a winning ticket that amounted to two hundred thousand gold rubles—the equivalent of several million dollars today. The couple was rich overnight, and for the first seven years of Balanchine's life, the family resided in various enormous apartments—one had twelve rooms—in St. Petersburg, while also building a stately country dacha in what is now Finland, three hours by train from St. Petersburg.

The household featured servants, nursemaids, and tutors, with lavish feasts accompanied by costumed entertainments, and much merriment. Derailed from his musical destiny by the fast fortune, Meliton dallied in various speculative ventures, most unsuccessful, from wine importing and purchasing land and a roof-tiling factory, to investment in Georgian restaurants.

By 1911, when Georgi was seven, the fortune was all but gone, the debtors came calling, and his father disappeared for a while, either to debtor's prison (Balanchine's version) or house arrest elsewhere, while his family gave up their St. Petersburg abode and moved to the dacha to await his eventual return.

Whatever his parental bloodlines were, Balanchine was Russian Orthodox through and through. Balanchine's paternal grandfather, Amiran Balanchivadze, was a priest in Georgia, and the young boy took religion to heart. When he was about six years old, he was taken to the Kazan Cathedral in St. Petersburg to witness the symbolic burial and resurrection ceremony of the archbishop of Tbilisi as he became a monk. Before the altar, the archbishop lay facedown on the ground, arms spread to the side, covered with a giant black shroud: the secular man interred, the holy man born. This was the great theater of Russian Orthodoxy. Balanchine never forgot and would re-create this haunting transposition seventy-five years later, in one of his final works, to the last movement of Tschaikovsky's *Pathétique Symphony*.

Balanchine's parents foresaw a career in the military for him, like one of his uncles and his half brother, Apollon, and took him in 1913 to apply at the prestigious Cadet Corps in St. Petersburg. The academy was full and suggested he wait and reapply the following year. That same year his older sister, Tamara, was taken to audition, for the second time, at the Imperial Theatre School. Both academies, military and dancing, were fully subsidized, not by the government but as part of the tsar's household. On this occasion, a school official saw the girl's quiet, proud little brother, likely lingering in a hallway, and suggested he audition too. Why not? How many male dancers began because of a dancing sister?

Tamara was again refused, but, after the two-day audition, Georgi was accepted. Founded in 1738 by Anna Ivanovna, empress of Russia, during her ten-year rule, the school, as an offshoot of the Cadet Corps, was a regimented boarding academy where the carefully chosen students wore elegant, military-like uniforms and were taught Russian, French, arithmetic, religion, and dance under both spartan (cold baths each morning) and imperial (gold-trimmed coaches) conditions in preparation for a career on the stage.

Georgi was nine years old, didn't like to dance, had never been to a school (the Balanchivadze children had tutors at home), and was, on the very same day as his acceptance, abruptly left by his mother, against his will, to become the school's youngest boarder. He "felt like a dog that had just been taken out and abandoned," he told his first biographer. Traumatized by this sudden separation, he immediately ran away from the school, taking refuge with an aunt who lived in St. Petersburg. But she promptly returned the little boy, and within a year he had fallen down the rabbit hole that is the theater, the ballet, that world that is better than the world, a place defined by a stage, an orchestra pit, a proscenium, and the great curtain that reveals and conceals. And those lustrous creatures who drifted about on their toe tips.

His first glimpse of this magic kingdom was from the stage of the sumptuous, glittering, gold, white, and blue Maryinsky Theatre when, during his second year at the school, he was chosen to play a role in Act III of *The Sleeping Beauty*. "I was Cupid, a tiny Cupid," he said. "I was set down on a golden cage. And suddenly everything opened!" An elaborate production, it is famous to this day for its two-hundred-member cast, multicolored lighting, real foliage, fountains cascading real water, live horses, and multiple moving, rising, descending, and turning stages all nestled inside the warm splendor of Tschaikovsky's ravishing score.

There was one more way that the busy students would have peeks, literally, of the profession they were training for. Though forbidden, one by one, they would take turns spying through a keyhole on the great ballerinas Tamara Karsavina and Mathilda Kschesinskaya as they rehearsed. They also would catch glimpses of these enchanting women as they departed the building swathed in their perfume and furs, like Hollywood divas.

Cupid in a golden cage onstage, but offstage Georgi was given the nickname of Rat because of the occasional tic, a sniff, that he had all his life, as if he were wiggling his whiskers, appraising the cheese. This sniff became an all-important symbol to his dancers, taking on over time the impact of his whole being, as he would observe with such speed and acuteness as to redefine a dancer's hopes in seconds. One sniff and he knew you better than you knew yourself.

In school, Balanchivadze memorized Pushkin, Lermontov, Griboyedov, and Mayakovsky and learned ballroom dancing, fencing, pantomime, and piano alongside ballet. And he played the piano better than anyone else. At night, in the dormitory, under the covers, he devoured detective stories featuring Sherlock Holmes, Nick Carter, and Nat Pinkerton, and the novels of Jules Verne. He loved the movies, in particular films from the German UFA studios with Conrad Veidt and Werner Krauss.

On his deathbed, Balanchine spoke of his years at the school with the wonder attending a lost world:

> This was a court school! We had special uniforms—light blue, very handsome, silver lyres on our collars and caps— and we were driven around in carriages. Two men in livery sat on the coachbox! Like Cinderella! . . . We were all the Tsar's dependents. We had servants and lackeys at the school: all handsome men in uniform, buttoned from top to bottom. We got up, washed, dressed, and took off. We didn't make the beds we left everything. The servants took care of it . . . We were presented to Nicholas II, son of Alexander III, Tschaikovsky's patron . . . The Tsar's box at the Maryinsky Theatre is on the side (not in the center) on the right. It had a separate entrance, a separate foyer, with a large private driveway. When you come in it's like a colossal apartment: chandeliers, the walls covered in light blue. The Emperor sat there with his whole family—Empress Alexandra Feodorovna, the heir, his daughters—and we would be lined up by size and presented . . . The Tsar was not tall. The Tsaritsa was a very tall, beautiful woman . . . The grand princesses, Nicholas's daughters, were also beauties. The Tsar had protruding light-colored eyes, and he rolled his R's. If he said, "Well, how are you?" we were supposed to click our heels and reply, "Highly pleased, Your Imperial Majesty."

. . .

This memorable event took place on the tsar's name day of December 6 in 1916, when Georgi was twelve years old. He was described by a fellow student at this time as "very thin, pale—almost transparent—with black smooth hair, wide-apart eyes, and a generous mouth." Eleven days later Rasputin was brutally murdered: the regime-changing revolution had begun. While the Theatre School had continued cocooned and curiously undisturbed through the first years of World War I (but for sugar rations one day a week), when the Bolshevik Revolution broke out three months later, in early March 1917, everything changed. The protected, opulent world of the tsar's rule crumbled forever.

The school closed, and the Balanchivadze family dispersed. Georgi went to live nearby with his aunt and brother and was soon joined by his mother, who worked outside the city in a war hospital. His father escaped to his native Georgia, while his sister stayed with an uncle in Kasimov, over six hundred miles away. A cholera epidemic raged, and pneumonia was prevalent. By early 1918 most of the Balanchivadze family had trickled back to Tbilisi, but Georgi was left in St. Petersburg (now renamed Petrograd) with his mother. Though mother and son received exit visas that October to escape to Georgia, they did not go. There is evidence that his mother was still in Petrograd three years later, though Georgi did not live with her.

There was no money and no food. Georgi went to work at odd jobs as a messenger, as a saddler's assistant, and playing the piano wearing gloves in unheated silent-movie theaters. He watched horses drop dead in the streets from starvation and people leap on the carcasses with knives to carve out their dinner. Looters were shot, and cats were killed and eaten and became scarce. "The worst part," Balanchine said, "was being hungry." The dancers performed anything, anywhere, for survival: "We did a Hindu dance at the circus," Balanchine recalled, "and for every performance we got a loaf of bread." Typhus, lice, and boils proliferated with the famine and brutal cold, weakening Balanchine's constitution for the rest of his life.

The school reopened in the fall of 1919 once Lenin had been convinced that ballet and opera were not inherently "decadent." The ushers at the theater were stripped of their uniforms with the tsarist epaulets. The audience at the Maryinsky changed too. "We had soldiers and sailors come," said Balanchine. "They smoked in the theatre, ate sunflower seeds, tapped their heavy boots in time to the music. They sat on the railings of the boxes, legs dangling . . . water froze in the pipes and they burst. Ice floated in the sinks. The corps de ballet wore long-sleeved T-shirts under their costumes. But what could the poor prima dancers do? They got pneumonia, one after the other."

Around this time, an ambitious young man of sixteen named Yuri Slonimsky went to the theater and came to know the teenage Balanchivadze:

> Balanchine possessed an astonishing ability to win people's favor, to inspire sympathy . . . This was due to his sincerity, his modesty, and above all, his kindness. I single out this final trait; it was one of the primary determinants of his behavior. He responded eagerly to any need and offered help without ostentation . . . Balanchine was happy for the opportunity to render any service.

Zinaida Serebryakova's painting of Georgi Balanchivadze in 1922, age eighteen

The stage door to the theater was a sacred, heavily guarded portal marked by a sign reading "Interdict" ("Forbidden"), but in one of his earliest choreographic forays, Balanchine, already the leader of his student peers, arranged for a group of them to surround his new friend Slonimsky "in a dense mass" and directed them to whirl in a tight turning cluster past the guards, bringing the concealed boy into the "holy of holies," the bustling, forbidden backstage area of the Maryinsky Theatre. "I trembled with happy excitement before an unfolding new world," wrote Slonimsky. "I found in one instant the enchanted world which would possess me for the rest of my long life." Slonimsky, who became a much-respected critic of Russian ballet and theater, remembered the boy who had spirited him across "the Rubicon" as being a "sorcerer's apprentice."

Balanchivadze graduated from the school with honors in 1921 and was offered a place in the corps de ballet at the Maryinsky Theatre. His graduation performance, on April 4, 1921, was attended by, among others, Agrippina Vaganova and Pavel Gerdt, two of the still-legendary great ballet teachers in the art's history. It was noted that the young Balanchivadze was an "especially reliable partner." The previous year he had also enrolled in the Petrograd Conservatory, where he studied music for three years, thus taking on a huge workload as both a professional dancer and a musician.

Balanchivadze had made his first dance at age sixteen, while still at the school. A four-minute pas de deux titled *La Nuit* set to lush, romantic music by Anton Rubinstein, it was described by Alexandra Danilova as a "sexy number" where "the boy conquered the girl, lifted her in arabesque and held her with a straight arm overhead, then carried her off into the wings—so, she was HIS!" The dance caused a small furor for its overt eroticism, with the female dancer wearing a Greek-like tunic, not a tight tutu, her loose hair held by a single ribbon, and legs and lifts with "tender transitions" extending in unexpected directions. There was talk of dismissing young Balanchivadze from the school, and he was "reproached for indecency"—though the ballet was performed for decades in Russia, long after Balanchine had departed.

There it was in his first dance, while he was just a teenager: his life's devotion declared to yearning, soaring music, a romantic encounter between a boy and girl, entwined limbs, extended legs—though this outcome of successful male conquest in Balanchine's oeuvre was short-lived. Soon, and for the rest of his life, it was the man who was conquered, ever pursuing the impossible beloved.

Within a year of graduating and becoming a member of the Maryinsky, Balanchivadze organized a small troupe of about fifteen dancers, his first company, his "accidental brain child," as one critic noted. They called themselves the "Young Ballet"—and young they were: ages sixteen to eighteen. The group met in their spare time, sewed their own costumes, rehearsed late into the night, and performed for free. He titled the first program with astonishing nerve bordering on impudence that now looks like premonition: "The Evolution of Ballet: from Petipa through Fokine to Balanchivadze." All the dances were choreographed by Balanchivadze and set to Ravel, Chopin, and even a musical composition of his own called "Extase"—"Ecstasy."

In the course of its year or so in existence, the group premiered about fourteen pieces by the ambitious young choreographer, whose lifelong credo—veneration for tradition while being fiercely progressive—was already evident: conservative and radical in equal doses. "This evening has demonstrated that slowly and painfully," wrote one critic, "as with all living things, ballet is being reborn"; "Balanchine is bold and insolent," wrote another, "but in his insolence one can see genuine creativity and beauty. Although in classical work he does misuse poses, he combines them in such an interesting way and creates such beautiful if unexpected transitions that one can grudgingly excuse this defect."

Balanchivadze was extraordinarily busy in 1923 with multiple jobs: in addition to the Young Ballet, at the start of the 1923–24 season, he was named balletmaster of the Maly Opera Theatre, where he made three new works while also performing in *Tannhäuser, Prince Igor, Swan Lake,* and *Le Corsaire* at the Maryinsky, as well as making a *pièce d'occasion* for the great ballerina Elizaveta Gerdt, at her request, for a benefit performance, and choreographing a program for a St. Petersburg cabaret called the Carousel. And he was still playing piano for classes at the school for three hours a day and studying music at the conservatory. He said yes to all, a multitude of apprenticeships. The one thing he did less and less of was dance himself.

The Young Ballet became the talk of St. Petersburg, and soon the name of Balanchivadze became known. In December, he appeared on the cover of *Teatp* (Theatre) magazine in an astonishing photo, looking like a mélange of Chopin and Lord Byron. He was nineteen years old and clearly putting some effort into cultivating a romantic, brooding countenance: his dark hair hanging long and straight over his forehead and down one side of his pale face, his dark eyes enhanced by dark shadow, his fingernails painted, he wore a black jacket and a cameo bracelet. "His whole presence projected the confidence of a leader," said one friend, "with his aquiline features, and Byronic hair, he seemed a combination of poet and general." He remained an elegant and idiosyncratic dresser to the end—though he gave up the eye shadow and shining nails sooner than later.

The previous year, in October 1922, he married the beautiful, educated Tamara Gevergeyeva, a student attending an evening program of classes at the ballet school. The bride and groom were, respectively, seventeen and eighteen years old. The bride's father,

A Byronic Balanchivadze, age nineteen, as he appeared on the cover of *Teatp* magazine, December 11, 1923

Levky Ivanovich Gervergeyev, was a rich and cultured businessman who owned a brocade mill that made vestments for the clergy. The family lived in a twenty-five-room mansion with a vast library of first editions of rare books and an impressive art collection. Tamara (later known as Tamara Geva), with fair hair, blue eyes, and high cheekbones, became the first of Balanchine's wives.

On April 4, 1924, five dancers of the Young Ballet—now calling themselves the "Principal Dancers of the Soviet State Ballet"—applied for permission from the government to do a concert tour in Europe and managed to convince the commissars that their tour would be good propaganda. Just prior to their departure, on June 16, one of their group, a feisty young dancer named Lidia Ivanova, mysteriously drowned in a boating accident while with some admiring fans. Her death, never resolved, was suspected by most, including Balanchivadze, to have been a setup, a premeditated murder—she had overheard something dangerous while socializing with Communist officials. With suspicious timing, the troupe's exit visas—minus one—arrived the day after Ivanova's death.

On July 4, the small, grief-stricken group, which included Tamara, dancers Alexandra Danilova and Nicholas Efimov, manager Vladimir Dimitriev, conductor Vladimir Dranishnikov, and musicians, set sail on a German ship. They arrived in the West four days later with Balanchivadze as their leader—and no scheduled performances. Once they reached Berlin, they received a telegram from Moscow instructing them to return immediately, and while the conductor and singers obeyed the order, the dancers did not. "We paid no attention to that telegram, as simple as that," said Balanchine, although he also made clear later that this was no dramatic leap to freedom due to "moral principle" or a stand against censorship—it was because they needed to find work.

They quickly hustled up some concert dates at spas in the Rhineland and a few gigs in London. During the tour, a telegram arrived with money from Serge Diaghilev. They had been summoned by the formidable Russian impresario—whose dictum was "Étonne-moi!" ("Astonish me!")—to audition for the Ballets Russes, the company that had taken Paris by storm in 1909 and changed the face of Western dance forever.

Safely ensconced in Europe just days before his twenty-first birthday, Balanchivadze, who had lived through fourteen years in the plush world of Russia's last tsar and seven years of poverty and privation under the Bolsheviks, and already had thirty-five works to his name, became Diaghilev's last choreographer, launching his career into the West.

13. THE AMERICAN

M atisse? Who's Matisse?" Balanchivadze asked when told that he would be working with him. Upon being hired for the Ballets Russes, along with his small group of dancers, he embarked on a crash course in early modernism: his steeping in imperial Russian culture received a gigantic jolt that would plunge him, within just a few short years, into the epicenter of his own genius.

Diaghilev—it was he who Frenchified his new protégé's name to Georges Balanchine—asked him if he could make opera ballets "very fast." He could. Between February 1925 and May 1929 he choreographed no less than fifty-eight dances—not just opera ballets but pas de deux, restagings, and full ballets. Nothing was above him, or beneath him, so long as it was theater: he choreographed, uncredited, the numbers for music hall maestro Charles Cochran's 1929 London revue *Wake Up and Dream* to Cole Porter songs, and moonlighted as "G. Bulanchin" in three dances for Balieff's *Chauve-Souris* (which was performed at Jolson's 59th Street Theatre in New York City in January 1929—though without "Mr. Bulanchin's" presence).

With Diaghilev, Balanchine was immersed among a virtual who's who of early-twentieth-century culture. In dance there was Pavlova, Karsavina, Nijinsky, Massine, Lifar, Dolin, Markova, Spessivtseva, Doubrovska, and Danilova; in music there was Ravel, Debussy, Prokofiev, and Stravinsky; and in design there was Picasso, Miró, Braque, de Chirico, Bérard, Chanel, Cocteau, Bakst, and Tchelitchev. Years later, however, Balanchine was dismissive of this onslaught of visual influence. "I don't get my ideas from looking at paintings," he said. "I worked with Georges Rouault, Utrillo, Matisse, and André Derain, but they had no influence on me." His later plotless, decorless, costumeless ballets are testament to his rejection of any interference or competition with the dancing itself.

In 1927, after a bad knee injury, Balanchine transitioned completely from dancer to balletmaster; his marriage to Tamara Geva dissolved and she left the company. He became lovers with Danilova, with whom he lived for some years and who has come to be considered the second of his five wives, despite the fact that they couldn't marry, as it was not yet possible, due to the political upheaval in Russia, for him to obtain his marriage papers in order to divorce.

Within the year, Diaghilev presented Balanchine with a new score by the forty-six-year-old Igor Stravinsky, and the lifelong collaboration of two of the century's titans began. *Apollon musagète*, with music like smooth glass, of celestial gravity (Diaghilev described it as "somehow not of this world, but from somewhere else above") had choreography to match: *Apollo* (as it was later called) "doesn't just demand good dancers," said Danilova, who was in the original production, "it demands goddesses." The ballet premiered in Paris on June 12, 1928, and was the twenty-four-year-old choreographer's first masterpiece. "*Apollo* is about poetry," wrote Edwin Denby, "poetry in the sense of a brilliant, sensuous, daring and powerful activity," referring to the ballet's "grace, its sweet wit, its force and boldness," its "limpid grandeur."

Balanchine later said, in a rare elucidation, that this ballet about the birth and education of the young god of music and poetry was a "turning point" in his life: "It seemed to tell me that I could dare to not use everything, that I, too, could eliminate," he explained. "I began to see how I could clarify, by limiting, by reducing what seemed to be multiple possibilities to the one that is inevitable."

The roles of the ballet were uncannily prophetic: the male artist and three female artists who become his muses was a theme that reemerged five years later in *Serenade*—and many times again after that. Balanchine's dictum was written early and at once.

Balanchine was not only Diaghilev's final choreographer but

also the only one—aside from Nijinska, a woman—who was not also the impresario's lover. Diaghilev referred, in fact, to Balanchine's "morbid interest in women." This morbidity received a new spin early in the following year when he choreographed his only dance to Sergei Prokofiev, *Le Fils prodigue* (*The Prodigal Son*), the biblical tale of the wayward son whose adventures in lust and greed and iniquity culminate in a stunning pas de deux between the Prodigal Son and the Siren, a woman who towers over him, seduces him, and all but suffocates him in the vise of her legs, leaving him broken, torn, and mystified: ripe for redemption. Agnes de Mille called this dance "one of the most important seductions to be found on any modern stage." Balanchine's first great octopussian Amazonian woman was born—she would have numerous incarnations—and his love of long, long legs would only grow with time.

In August 1929, seven months after the premiere of *Prodigal Son*, the twenty-two-year-old son of a prominent Jewish family from Boston, just graduated from Harvard, was touring Europe—a classic Jamesian American searching out the cultural history and masterpieces his own young country had yet to produce. Lincoln Kirstein had been intrigued by the ballet he had already seen performed stateside by touring companies. "Their thrilling dances then gave me a sharp pang or yearning to get a closer view of things immeasurable and unattainable," he wrote, "which I attribute to the silent and nebulous precision of all they do."

On this particular day, Kirstein was with a friend in Venice, looking for the El Grecos at San Giorgio dei Greci, when he happened upon the funeral of Serge Diaghilev. "In the center of the floor was a bier guarded by four large wooden gilt candles," he wrote soon after in his autobiographical novel, *Flesh is Heir*. He continued:

> This gathering was the end, the last noble congress that was to sit a period at the end of an epoch. A dynasty had ended, the king [Diaghilev] was interred on the Island of Saint Michael among the marble headstones and the cypresses . . . It was the end indeed, the end of youth for a distinguished

company of human beings, the end of power and endeavour, the end perhaps of the first quarter of the twentieth century . . . This must have been the immemorial atmosphere that hovered above the death beds of all kings from Egypt from Versailles when there was no heir and blackness faced the succession . . . "Fin du siècle . . . Fin d'un epoque? Non, m'sieu—Fin du monde."

"The end of the world"? With "no heir"? The fact that this young man who within just a few years would bring ballet to America in the person of George Balanchine had landed, by chance, before the coffin of the Russian impresario who had given rebirth to ballet in Europe is, as history testifies, a verifiable act of destiny, a passing of the mantle. Or perhaps the grasping of it.

After Diaghilev's death, the Ballets Russes promptly disbanded, bankrupt, and Balanchine spent the next few years bouncing around Europe doing numerous choreographic odd jobs for British music halls, the Royal Danish Ballet, and the Ballet Russe de Monte Carlo (one of myriad short-lived "Ballets Russes" that popped up post-Diaghilev). While working at the Paris Opera Ballet, Balanchine contracted pneumonia and pleurisy that turned into tuberculosis. He was sent to a sanatorium in Haute-Savoie, where, like a dancing Hans Castorp, for three months his life hung in the balance, his frailty enhanced by the years of cold and starvation in Russia. He refused surgery and emerged with portions of each lung permanently impaired. After this he liked to say that the remainder of his life was a second life, one unintended: Balanchine was a dead man dancing.

In early 1933, back to work, he assembled a small company, for which he made six new ballets. Les Ballets 1933 lasted for just two brief seasons in June and July—one in Paris, one in London—and cost its British benefactor, Edward James, a fortune in a failed attempt to please his wife, Tilly Losch, who starred in two of the works. By mid-July the company had already disbanded. But Kirstein had seen enough: "I knew I must find Balanchine if I was serious about anything." Through Romola Nijinsky, wife of dancer Vaslav Nijinsky, Kirstein, an unknown twenty-six-year-old, wangled an introduction to the choreographer in London.

Lincoln Kirstein, photographed
by Walker Evans in 1931, age
twenty-four, two years before
bringing Balanchine to America
*(The Museum of Fine Arts, Hous-
ton, Museum purchase funded by
Louisa Stude Sarofim © Walker
Evans Archive, The Metropolitan
Museum of Art)*

I asked Balanchine if he would like to come to America
to found a school and a ballet company . . . He replied that
something like that had always been his hope, but at the
present he had a good offer to become the balletmaster of
the Royal Opera House, Copenhagen, where he had already
served, and also the Paris Opéra wished to have him. But
he readily admitted that America was far more tempting . . .
My mind jumped forward in time and I saw the completed
school achieved and functioning, and even more, a great
stage swarming with dancers the school had trained, situated
somewhere in America. It was exasperating and exhausting
to think concretely of ways and means to make the mirage
a miraculous reality.

On July 16, Kirstein wrote from his London hotel a sixteen-page
letter to his friend Arthur Everett "Chick" Austin, a Harvard cohort
and then the director of the Wadsworth Atheneum in Hartford.
This document, a rarity in the relatively letterless domain of ballet history, also marks an actual moment that changed that history,
and shifted Kirstein's "mirage" into "miraculous reality." Here it is,
in part:

Dear Chick,

This will be the most important letter I will ever write you
as you will see. My pen burns my hand as I write: words will
not flow into the ink fast enough. We have a real chance to
have an American ballet within 3 years time . . . Do you know
Georges Balanchine? If not he is Georgian called Georgei
Balanchivadze. He is, personally, enchanting—dark, very slight,
a superb dancer and the most ingenious technician in ballet
I have ever seen . . . he wants to proceed, with new ideas and
young dancers . . . Balanchine is willing to devote all his time
to this for 5 yrs. He believes the future of ballet lies in America
as do I. I see a great chance for you to do a hell of a lot here . . .
This school can be the basis of a national culture as intense
as the great Russian Renaissance of Diaghilev . . . No first
dancers. NO STARS. A perfect ESPRIT DE CORPS . . . It
is absolutely necessary to keep Balanchine to ourselves . . . He
is an honest man, a serious artist and I'd stake my life on his
talent. In two years . . . he could achieve a miracle, and right
under our eyes: I feel this chance too serious to be denied. It
will mean a life work to all of us . . . I wish to God that you
were here: that you could know what I am writing is true, and
that I am not either over-enthusiastic or visionary. Please,
please, Chick, if you have any love for anything we do both
adore, rack your brains and try to make this all come true . . .
I won't be able to hear from you for a week, but I won't sleep
till I do . . . We have the future in our hands. For Christ's sweet
sake let us honor it.

Yours devotedly,
Lincoln

Thanks to the passion—and hastily pooled finances—of a
few ambitious, well-educated, cultured, too-big-for-their-britches
American boys, steered by Kirstein, the deed was done. "I began to
sense that somehow I was now fatally aligned," wrote Kirstein, "with
a commanding historical process." After a flurry of telegrams, wired
money, lost wired money, lost addresses, missed connections, and

endless paperwork, Balanchine, twenty-nine, arrived in America on October 17, 1933. But he was not alone: he had insisted on bringing his right-hand man, Vladimir Dimitriev, who managed, and mismanaged, things for Balanchine and the fourteen-year-old prodigy "Baby Ballerina," Tamara Toumanova—called the "Black Pearl" of the Russian Ballet, "the loveliest creature in the history of ballet"— and her formidable Mama.

The glamorous Toumanova went on to an illustrious career as a ballerina and her dark, sensual beauty was so arresting that she was asked to appear in six Hollywood movies—always as a dancer— working with Billy Wilder, Alfred Hitchcock, Gregory Peck, and Gene Kelly. Her love for Balanchine was lifelong, as for so many of his dancers—she had known him as a child, he had "discovered" her in Paris, and like him, she had Georgian blood, they were all but family. "All the ladies were in love with him," she said later. "He was like the ocean. I think the waves kept coming to him. . . . What Balanchine gave . . . was the likeness of the sun and the moon. Both."

Upon disembarking from the *Olympic* ocean liner, surviving sister of the *Titanic,* the unlikely group was immediately detained by immigration officers at Ellis Island. "They didn't want to let us into America," Balanchine said later, "but Lincoln Kirstein took care of everything"—as he would continue to do for the rest of the choreographer's life, removing endless obstacles and enabling George Balanchine to do his work.

Within a few months of landing in New York, he was showing American girls where to stand in the studio on Madison Avenue in what would become *Serenade.* "I became a choreographer," he said simply, "because I wanted to move people around." Before he was thirty, Balanchine had known abundance and aristocracy as well as illness and deprivation. And total separation from his family—this man who kept almost nothing in the material world kept all the letters from his mother until his death. He knew loss on both grand and small scales, and his ballets for the next fifty years would be filled with this loss, his loss, the unutterable, thus danceable, beauty of loss, none more than *Serenade,* a ballet about ghosts. But the ghosts were lively ones, in tight topknot buns, with swooping black eyelashes and the high-strung bodies of thoroughbreds at the starting gate.

. . .

We are now near the end of the second movement, seventeen of us dispersing after the giant crossing, randomly—a rare time where direction is not precisely prescribed, though time is always precisely prescribed—around the stage in the "drags" in the final moments of the Waltz, leaning deeply sideways at the waist, as if being pushed to one side, then the other by an invisible force, one of many such forces, arms alternately overhead, completing the curve of the side semicircle. Twelve girls "drag" themselves all the way into the wings and offstage, while the Russian Girl and four of us—the Russian Girls—assemble into a tight group center stage, beside one another but staggered so as to be even closer to each other than side-by-side would allow.

Our feet are in B+: we are standing on a straight right leg, with the left leg bent at the knee and locked tight to the knee of the straight leg, while the left foot is extended behind, crossed over, in an upside-down arched pointe, toe shoe tip curled under, gently resting on the stage floor. B+ is a NYCB term—meaning literally "Balanchine cross"—a shorthand developed by necessity from such frequent use of this position.

We each bring our arms down, softly rounded in ovals, fingertips all but touching those of the other hand, and, on the final beat of the violins, we raise our arms in unison above our heads in slightly overlapping circles—the result of our staggered lineup—au couronne, "crowning" our bodies, while our elbows barely crisscross each other's, no space between. As our arms rise, we turn our heads softly to the right. Not flat right, but tilted so the left cheek is just barely offering itself outward, upward. This is the head position Mr. B spoke so frequently about, "as if waiting for a kiss." While I never saw him plant such a kiss on a sloped cheek, it was enough for us to all imagine. We understood and remembered easily. It was a placement of the head dictated entirely by love, by desire—thus our immediate and accurate execution. And Mr. B getting exactly what he wanted: a stance of beauty, filled with just a little yearning, the barest of offerings, neck slightly exposed and extended. He enticed romance from us, though we only concentrated on getting positions correct for him.

The second movement is over. Minute 14:31.

Serenade is now all but half completed in actual time, but the drama—the man-woman one—has yet to begin. Despite the two brief entrances of a single male dancer in this movement, we have begun and ended without him, without his appearing to be much more than a phantom supporting partner to the Waltz Girl. All this is about to shift into mysterious intimacies in the next movement—the Russian Dance, *Tema russo*—a section of the ballet that once wasn't even there.

14. THE COMPOSER

n 1934, Balanchine choreographed just the first three of the four movements of the musical score.* Then, when he did add the missing movement—*Allegro con spirito*—six years later, he placed it third, not last, as Tschaikovsky composed it. And he left it there.† Well, it takes a lot of chutzpah to change the order of a composer's score, particularly when he is one of Tschaikovsky's stature, but with Balanchine, authority—the authority I witnessed daily—was so deep, so natural, it just flowed, like water, a given fact, not a learned, or earned, much less assumed, attribute. I have never known a man so clear.

Besides, Mr. B was close to Tschaikovsky, and had, he explained to us, frequent consultations with him, including, apparently, the occasional phone call, and the composer often "helped"—and, with curious frequency, approved!

Bernard Taper, Balanchine's first biographer, reports an exchange

---

* In 1915 at the Maryinsky, Michel Fokine choreographed a ballet named *Eros* to the same first three movements of *Serenade*. Balanchine likely saw a revival in 1922, and stated later, "I didn't like it very much, so I did *Serenade* my own way." Fokine's version included the roles of a youth, a young woman, Eros, an angel, and a corps of nymphs in white tunics. The ballet was condemned by critics of the day.

† Of more than 217 musical recordings of *Serenade,* only longtime NYCB conductor Robert Irving's holds to Balanchine's altered order of movements.

that illustrates Balanchine's effortless rapport with Tschaikovsky. After deciding on the metronome tempo of sixty-nine for a recording being made of *Serenade*'s final movement, Balanchine asked our superb conductor, Robert Irving, "What does Tschaikovsky say?" After checking the composer's arrangement, Irving reported, "Ninety-six." "It must be a misprint," Balanchine replied—and decided on sixty-six, even slower.

Tschaikovsky's death, just over ten years prior to Balanchine's birth, provided little impediment—and perhaps considerable assistance—to their bond: they were St. Petersburgers! "Petersburg is a European city that arose in Russia by miracle," Balanchine explained, and "I was born in the Petersburg that Tchaikovsky had walked in." Tschaikovsky, he said, was a "Russian European." Like Balanchine.

So great was Balanchine's reverence for his compatriot that he agreed to meet, in the final months of his life, over thirty times with the Russian writer and musicologist Solomon Volkov to speak (in Russian) about Tschaikovsky. At a time when most of us will talk of ourselves, setting the record or setting it straight, Balanchine wanted to talk about Tschaikovsky. He loved him, really loved him—the music *and* the man.

"I don't quite understand how they examine the life and the works separately," Balanchine told Volkov. The result is a telling twinning: Balanchine's life and work filtered through Tschaikovsky's life and work. "Tchaikovsky is Pushkin in music," said Balanchine, "supreme craftsmanship, exact proportions, majesty." One can, I believe, with neither exaggeration nor melodrama, conclude, by evidence of *Serenade* alone, that these two "Russian Europeans" indeed have a truly mystical bond—of country, culture, soul, and sound—that was sealed onstage, night after night, in Balanchine's theater.

Pyotr Illyich Tschaikovsky is the musical father of classical ballet. "Tchaikovsky was convinced from the days of his youth," said Balanchine in 1982, "that ballet was an art, equal to the other arts and this was a hundred years ago! Most people are only coming to that viewpoint now." As composer of three of the four cornerstone ballets of the classical canon—*Swan Lake, The Sleeping Beauty,* and *The*

Nutcracker (the fourth is *Giselle,* composed by Adolphe Adam in 1841)—Tschaikovsky reigns supreme. "The stage, with all its tinsel," the composer wrote of his love of composing music for the ballet, "continues to attract me." His music raised the standards in the last decades of the nineteenth century, from the rather rinky-dink tunes with perfunctory, predictable rhythms that often characterized "ballet music" to that of symphonic music, with orchestral scores that stand alone in concert yet still brim with drama, romance, emotion, and pathos. And such splitting sweetness. His music is the colossus, upon which the art of ballet stands. "If it were not for Tchaikovsky," Balanchine stated unequivocally, "there wouldn't be any dancing."

In Balanchine's aqua analogy, where dancers are like fish, Tschaikovsky—his name synonymous with his music—provides our most essential, most eminent aquarium, a liquid land of misty opulence.

And such melodies!

Ballet doesn't exist without music. It has been tried, naturally, but is a dead event. We cannot move without music; it is our animator, our propulsion, our raison d'être. "I couldn't move without a reason, and the reason is music," Balanchine said. He considered the music first and his choreography second in importance—thus his insistence on a first-rate, live orchestra. He liked to say that it was fine to close your eyes at a ballet performance and just listen. And to our frequent, only slightly amused lament, unlike in most dance companies, Mr. B told us to keep pace to the conductor's tempos and not the reverse. We followed the music; the music did *not* follow us.

Balanchine's catalogue lists a total of twenty-six works choreographed to Tschaikovsky, spanning five decades of allegiance, with fifteen of them extant. Balanchine's musical compass was entire, and he was no snob despite being a trained classical musician; though he did stop short at pop music, admitting, "I can't understand rock 'n' roll." He choreographed dances to music from over fifty composers, from classical to jazz to Hollywood and Broadway show tunes. He made dances to Bach, Mozart, Stravinsky, Bizet, Schumann, Handel, Brahms, and Schubert; to Verdi, Puccini, and Wagner; to Hindemith, Chabrier, Ravel, Rossini, Rachmaninoff, Offenbach, Chopin, Saint-Saëns, and Rimsky-Korsakov; to Grieg, Rieti, Donizetti, Mussorgsky, Gounod, and both Strausses (Johann and Richard); to Liszt, Delibes, Borodin, Glazunov, Minkus, and Franz Léhar; to Kurt Weill, John Philip Sousa, Charles Ives, George Gershwin, and Irving Berlin; to Vernon Duke, Richard Rodgers, Frederick Loewe, Harold Arlen, Paul Bowles, and Johnny Mercer.

But again and again he returned home, to Tschaikovsky, the Russian composer of his boyhood debut in *The Sleeping Beauty*. And at the end of his life, at age seventy-seven, he came back, yet one last time, to Tschaikovsky, in his transcendent masterpiece *Mozartiana*, which he positioned—no, he did not say this, but how clear it is!—in heaven, a joyous place filled with wit, elegance, and explicit prayer, with dancers dressed in black, trimmed in white lace. So Balanchine closed his travels with Tschaikovsky in a perfect circle: this 1981 version of *Mozartiana* was an entirely new ballet to the same music that had marked his first full ballet to Tschaikovsky, in 1933, at age twenty-nine.* But in his final version, Balanchine, rascal to the end, changed, as he did with *Serenade,* the order of the composer's score.

Serenade thus became Balanchine's second complete ballet to the composer's work, and it is interesting to note that in both of these scores Tschaikovsky paid homage to his musical god: "I not only love Mozart, I worship him." I view *Serenade* as Balanchine's communion with Tschaikovsky, a spiritual union that endured, fully alive, for the remaining fifty years of Balanchine's life. The last festival he conceived, in 1981, two years before he died, when he was already in declining health, was to celebrate Tschaikovsky; it featured over twenty works by the composer. Alas, Tschaikovsky never knew, never saw, the beauty Balanchine shaped to his work, or the incalcuable effect that these ballets have had in bringing his music to a whole new audience in their visualizations—nor did he hear the changes his compatriot made in his music!

I, too, love Tschaikovsky. For most dancers, his music is the pervasive aural aura of our earliest years at the barre, in class varia-

---

* *Serenade* was, in fact, Balanchine's fourth foray into Tschaikovsky's world. Prior to *Mozartiana,* he had two brief flirtations on London music-hall stages—a pas de deux made for Charles B. Cochran's 1930 Revue in March 1930, and an improbable ensemble staging of the *1812 Overture* for Sir Oswald Stoll's Variety Shows the following year.

tions, in teenage school performances. And, for me, it became the physically inculcated soundtrack of my young life when, starting at age eleven, I danced, year after year, in *The Nutcracker*. (I did know who the Beatles were and had heard of the Rolling Stones and of someone who growled unintelligibly called Bob Dylan and another who groaned unintelligibly called Leonard Cohen—but they were all of less than little interest.) Here lies a great obstacle for me: using words on a page to convey the experience of *Serenade*. The music, the music, the music. While I certainly can accurately describe these thirty-three minutes of celestial sound as lyrical, melancholy, delicate, anguished, sacral, otherworldly, exalted, vivacious, joyous, and elegiac, this will transmit to you little actual feeling. What I cannot convey is the effect of these sounds, rhythms, moods, or swaying melodies. Music enters the mind instantly like no other medium, and, if a connection is made in the core, can pierce the heart. It carves out a different route than language, blessedly bypassing intellect. "Tenderness" is perhaps the single word—should I have to choose one—to describe Tschaikovsky's *Serenade*, tenderness punctuated by sorrow. The sorrow. The rapture and the loss, inseparable. And the violins—ah, the violins!

Unlike Balanchine, who left us only his ballets as his autobiography, Tschaikovsky was quite the correspondent and wrote not only voluminously—over five thousand letters to almost four hundred recipients—but eloquently, intimately, often with brutal honesty.

How beautifully Tschaikovsky breaks—as does Balanchine—the much-adored romanticization of the great artist with a raging ego and selfish temperament. His letters demonstrate compassion and kindness, generosity, penetrating self-knowledge, warmth, frequent gratitude, and a moving humility. He called himself on one occasion "merely a talented person, but no extraordinary phenomenon." But he also revealed his irritability, shyness, reclusiveness, sensitivity, and moody, highly emotional states; he wept easily, frequently. He offers numerous damning judgments: he detested Brahms—"What a giftless bastard!"—calling him "a pot-bellied boozer" and "a conceited mediocrity"—all the while also enjoying the occasional inebriated socializing with him. And he wrote much about the day in, day out relentless struggle, particularly as his celebrity grew, to obtain the right conditions, to be alone, to work.

"I love fame and strive for it with all my soul," he wrote the year he composed *Serenade*. "But from this, though, it does not follow that I love the manifestations of fame that take the form of banquets, suppers, and musical soirées, at which I have indeed suffered, just as I always suffer in the company of people who are alien to me . . . I want, desire, and love people to take an interest in my music and to praise and love it, but I have never sought to get them to take an interest in me personally, in the way I look or in what I say."

His description of the delicate, thrilling process he calls "inspiration" is unmatched in its clarity:

> The SEED of a future composition usually reveals itself suddenly, in the most unexpected fashion. If the soil is favourable . . . this seed takes root with inconceivable strength and speed, bursts through the soil, puts out roots, leaves, twigs and finally flowers. I cannot define the creative process except through this metaphor . . . All the rest happens of its own accord. It would be futile for me to try and express to you in words the boundless bliss of that feeling that envelops me when the main idea has appeared . . . I forget everything, I am almost insane, everything inside me trembles and writhes . . . one idea presses upon another. Sometimes in the middle of this enchanted process some jolt from outside suddenly wakens you from this somnambulist state . . . and reminds you that you have to go about your business. These breaks are painful, inexpressibly painful . . . But there is no other way. If that state of the artist's soul . . . were to continue unbroken, it would not be possible to survive a single day; the strings would snap and the instrument would shatter to smithereens. Only one thing is necessary: that the main idea . . . appear not through SEARCHING but of its own accord as the result of that supernatural, incomprehensible force which no one has explained, and which is called INSPIRATION . . . I consider it is the duty of the artist never to give way, for LAZINESS is a very powerful human trait. For an artist there is nothing worse . . . Inspiration is a guest who does not like visiting those who are lazy. She

reveals herself to those who invite her. YOU MUST, YOU HAVE TO OVERCOME YOURSELF.

Such eloquence throws into stark relief the virtually total lack of writing of any kind left to us by Balanchine, who said, "I am silence." He left no diaries, no memoirs, a bare handful of short notes—a rarity among artists of all disciplines. Truly he was a cloud passing over and wanted it so.

Pyotr Illyich Tschaikovsky's life was defined by his relationships with three women: his mother, his wife, and his patron. Born in 1840 in Votkinsk, a small town about nine hundred miles southeast of St. Petersburg, Tschaikovsky was the second son of a family with six children and many generations of men dedicated to military and government service. His Ukrainian Cossack great-grandfather served under Peter the Great. And the civil service was to be young Pyotr's destiny—as it was to be Georgi's. Tschaikovsky's mother, eighteen years her husband's junior, was, also like Balanchine's, his father's second, much younger, wife.

At age ten, the boy was abruptly separated from his family, when he was shipped off (again, like young Balanchivadze) to board at the prestigious Imperial School for Jurisprudence in St. Petersburg, to train as an imperial administrator. Four years later his mother's sudden death from cholera began his lifelong mourning.

"Tchaikovsky loved his mother more than his father," Balanchine told Volkov. "Even when he was a grown man he couldn't talk about her without tears . . . It was an open wound for the rest of his life . . . Childhood impressions are . . . always the most powerful. This holds particularly for musicians and dancers because they usually start studying music and ballet at a very early age."

While the young Tschaikovsky had been an outstanding student—in addition to Russian, he spoke Italian, French, English, and German—he also excelled at piano and composition. After completing his course at the School of Jurisprudence, he decided, at age twenty-two, to devote himself to music, and his talent, soon recognized, resulted in a teaching position at the newly established

Pyotr Illyich Tschaikovsky, 1867 *(ullstein bild Dtl./Getty Images)*

Moscow Conservatory. By his midthirties he had already become a well-recognized composer of singular, occasionally controversial, accomplishment. When he composed *Serenade,* in 1880, he was just forty years old, but the preceding few years had been the worst of his life—defining years, precipitated by his marriage.

Tschaikovsky was homosexual at a time in Russia when it was very dangerous and illegal, and the attendant shame and secrecy were particularly threatening to one of budding fame and ambition, so he decided at age thirty-six that he must abandon "forever my habits." (He never did.) He wrote to Modest, one of his brothers, who was also homosexual: "I find that our inclinations are for both of us the greatest and most insurmountable obstacle to happiness, and we must fight our nature with all our strength."

Fate soon provided. In May 1877, the composer received several unsolicited, passionate letters from a twenty-eight-year-old woman, Antonina Ivanovna Miliukova, who had briefly attended the Moscow Conservatory. She had been secretly in love with Tschaikovsky for four years, since a chance meeting that he did not recall.

"I am dying of longing," she wrote to the composer. "My first kiss will be given to you and to no one else in the world . . . I cannot live without you, and so maybe soon I shall kill myself. So let me see you and kiss you so that I may remember that kiss in the other world." Thus began the disaster.

"I have decided to marry," wrote Tschaikovsky to Modest. "It's unavoidable. I have to do this, and not only for myself, but also for you . . . for everyone I love. Especially for you! . . . Homosexuality and pedagogy cannot get along together."

Miliukova and Tschaikovsky had met for the first time at his instigation on June 1, and three days later he proposed, telling her what she could expect from him "and on what she should not count," namely he offered her "brotherly" love. He told her that he required complete "freedom," though it is quite possible, given the times, that his bride-to-be still did not comprehend that he was homosexual— or perhaps she did not regard this as a hindrance.

"Why did I do this?" he wrote three days before the wedding. "Some force of Fate was driving me to this girl . . . I told my future wife that *I did not love her* . . . It is very distressing, through force of circumstances, to be drawn into the position of *a bridegroom* who, moreover, is not in the least attracted to his bride." But Tschaikovsky was, of course, inherently romantic—not about conjugal bliss but about "Fate" as a living force.

At the altar—one of the two witnesses was Tschaikovsky's most recent young lover—he cried when asked to kiss his bride. Within days of cohabiting, he wrote of his "*intolerable spiritual torments.*" The thought of her bathing he found so "*totally repugnant*" that he left their apartment and went to church to Mass to pray. "It appeared to me," he wrote, that "the only good part of myself, that is, my musical talent, had perished irretrievably. My future rose up before me as some pitiful vegetation and the most insufferable and pedestrian comedy . . . death seemed the only way out." He found his wife to be "an unbearable encumbrance," "a terrible wound," and spoke of drowning himself.

The couple separated in the fall after having lived together a total of thirty-three days: the marriage remained unconsummated. Tschaikovsky descended into an unprecedented state of emotional anxiety, a breakdown—possibly exaggerated by him and his family to justify his hasty escape.

Though she twice refused his requests to divorce, the couple never lived together again, but he supported her financially thereafter. By 1884 she had given birth to three illegitimate children with a lover, but she gave them up to an orphanage for pecuniary, health, and legal reasons.*

All three children died before age eight.

Antonina Tschaikovskaya outlived her famous husband by twenty-four years, spending the last twenty of them in an insane asylum with "*paranoia chronica*" that included hallucinations and delirium. The lifelong pension from Tschaikovsky's will paid for her keep. Her grave has long since disappeared.

. . .

* Though Tschaikovsky continued his financial support of 100 rubles a month, it was insufficient for a large family. Had his estranged wife kept her children they would have needed to be registered, legitimately, as Tschaikovsky's, causing numerous further difficulties. She did, however, ask him in 1886 to adopt her youngest, a girl, a request he declined by not responding, though he voiced concern that the children were in an orphanage.

A bare six months before his nuptials another woman had made herself known to Tschaikovsky. Nadezhda Filaretovna von Meck was no dreamy, naive young woman in love but a formidable force who would change the composer's life forever and is now inseparably melded to the music he left us.

Von Meck, at age forty-five, was nine years older than Tschaikovsky and recently widowed, leaving her an incredibly wealthy woman, when she first wrote to the musician whose work she much admired. Music was von Meck's great passion, and she wanted something for herself—she was a pianist—and her in-house violinist to play for her own pleasure. The remuneration was handsome; inept with money, Tschaikovsky was ever in need and immediately complied, inaugurating a fourteen-year friendship.

After an elaborate confession to von Meck of his marital debacle, she offered Tschaikovsky a very generous yearly stipend of six thousand rubles (a civil servant at the time earned only three to four hundred rubles a year), which allowed the composer to renounce his teaching at the Moscow Conservatory and devote himself entirely to his composition.

"You know how I love you, how I wish you the best in everything," she wrote with graceful insistence. "You know how many happy moments you have afforded me, how deeply grateful I am to you for them, how necessary you are to me, and how for me you must be exactly that which you were created to be. Consequently I am not doing anything for you, but everything for myself . . . so do not prevent me from giving my attention to your housekeeping, Pyotr Ilich!"

"Every note that will now pour out from under my pen," he wrote to the woman he called "my own Providence," "will be dedicated to you. Never, never, not for one second, while working, I will not forget that you give me the opportunity to continue my artistic vocation." On another occasion, he demonstrated with startling directness their ease with each other, stating, "You are the only person in the world I am not ashamed to ask for money. First, you are very kind and generous; second, you are rich."

While one cannot measure the exact effect this financial stability had on his output for the remainder of his life, it can be safely assumed that von Meck's support gave us much music that perhaps

Nadezhda Filaretovna von Meck. "Music puts me in a state of intoxication," she wrote. "One is mysteriously propelled ... into a world whose magic is so great that one would be willing to die in this condition."

otherwise would not have been made. This was patronage of the highest order—though it came with peculiar strings attached, or, more accurately, unattached.

Von Meck requested from the very start that they never meet in person. Tschaikovsky, suffering similarly from their mutual "illness" of "misanthropy," agreed.

"My ideal man is a musician," she explained. "The more I am enchanted by you, the more I fear acquaintance ... I prefer to think of you in the distance, to hear your music, and to feel myself at one with you in it. Of my imaginary relationship with you ... I will say only that this relationship, however abstract it may be, is precious to me as the best, the highest of all feelings of which human nature is capable." She did, however, ask for a photo of him, and spoke of being "delirious" over his music.

Tschaikovsky, in accord, wrote back of "that disenchantment, that yearning for the ideal that follows upon every intimacy . . . I am in no way surprised that, loving my music, you are not attempting to make the acquaintance of its author . . . you would not find . . . that complete harmony between the musician and the man."

On a single occasion, due to missed messages about a change in her daily schedule, they came face-to-face when he was out on one of his frequent walks while staying, at her invitation, in his own well-appointed house on one of her enormous estates. She, in her carriage, froze, and he just tipped his hat. Not a word was spoken, and both were shaken by the chance encounter.

"I am very unsympathetic in my personal relations," von Meck wrote to her "beloved friend." "I do not possess any femininity whatever; second, I do not know how to be tender." This from the woman who had once written to Tschaikovsky of his marriage, "the thought of you with that woman was unbearable. I hated her because she did not make you happy; but I would have hated her 100 times more if she had." Her years of devotion to Tschaikovsky belie in a stroke her claim that she lacked tenderness.

For over thirteen years, they wrote to each other weekly, sometimes daily, often at great length, resulting in an astonishingly intimate epistolary outpouring that produced (due to Tschaikovsky's noncompliance with her request to destroy the letters) over twelve hundred letters that fill three volumes and offer an unprecedented window into the man behind the music.

In June 1880, Tschaikovsky received the suggestion to write a commemorative piece for an upcoming Moscow Exhibition to celebrate the Russian defeat of Napoléon in 1812. He was disgruntled at both the request to produce music glorifying "what [delighted him] not at all," and the imprecise remuneration.

"My dear chap!" he wrote to Pyotr Jurgenson, his publisher. "You seem to think that composing ceremonial pieces for the occasion of an exhibition is some sort of supreme bliss, of which I shall rush

to take advantage, and immediately begin pouring out my inspiration ... I won't lift a single finger until something is <u>commissioned</u>
from me ... (for a commission I'm even prepared to set Tchaikovsky
music to the pharmacist's advert for corn medicine) ... There are
two inspirations: one emerges directly from the heart with free
choice of this or that motive for creativity; the other is to order. The
latter requires motivation, encouragement and means of inspiration
in the form of precise instructions, fixed periods of time and the
prospect in the more or less distant future of (many) Catherines!"*
After considerable haggling, the composer agreed to the job.

On October 3, Tschaikovsky wrote to one of his brothers, Ana-
toly, that he had "started to write something"—but this was not the
dreaded music for the Exhibition; this was *Serenade*. Uncommis-
sioned, "from the heart with free choice." Thanks to Tschaikovsky's
copious correspondence, one can track his progress to the day—and
be astonished not only by the incredible speed of composition but
also by the simultaneous juxtaposition of it with his work on the *1812
Overture,* complete with its "platitudes and noisy commonplaces."

On October 7, he told von Meck that he was writing a "suite for
string orchestra," and had already finished three movements. The
first three movements of *Serenade*—Sonatina, Waltz, and Elegy—
were thus composed in little more than four days! On October 12,
he began the commission and finished that in just six days. Tschaikovsky acknowledged to his patron that he was on a roll: "Imagine,
my dear friend, that my muse was so kind to me lately, that I wrote
two things with great speed, namely: 1) a large solemn overture for
the exhibition, at the request of Nick[olai] Gr[igorievich], and 2)
a Serenade for String orchestra ... The overture will be very loud,
noisy—but I wrote it without a warm feeling of love, and therefore
there will probably be no artistic merit in it. On the other hand, I
composed the Serenade out of an inner urge; I felt it and therefore,
I dare to think, is not devoid of real dignity."

By November 4 *Serenade* was orchestrated—one month from
start to finish—and a few days later he wrote to his publisher, "Pyotr
Ivanovich! You have an unpleasant surprise in store. I accidentally
wrote a Serenade for String Orchestra in 4 movements, and I'm

* A "Catherine" was a 100-ruble note that carried the image of Catherine the Great.

The first page of Tschaikovsky's handwritten score of *Serenade*. His note at the bottom reads: "The more numerous the instruments in the string orchestra, the more it will please the composer."

sending it to you the day after tomorrow in the form of a score and 4-handed arrangement. I can see from here how you'll be leaping up and exclaiming: thank you, I wasn't expecting this! Whether because this is my latest offspring, or because it actually isn't too bad, I just love this Serenade terribly, and I'm dying for it to see the light of day as soon as possible."

On December 3, two months to the day that he began composing "something," he was invited to a private concert at the Moscow Conservatory, his former place of work. "This piece [*Serenade*], which at the present time I consider the best of all that I have written," he reported to von Meck, "was played by the professors and students of the Conservatory very satisfactorily and gave me considerable pleasure too."*

The great Russian pianist and composer Anton Rubinstein, long one of his severest critics, declared *Serenade* "Tchaikovsky's best piece." Tschaikovsky himself conducted his "favorite child" numerous times in his remaining years, including in Philadelphia and Baltimore during a celebrated tour to America in 1891, a trip occasioned by his invitation to the opening of Carnegie Hall.

The "detestable" *1812 Overture* did not receive its premiere until August 1882, due to various delays, and it went on to become his most recognized work—thanks in part to Arthur Fiedler's 1976 association of this very Russian, over-the-top-cannons-and-all pièce d'occasion with the totally unrelated American Independence Day of 1776. This is the score that made the Tschaikovsky estate very wealthy.

In 1890, von Meck mysteriously, suddenly, stopped Tschaikovsky's yearly stipend and asked for no further contact. Having been given the honor of a yearly pension of three thousand rubles by Tsar Alexander III in 1888, Tschaikovsky was by now also making considerable money from his music, so while this did not threaten pending poverty, it was an incomprehensible cessation of the deep friendship that, he once wrote her, would "always be the joy of [my] life."

---

* He dedicated the work to his good friend Konstantin Albrecht, a cellist and colleague from the Conservatory.

While she referenced "bankruptcy" and various pressures from her family, she declined to mention that she was ill and her right hand had atrophied, making writing all but impossible.

In his final letter, he called her "the anchor of my salvation."

Two years later, at age fifty-three, just nine days after conducting the premiere of his last masterpiece, *Symphony No. 6 in B minor*—the *Pathétique Symphony*—Tschaikovsky died. His cause of death continues, to this day, to be debated: the official Russian version has long been that he died of cholera (like his mother), but there is much evidence to suggest that it was suicide, related to the possible impending revelation of a homosexual liaison. Still further, there is credible evidence not only that he killed himself by purposefully drinking unsafe water during a cholera epidemic but also that he was ordered to commit suicide by an "honor court" of his peers from his days at the School for Jurisprudence. But whatever the truth, likely never to be known definitively, his reputation remained intact as the man who brought respect and fame to Russian music (as Tolstoy had brought respect and fame to Russian literature), and he had laid the musical foundation for the entire art of classical ballet. He was given a magnificent funeral, paid for personally by Tsar Alexander III, with a train of mourners over a mile long.

Balanchine believed fervently that Tschaikovsky had been persecuted due to his sexual orientation: "I believe that he wrote the *Pathétique Symphony* as a kind of suicide note," he told Solomon Volkov. "He wrote it, then conducted the symphony himself; it was like coming back to life to see what people would say. He was preparing himself for his death . . . Tchaikovsky was a noble person. He did not want to involve people dear to him in a scandal. He couldn't stand gossip around his name. Tchaikovsky gave in to society's pressure, accepted its cruel laws—and left this life. They forced him to die."

Nadezhda von Meck died just two months after her beloved Tschaikovsky. When her daughter-in-law, who was Tschaikovsky's niece, was asked how von Meck had endured his death, she replied, "She did not endure it."

15. TRANSITIONS

Balanchine inserted the Russian Dance between the Waltz and the Elegy in 1940, when he staged *Serenade* for the Ballet Russe de Monte Carlo, an established company, where he had more dancers, stronger dancers—not the scattershot group of the first students at the School of American Ballet six years earlier—and enough rehearsal time to make the addition. But even here he did not add the entire movement as composed. This new section of the ballet is the most technically demanding of all the movements. We are already tired from the Sonatina and the Waltz, with very few short offstage breaks, but now things speed up even more, with a great deal of jumping—all over the stage with no time out to breathe or recover. Jumping while also "traveling" is a far greater exertion than jumping in place, which requires the defiance of gravity in just one dimension rather than in multiple dimensions.

For the Ballet Russe version, he used one ballerina and a soloist for parts split earlier between several dancers, and added a second man and four demi-soloists for the Russian Dance. He had already changed the orchestration around 1935 from that of George Antheil's 1934 version—*"ces affreux trompettes!"*—to the composer's own scoring. He tinkered with *Serenade*, returning to it like a touchstone over the course of his life, until every note of Tschaikovsky's score was finally visible onstage. In 1977, more than forty years after first making the ballet, Balanchine said *Serenade* "took me a long time. Just two years ago I finished it completely, so not one bar is left out, all cuts are restored. I made the full ballet now."

The first costumes changed too, as they would several more times over the next decades. Early ventures included "pink Latex which tears easily," Kirstein noted in his diary in late 1934, "and spirals of black material sticking out stiffly from it." While the costumes of the solo dancers were "made in white and gray bath-toweling—as [Helen] Leitch said 'one dirty and one clean towel'—snipped at by scissors to look ragged; they were fierce and finally scrapped. Great row as to whose fault it was—Balanchine's or Okie's who 'designed' the costumes."

Later costumes included long, totally transparent skirts; short, puffy skirts; two-colored, paneled, multi-flapped skirts in several tones; mid-thigh tutus with petal-like flaps over tight pleats; thick-roped braiding trim; off-one-shoulder attached sashes; bodices with dark, webbed veins; white head bandannas and opera-length gloves—until Karinska's final version in 1952 put a stop to the atrocities.

The *Serenade* blue, however, is to be found doggedly popping up in both costumes and scenery from the very start. It's a wonder the ballet itself survived beneath what can only now be seen as unflattering, highly distracting hoopla. Even Karinska's final design has undergone small refinements: the fabric of the bodice went from unyielding satin to stretchy Lycra; the two beige leg panels were added, and the hem went from being even all around to what I danced in, where the hem was shorter in front, just above the ankles, so all the pointe work was visible, and longer in back, to the ankles, to give a slight illusion of a flowing train behind us as we moved.

Various early stage sets were also weird, some appalling. The first designs for the 1934 premiere in Hartford, Connecticut, sported an imposing, swirling, trompe l'oeil cyclone, jabbing its modernism out on center stage from a navy blue background. It was never used.

For a 1941 tour of South America by Ballet Caravan, the backdrop featured "the sky over the Southern Hemisphere with the start of the Southern Cross intertwined with two meteors." A quixotic Paris Opera production in 1947 boasted a stage set that included a life-size nude statue of the virile young god Eros officiating over the proceedings from a high pedestal center stage with soft curtains swathed all around, while the dancers wore short, soft skirts with Russian-style diadems and trailing veils crowning their heads: a Gallic pastiche of a mythical Slavic bedroom.

Eventually the scenery was reduced to the barest possible: simple black wings and borders, and a deep blue scrim with a dark blue backing that is lit from a lighting trough upstage that throws up an even, vertical sheet of light onto the scrim. "It's all reflection," says Perry Silvey, our adored, ever-calm NYCB stage and production manager, who kept things running backstage and onstage for over forty-two years. "What you see [from the audience] is all reflected light—six lamps in every wing of deep blue and ten more lamps of steel blue and deeper medium blue. I always thought the blue corresponded to sky, but he never said that." Throughout the ballet, the lighting undergoes slight shifts in tandem with the choreography: "After the Waltz Girl falls [in the Elegy], there's a cue that changes very subtly that adds a little color, and at the end, when she is up in the air on the man's shoulders, there's a slow cue upstage right so the light is on her, up high," Perry explains. "Mr. B was notorious for going out front to the lighting board. We had to signal the lighting operator as he was scared to death because Mr. B would walk into the booth, during an actual performance, and change the lighting in the middle of a ballet sometimes, a possibly disastrous move. One of us would always run after him as he headed out front."

Balanchine altered and added to *Serenade* in numerous smaller ways too (hair in high bun, low bun, in-between bun), alongside larger musical and choreographic additions and alterations. He was still making significant changes just before he died. During my time—his last years—he was always in the front wing watching *Serenade*. I can only wonder what it would have been like for him to see us, his ultimate thoroughbreds, dancing that same dance he put together in 1934 with that brave and rather motley crew of early voyagers.

The music of the Russian Dance begins so softly, with a few high, sweet notes, that we can barely hear it, though we are only feet from the orchestra pit. But we can see the conductor clearly and follow his baton. I am standing just to the right of the Russian Girl, who is the center of our little band of five, echoing the five of the Aspirin dance, though we are different dancers and we do not have headaches.

This was one of the first roles I learned when I got into the company. It is sometimes referred to as a "demi-solo" role: the four Russian Girls dance everything the rest of the corps dances plus this dance—which means they have the most time onstage of any role in the ballet. By the end we are beyond exhaustion, having danced ourselves into an altered realm.

After a breath in, we close our B+ on the exhale, pulling the extended left foot into a tightly sealed fifth position, feet in 180-degree opposing directions but suctioned together along their sides. Mr. B did not like a loose-fitting fifth, not at all. We came to know that it was messy, slack, unfinished, a cheat: psychologically, one remains on two feet, while he wanted a newly created single high-reaching column comprised of two legs, and two feet bonded as one.

Breaking this bond, we extend the front, right leg forward and begin a very slow slide all the way down to the stage floor. The move is led by a full, beautifully pointed foot forward, toward you, but, in practice, when the edge of the hard box on our pointe shoes hits the stage it sticks and halts the slide, so we all know to keep our arches pointed but simultaneously relax the ball of the foot so that the forward underside of the shoe, not the tip, hits the stage and glides easily. A few inches into the descent, gravity, momentum, and body weight take over and we point our toes again as we slide smoothly, gradually, into full splits on the stage floor. While it is clear to the audience that we are in five aligned acrobatic splits, because they are forward-facing and topped by mounds of tulle, this classical anachronism looks, well, classic, though it certainly is not. No one got this low, in quite this way, in nineteenth-century ballet.

Arms open wide to the side, softly we place our right hand down and imperceptibly push into the stage floor, using the leverage to lift ourselves up and back, until we are each sitting on our bent left leg, right leg straight, pointed forward. And over we go, arms and torso extended forward over our front leg. We are now, five of us, dying swans all.

This folding, one of ballet's most recognized poses, was burned

Anna Pavlova in *The Dying Swan,* 1905 *(© National Portrait Gallery, London)*

into history in 1905 by the legendary Anna Pavlova in her four-minute solo, by Michel Fokine, called *The Dying Swan.* Pavlova performed this short dance to enormous acclaim over four thousand times around the world—it was her signature piece—and this moment of the Swan weakening, folded over her own legs as she is losing life, is its iconic image. "Nobody cared about the dancing, really," Balanchine said in a feisty interview in 1963 about this solo. "They are just waiting for her to die. 'Ah!' they say. 'Great die!'"

But this pose was not new on Pavlova in 1905: it had appeared ten years earlier in the Petipa-Ivanov *Swan Lake,* at the start of the Act II pas de deux, where Prince Siegfried reaches down to gently raise Odette up from the same stance: she is a Swan Queen awaiting her prince. Was Balanchine making a bow, literally, to his forefathers in the Russian Dance of *Serenade*? Perhaps, perhaps not—but it is there, a nod to our tradition in the pose. We, though, are not Swans with birth, love, and death stories; we are simply women doing beautiful movements, honoring our heritage while advancing it.

16. THE OTHER BALLETMASTER

M r. B would often pause in class while focusing on a minute detail—a particular transition, a particular foot position as it molded itself about the opposite ankle and say to us all, "You *see*! It's all Petipa!" Balanchine knew this great balletmaster to be his choreographic father and delighted in showing us, repeatedly, that all we danced, all that he taught us, was also Petipa.

Victor Marius Alphonse Petipa—later Marius Ivanovich Petipa—is the undisputed, towering figure of nineteenth-century classical ballet. His work looms ubiquitous and immortal, his intricate ballerina variations and gigantic set pieces all but law. Even his very name—petit pas—is a ballet step, albeit a small one. So pervasive is Petipa's presence that his name connotes, the world over, ballet as we know it today. He set the whole unlikely thing up, and his legacy is ever present in every step we take, inborn, irradicable. How, in such an evanescent practice, did this maître de ballet come to be a fortified edifice? And within the citadel walls still reside his diamantine ballets, though these are a mere fraction of all he made (he claimed 105 works)—*The Sleeping Beauty, Swan Lake, The Nutcracker, La Bayadère, Raymonda*. We also have his staging of *Giselle*, and numerous pas de deux.

Three days after Petipa's death, at age ninety-two, one obituary claimed that the balletmaster might well have declared, without dispute, echoing Louis XIV: "Russian Ballet—c'est moi." The irony is precise, for Petipa, father of Russian ballet—and the reason for the frequent though mistaken notion that ballet originated in Russia—was a Frenchman through and through, despite a life lived, for over sixty years, in St. Petersburg, the city of his artistic confreres, Tschaikovsky and Balanchivadze. Upon the occasion of his first marriage in Russia, Petipa was granted special dispensation by the authorities to retain his French citizenship and his Catholicism; in return, he pledged to raise his future children—there would be eight of them, with one illegitimate son already existing—in the Russian Orthodox faith. His last child, a girl, was born when he was sixty-seven.

In his despairing, precise—he accounted daily for every ruble he spent—and occasionally self-pitying diary entries, written during the last years of his life, he wailed, upon learning of the death of his sister, the last member of his French family, "All my relatives now are Russians!!!" He subscribed to French journals, wrote his brief unreliable memoirs in French, and never properly learned Russian. The dancers giggled when he tried. But given that the language of ballet is French, and many Russians at the time learned the language, this was no great impediment to the balletmaster's work.

Classical ballet has had three major centers, three cultures, three cities—it is an urban art—that mark the most innovative of its flowerings, both onstage in choreographic outpourings, and backstage, in the teaching and technique of the craft itself. Paris saw the founding and codification of this inordinately costly art funded by the court of Louis XIV in the late seventeenth century; St. Petersburg, under the direction of Petipa, was entirely subsidized by the imperial Russian purse in the mid-nineteenth (Petipa outlived three tsars, Nicholas I and Alexanders II and III); and in the mid-twentieth, New York City, under Balanchine, the only great innovator to flourish without monarchical support, ballet thrived via the more precarious, and substantially reduced, coffers of capitalism, as expertly maneuvered by Lincoln Kirstein.* And so, fittingly, in this nomadic art,

* Copenhagen, a close-stepping fourth city, under the long creative rule of the great choreographer August Bournonville—at the helm of the Royal Danish Ballet in

it was a Frenchman who made ballet Russian, and a Russian who made it American. Where next?

Incredibly, only recently, two hundred years after his birth, have the details about Petipa's life emerged, thanks to the publication of the first full-length biography in English by Nadine Meisner. Imagine if only now the first serious biographical information was emerging on Nietzsche and Dostoyevsky, or Cézanne and Rodin, or Dickens, Flaubert, and Baudelaire? Ballet remains the unwritten art.

Like Beauchamps, Taglioni, and even Louis XIV himself, Marius Petipa was born into a theatrical dancing family, in 1818, in Marseilles. His mother, Victorine, was an actress, and his father, Jean-Antoine, was both a lead dancer and dancemaker of considerable accomplishment and verve who spent years variously as dancer and director of the ballet company at Théâtre de la Monnaie in Brussels, and later in Nantes and Bordeaux, and even embarked on a brief, bankrupting tour of America.

Eight days after his fifth birthday, Marius, like his father before him (and like young Balanchivadze) made his stage debut as a little Cupid, *"un petit Amour"*—not, as did Georgi, in *The Sleeping Beauty*, which Petipa would choreograph sixty-seven years later, but in a ballet called *Psyché et l'Amour*. (So many Cupids—as if Terpsichore herself ordained that balletmasters must begin their labors in her employ as the winged god of love.)

Marius was the second child of six, and his older brother, Lucien, age eight, true to form, played another Cupid in the same performance—and he was such a beautiful child that he was chosen as a model by the French painter Jacques-Louis David, then in self-imposed exile in Brussels. Lucien Petipa is now immortalized in the gigantic, final painting by David, *Mars désarmé par Vénus*, as the rosy-skinned cherub, crowned with shimmering curls and white, gold-tipped wings, who is mischievously untying the straps on a sandal of the sexy young Mars, god of war, as he readily yields to the voluptuous temptations of Venus. Cupid's darts of love encircle his

---

the mid-nineteenth century—ran parallel to Petipa and was similarly funded by the Danish monarchy.

body in their phallic quiver, and with his gilded bow to one side, his gaze turns to us, knowing beyond his years.*

Handsome Lucien, though now all but forgotten, was, in fact, a superior dancer to Marius and became the lead male dancer at the Paris Opera. "We must pay tribute to [Lucien] Petipa," wrote French poet Théophile Gautier in 1843. "How devoted and attentive he is to his ballerina, and how well he supports her! He does not seek to attract attention to himself . . . he does not put on the artificial graces and the revolting mincing manner that have turned the public against male dancing." Lucien holds the unique honor of being the first Albrecht in history, in the premiere of *Giselle* in 1841, partnering onstage (and apparently off, despite her long liaison with famed balletmaster Jules Perrot) the great Austrian-born, Italian-trained ballerina Carlotta Grisi.

Meanwhile, Marius, now twenty-six, secured a contract in Madrid, where he soon attained a measure of fame both professionally and privately. He debuted, also in *Giselle,* in the summer of 1844, and initiated a clandestine affair with the daughter of Maria de la Concepción, the marquesa de Villagarcia, a member of the nobility. The daughter, Carmen, was not only considerably above Petipa's rank (as a dancer, he had no rank at all) but, at twenty, was still underage according to Spanish law. The affair quickly devolved into a Feydeau farce, avant la lettre, though with unamusing consequences.

Within three months the dangerous liaison was discovered by Carmen's mother's lover, one Count de Gabriac, also a Frenchman, who erroneously deduced that Petipa was sneaking into the grand house to see his own lover, the marquesa, rather than her daughter. News of the scandal traveled far and wide and all opined. "I thought that M. Petitpas [*sic*] was after the marquesa de Villagarcia herself," wrote Prosper Mérimée. "They say that he's a man without prejudices who eats the mature fruit first and the green fruit later."

In September 1844 Petipa challenged the count to a duel rather than submit to the beating the count proposed. The two men and

---

* The ballerina Mlle Marie Lesueur was the model for the graceful Venus, though the painter selected a servant girl to model the goddess's naked feet as Mlle Lesueur's were rather the worse for wear from life in her pointe shoes.

their seconds met the next day. The count's first shot misfired, but when Petipa took aim he shot off his opponent's left jaw, and the bullet pierced his neck. A doctor was able to remove the bullet and the count, implausibly, survived. In Petipa's version of the event, when called to the police station to account for participating in an illegal duel, he denied that it had happened at all, and was released without punishment. This bizarre incident is documented by the tenacious Meisner and by Petipa's Spanish biographer, Laura Hormigón. One German newspaper reported that Petipa dishonorably took his shot while the count was reloading his pistol.

All this drama did not prevent young Marius from pursuing his lover, and in January 1847, more than two years later, the scoundrel took flight with Carmen in tow. In doing so, he went missing from his performance in a ballet called, aptly, *The Devil in Love*. The ensuing uproar produced a full-scale European manhunt. One Spanish newspaper suggested that the authorities should take heed that Petipa, the "kidnapper," was a man with "a truly amazing lightness of foot."

The distinguished Spanish writer and diplomat Juan Valera reported the "notable event" to his father, saying that Carmen had left her mother a note in which "she cited the excessive burden of the intense love she felt for the aerial and vaporous lover with whom she has eloped." Letters flew back and forth from the Spanish embassy to the French embassy in an attempt to save the girl's honor, or some of it, and the lovers were located two months later by the French police, hiding out in a village near Rouen. Carmen was arrested and returned to her family, while Petipa once again apparently evaded legal retribution. He was, however, left penniless, jobless, and girl-less.

A propitious invitation to dance in St. Petersburg—possibly obtained through Lucien's influence—saved the day. The peripatetic Petipa arrived, with a clean slate, in St. Petersburg some weeks later and never left: one of the most vital turning points in all ballet history thus having transpired due to the unsuccessful amorous escapades of a passionate, and unscrupulous, young Frenchman. Marius Petipa was twenty-nine when he appeared on Russian soil, and during the ensuing sixty-three years ballet did indeed become "Russian."

But it was a very long slog for the balletmaster. The byzantine bureaucracy and intrigue of the imperial court knew no bounds, and it took the ambitious and persistent Petipa, working nonstop, sixteen years to attain the position of second balletmaster, and, by 1870, that of first balletmaster, the boss. As director of the Imperial Theatres, he had charge of a veritable cultural multiplex that included the Bolshoi and Maryinsky theaters, the Imperial Russian Ballet, its dance academy, and five smaller court theaters. Long led, notably, by the great French balletmasters Charles Didelot, Jules Perrot, and Arthur Saint-Léon, the court spared no ruble to import French influence just as the art was seeing a decline into "floppiness" in Europe. They succeeded most unequivocally with their last, least prestigious import, Marius Petipa—"whom fate," wrote Akim Volynsky, "bestowed upon Russia," and whose staying power and insistence on unification in a world of intricate imperial machinations cannot be understated.

Not least of Petipa's formidable qualities was an impressive capacity for enduring failure—decades of it—marked by only occasional success. "The chart of his career shows a broken curve," wrote Slonimsky, "with deep falls and rare ascents." But it was in big, big ballets, ones that would, foremost, entertain the tsar and his family, that Petipa succeeded.

His first great triumph, in 1862, made in only six weeks, according to the ever-reliable Petipa, was a full-evening ballet called *The Pharaoh's Daughter*, where his "tendency to monumentality" was in flaming form. It boasted a prologue, three acts, and an epilogue, with some scenes featuring as many as seventy-five dancers onstage at one time—"there are so many people here," wrote Volynsky, "necessary and unnecessary!" With lavish costumes, scenery, and props, the ballet adhered to an absurd Egyptian-themed libretto, but the extravaganza was a superhit, and Petipa was "crowned with glory." Ballets on this imperial scale had not been seen since the ballets de cour at the French court more than a hundred years earlier. So much for such success: *The Pharaoh's Daughter*, like *Ballet de la Nuit*, resides with us now as but a historical fantasy.

During his six decades of work in Russia, Petipa produced more than fifty ballets, restaged nineteen others, and made dances for as many as thirty-seven operas, along with multiple pièces d'occasion,

Marius Petipa, 1878

and continuous revisions to all the aforementioned. And of these, we have but a precious handful, and it is ever unclear how true to their original source they are as performed today. Ballet, like Mother Nature herself, is an art defined by evolution.

Notably, the Petipa ballets that have survived were made in his later years, most after he turned seventy, a testament against the notion of the aging artist's fading talents. More important, and inseparable from their sustained success, is that these same ballets all came about once Pyotr Tschaikovsky, already a well-known composer of classical music, was invited (not by Petipa, but by the unusually cultured director of the imperial theaters at the time, Ivan Vsevolozhsky) to compose the scores. Until then, ballet composers produced a decidedly lower caliber of music. "It is particularly painful to consider," wrote Volynsky, "the balletic compositions of Delibes, Pugni, Minkus, and others. One feels their shallowness and obvious poverty."

Tschaikvosky, in agreeing to take detailed orders for each dance, for its length, rhythms, tone, and even which instruments to feature—most classical composers thought such instruction beneath them—changed ballet forever.* Prior to Tschaikovsky, the form was ever trailing behind opera and classical music in its prestige: now, Petipa, with Tschaikovsky's magnificent music, lifted ballet to the front of the stage and firmly established the ballerina. "Petipa turned the art of ballet largely into a woman's art," wrote Volynsky. "Sexual fire burned in this Frenchman's emotional blood, and he could not but impose his own intense individuality onto the dance . . . he bestowed upon the female dancer the Gallic quality of a coquettish Aphrodite." Balanchine, in the following century, with his compatriots Tschaikovsky and Igor Stravinsky, would elevate both the music and the female dancer yet higher, projecting to its zenith the only art where woman is sovereign.

Petipa's life, however, belied his art. One episode, only revealed recently in full—and reliably sourced by Meisner in her 2019 biography—cannot pass unmentioned. For close to a hundred and fifty years its ready evidence lay in the Central State Historical Archive in St. Petersburg awaiting discovery. On February 18, 1867, a formal complaint was filed with the St. Petersburg magistrate by the thirty-one-year-old wife of Petipa, the ballerina Maria Surovshchikova, mother of two of his children. The detailed document outlines in clear and cogent terms the ten years of physical and verbal abuse she endured at the hands of her husband. While known for his strict, often ruthless, and dictatorial nature with his dancers, this report disclosed something else entirely. The "aerial and vaporous lover" had feet of clay.

Petipa had married Maria when he was thirty-six and she was eighteen—just after her graduation from the ballet school as the most promising talent in her year. He encouraged her, taught her, and featured her as his muse in many ballets. Particularly beautiful, she had many admirers, as ballerinas so often do. Worse, for her jealous husband, she was sexy.

* For the famous dance of the two cats in *The Sleeping Beauty*, Petipa gave Tschaikovsky the following note: "Repeated mewing, denoting caressing and clawing. For the end—clawing and screaming of the male cat. It should begin ¾ amoroso and end in ¾ with accelerated mewing."

"Madame Petipa is the model of all that is pretty, sweet," wrote a smitten Jules Le Sire, upon seeing her dance in Paris in 1861. "Her slightly upturned nose, her white teeth between pink lips give her face something strange, wild, tartar, added to which is hair of reddish brown with waves that refract, here and there, flashes of fire.... You have no idea of the passion of her dancing." She was the toast of Paris, photographed by Nadar and portrayed in lithographs, engravings, and monographs.

Here, in part, reads her statement:

> In the duration of my ten-year married life literally not one week has passed when my husband has not subjected me to severe assaults....
>
> From my side there has not been the slightest reason for such treatment by my husband. Knowing his character to be irascible and jealous to the point of fury, I would carefully avoid anything that might arouse in him ... a feeling of jealousy ... I would keep silent before him when, backstage, he tore apart the bouquets brought to me by the public, accompanying this with outbursts, which don't bear repeating in writing.... His treatment of me grew more cruel day by day, the physical abuse was repeated more and more often and with even more violence than before. In this way my situation was unbearable, but out of my feelings as a wife and mother I was hesitant to use the power of the Law for mediation between me and my husband, and perhaps would not have turned to the Law, if it were not for an incident on 13 November which broke the limit of my endurance. On this day, when I was returning from the theatre in a carriage with my maid, my husband, having caught up with the carriage, stopped it, dragged my servant out of it, sat in her place, seized me by the throat and began to throttle me and spit in my face. I was not able to bear this latest insult [and resolved] to find protection in the Law from my cruel husband ...
>
> Fearing to weary your attention with a catalogue of each of my husband's actions—since they, recurring without interruption in the course of ten years, form too long a list

and do not stand out from one another in character—I consider it enough only to say what precisely they consisted of.
Wishing to get even with me for whatever misdeed created
by his imagination, he would seize me by the hand, drag me
into the bedroom, lock it, and start to hit me, in the majority of cases to the point that I would fall unconscious, and it
was in this state that the serving girls, Elena Sokolova, Olga
Andreeva, and the laundress Solomonida Smirnova, would
find me when they entered the bedroom after my husband
had left. Later my husband stopped being inhibited by the
presence of the children and the maid and assaulted me in
their presence, which the aforementioned laundress Solomonida Smirnova can confirm.

For verification, Surovshchikova provided the addresses of all
the people mentioned in her statement. The evidence was convinc-
ing enough to the magistrate that he immediately opened a criminal
investigation that could have resulted in Petipa serving time in the
terrifying Litovsky Fortress. Perhaps due to this threat, an agree-
ment was reached out of court and Maria never lived with her husband again. Curiously, it was decided that their daughter, then ten
years old, would live with her father, while Maria retained custody
of their eight-year-old son. She retired from the stage two years later
and died of smallpox at age forty-six. After her death Petipa married
his second dancer wife, who was thirty-six years his junior and with
whom he already had had four of the six children he would have
with her.

I am so disappointed by a man to whom, heretofore, as a dancer, I
was beholden. His abhorrent behavior is particularly haunting news
in a profession that so explicitly honors the nobility of good behavior. The vision of a balletmaster humiliating and hitting a ballerina—
those creatures of such delicacy and devotion—is a blight on Petipa's
memory. And how brave was this woman, well over a hundred and
fifty years ago, in tsarist Russia, to have had the self-respect, even in
her desperation, to go to the authorities and report her husband's
criminal behavior. Then was not now.

"My work is wasted," Petipa, age eighty-five, wrote in his diary,
on January 22, 1904, after learning that his latest new ballet had been

Maria Surovshchikova,
ballerina and Petipa's first wife

canceled before its premiere. He was being pushed out of his position of power at the theater and, in what one writer termed his "choreographic death agony," he made no more. That very same day, just
across town in St. Petersburg, Georgi Melitonovich Balanchivadze
was born. Petipa died six years later, aged ninety-two, embittered
and itching, having acquired an excruciating skin disease that gave
him daily misery. By then the six-year-old Georgi was already choreographing his phantom congregation of obedient chairs.

From the Dying Swan pose, we bring our torsos upright but remain
sitting on our folded back leg. The center girl, crossing her arm over
her body, offers me her left hand; I similarly cross my arm over my
body and take hers with my right hand, then offer my left hand to
the girl on my right. She takes my hand with her right and, being the
end of our line, offers her left hand to the air, to others who are there
but not there: continuity. This sequence is then repeated on the left
side of the center girl, with the last girl offering her right hand to
the air. In the first years of the Russian Dance, the outside two girls
offered their hands back inward, closing the circle, but sometime,

Opening the ring from five to infinity (from left: Roma Sosenko, the author, Lisa Hess, Darla Hoover, and Delia Peters) *(© Steven Caras)*

probably in the late 1940s, Balanchine changed it, opening the ring from five to infinity.

Thus we weave ourselves together, an open daisy chain. And we do not let go of one another's hands throughout our next movements, including when we stand up to full pointe.

The two outside girls step out on a flat foot and each begins winding herself about her friend with small steps, heels never touching the ground. The group keeps winding and winding around ourselves until we are a tight cluster of blue tulle, all on pointe, and we turn together as a whole, then unwind in reverse, hands never letting go. No pyrotechnics, no jumps, runs, or turns, just girls weaving around each other, finishing with all five facing the front of the stage, hands held up high to our sides, a zigzag of upward arms.

The center girl then begins yet another reverse pivot until we are all pulled in close, arms still held high and crisscrossed, facing the back of the stage. On the next two notes, we turn, drop our heads in unison sideways, ears down to the right . . . and then to the left, holding there a beat. We pivot to face front and repeat, pausing on pointe, arms held high, hands joined, head to the right, then left. We hold it there a beat. Such small head movements with such effect.

This opening of the Russian Dance has taken one minute and

An iconic moment in the Russian Dance *(© Steven Caras)*

forty-six seconds. It is the slowest, quietest, and most intimate sequence in the ballet, a witnessing of women in allegiance, no cause, no common adversary, just five women bonded in music, beauty, and bourrées.

Our link is finally broken when the lead Russian Girl lets go and takes three large, slow steps, down center stage, stopping in a majestic B+, thus distinguishing herself again as a solo dancer. We four loosen hands, the two inner girls taking three steps back, the two outer girls three forward. And we pause. Then all hell breaks loose. Minute 16:15.

17. HOPPING

IIIIIIIIIIIIIIIIIIIIIIIIIIIIIIIIIIIIIIIIIIIIIIIIIIIIIIIIIIIIIIIIIIIIIIIIIIIIIIIIIIIIIIIIIIIIIIIIIIIIIIII

After a series of zingy hip-forward juts; crazy, high, legs-akimbo jumps; a bunch of other jumps landing on a straight leg on pointe in arabesque to alternating sides; speedy, bendy bourrées; madly off-balance backward-leaning arabesques; and multiple bouncing chugs—chug, chug, chug—traveling about the stage, followed by eighteen traveling jumps, one leg in front followed by the other leg in back (we call these the "flies"), we five Russian Girls exit the stage. Whew! But we don't go anywhere, staying just out of sight in our far-upstage-left wing, bending over at the waist, hands on knees for support; we are breathing hard, gasping for air, while quickly wiping our fingers just above our eyebrows to stop drops from falling into our thick eyelashes, where they can gather and be momentarily blinding.

We have just been onstage for six minutes and fifty-two seconds, from the second movement straight into the third without an exit. This is an incredibly long entrance for any dancer in any ballet, and the final minute, when we are already tired, is the most physically strenuous of all. While ballet dancers are certainly the ultimate athletes, we are sprinters, not long-distance runners. (This brief "spurt" of energy quality is one of the reasons so many dancers over the years have been able to smoke and yet can still dance—though during my years at NYCB there was no smoking that I saw; a former smoker,

Balanchine did not approve.) After a six-second respite—yes, only six seconds—we charge, full force, back onstage, joining three other groups of four that have spun onstage to make us sixteen once again.

Following this controlled mayhem, we align ourselves in four rows across, each four dancers deep, and do the first series of "hops." Though we hop in opposite directions: the two rows on stage right hop in arabesque away from center toward the right wing, while the two rows on stage left do the same toward the left, parting into two groups and emptying the whole center of the stage. Creating a vacuum. It was at this very moment in the ballet that I executed the worst onstage faux pas of my entire career.

It is one thing for a dancer to slip and fall, for her headpiece to come loose, or for a seam in her costume to rip. But to actually do the wrong choreography is something else again: rather than a chance mishap, it is a kind of moral failing, especially if it's the choreography of George Balanchine that you bungle.

When I was asked to join the company after a year of being an apprentice, I was immediately assigned to be an understudy for one of the four Russian Girls—an exciting honor for a new recruit. The transition from lead dancer in the School to bottom-of-the-totem-pole in the company was abrupt. Occasionally the brief, but intense, attention on the "new" girl translated in Balanchine's world into immediate recognition within the company, evident in casting. A few of us—very few—would then commence an inexorable climb to the top, while most of us stayed in the corps de ballet: top dancers all, but without ascending to that higher plane where ballerinas reigned.

Along with learning a Russian Girl, I was soon also called to rehearsals to learn several roles in Jerome Robbins's ballets, danced by Patricia McBride and Gelsey Kirkland, who had recently left the company (I was in the petite, quick, good-jump category like them): *Scherzo Fantastique, Dances at a Gathering,* and *Goldberg Variations.* Elation and panic in equal measure. The powers that be—in this case Robbins, a company balletmaster alongside Balanchine—were always testing out newcomers. In the end, I never danced any of these principal roles that I learned, and within a few months I was no longer even called to their rehearsals. I never knew what had happened but could only conclude that somehow I had not been up to snuff. I never asked anyone why, being too timid among the greatness all about me—likely the problem itself. Though I, like many of us at NYCB at that time, certainly did not feel that Robbins was top-notch: he was a second-, if not third-rate, artist—and man—beside Balanchine, and unlike the world at large, we all knew it. He got no special attention in a crowded theater elevator, while the waters parted if the door opened and Mr. B stepped in. But Robbins was also less approachable than Mr. B, known for his temper and vicious outbursts at dancers. I kept away. Meanwhile, I was learning and dancing in about twenty Balanchine ballets, so onward was the call.

But I remained an understudy for *Serenade*—this was Balanchine casting, not Robbins—and spent the rehearsals for the next months in the back of the studio alone, learning the role of the specific Russian Girl I was told to watch. However, I never danced the role with the whole cast, much less in a performance.

Then, as was a not-infrequent occurrence, the Russian Girl I understudied hurt herself midafternoon one day and suddenly I was "on." A hastily tossed together rehearsal was called for me onstage after regular rehearsal hours at 6:00 p.m. Show at 8:00. Per usual in an emergency rehearsal, not everyone in the ballet showed up, and certainly not any of the three lead dancers. Since it is a run-through with only one purpose—to put in the new girl—many arrive in robes and soft toe shoes, hair down, and simply mark the dance by walking it and indicating the steps by waving their arms and hands about: everyone is tired after an already long day.

This single, straight run-through of the whole ballet was the first time I actually danced the role with everyone else. Whoa! This was an entirely different experience from just practicing the steps in the back of the studio by yourself. It felt like an onslaught at Grand Central with the after-work crowd rushing to the same train about to leave the station, all aiming for different compartments. The thirty minutes was focused not at all on actual choreography, the steps—I was supposed to know all that by now, and I did—but entirely on placement on the stage, so no actual collisions would happen during the endless entrances, exits, running, crisscrossing, and weaving. And hops.

After the run-through, a quick costume fitting—I would need to wear the costume of the girl I was replacing, and any last-minute adjustments, like shortening the shoulder straps, would be made immediately by the ever-on-hand costume ladies. Back at my dressing room cubby, I down three bites of tuna fish and a few more of my breakfast corn muffin, brush my teeth, take a quick shower after a whole day in the theater rehearsing, sweating. Then whip my hair up into a tight bun, put on my lashes, pancake makeup, blush under the cheekbones, and pale pink lipstick. Finally, a long search, sitting on the linoleum floor in front of my theater case, for the right pair of toe shoes—hard enough boxes for a lot of difficult dancing on pointe, but soft enough to not make a sound onstage, the ever-precarious balance. At 7:00 p.m., a twenty-minute warm-up at the barre in the little fifth-floor studio in three layers of leg warmers, then down to the stage-level greenroom at 7:45 p.m. to get cinched into the beautiful costume.

We drop our robes over the backs of various chairs, emerging in our pink tights—and occasionally pink tunic pants, if the costume's crotch is just thin netting, as it was with most tutus. We then find our costume on the rack, hanging in alphabetical order—our last name written on the inside waistband label reading "Karinska." I look for the name of the girl I am replacing. Stepping carefully with pointed feet into the two leg holes, we pull up the front and put our arms through the thin elastic straps, usually pink or beige, designed to disappear onstage. We wait our turn for one of two or three greenroom ladies to hook up the back of the bodice as we hold both arms up to the sides, clearing the way for their job. There are as many as thirty hooks on the outside, along with some larger, strategic ones inside to keep the waistband anchored in its place despite the endless movement that threatens to raise it. Mme Pourmel, a short, immaculate Russian woman, a tight, gray bun at her neck, is boss here, sweet like a grandmother but totally vigilant about our costume etiquette.

These Russian ladies peopled Balanchine's world, our world, from our teachers at the School to the costume shop. If Mme Pourmel, or any of her staff, caught you with your hands on your hips in your costume, they were quickly tapped down—she was like a beloved but strict Mother Superior: Karinska's costumes were expensive, handmade works of art that had to endure huge amounts of wear, tear, and sweat onstage, so backstage fingerprints from touching rosin or smoothing our hairsprayed hair were forbidden.

After retying my toe shoe ribbons several times for exactly the right tension—tight enough for total support but not so tight that one's ankle is strangled and goes numb—and sewing in the ends with a few quick stitches, I move on to the rosin box ritual: rosin on the heels of my tights, inside the toe shoe heel, and then all over the bottom and front tips. Onstage at 7:55 p.m. to practice a few pirouettes and do my own run-through of the thirty-three-minute ballet in the ten minutes before the curtain would rise: a last Hail Mary. We can hear the orchestra tuning up and some general rustling of coats and programs and chatter as the audience files in and takes their places on the other side of the enormous brocade gold curtain. Perry calls, "Places, please!" and I take my place all the way downstage left, in front, no one in front of me to follow should my memory falter. The orchestra begins, the audience is silent, the strings of the violins cut the air. Final toe shoe ribbon check, feet in tight parallel, right arm lifted, palm out, fingers separated and soft. The curtain rises. My God, it is exciting. Absolutely terrifying. But I look calm.

All had gone well until now—I'd made it through half the ballet with no mishaps—until these hops. I was one of four girls in the front row, splitting center. But now, as the sea of sixteen clouds of tulle parted, moving toward opposite wings, my posse hopped away from me, while I distinguished myself by hopping, big and proud, right at the front of the stage, in the direction of the group that was not mine. I recognized instantly—mid–first hop—my colossal blunder, but it was too late. I was center stage, alone. All alone. All wrong. Mortified. I might as well have been standing in court, all eyes on me, just convicted of a gruesome crime. Unlike most small choreographic mistakes, which much of the audience might well miss among the masses of moving dancers, I was, at this very moment, the only dancer on center stage, like a character in a *Saturday Night Live* skit of ballet bloopers. But this was no comedy. This was Balanchine and Tschaikovsky, our immortals, and I was AWOL.

Explaining the feeling of realizing what one has done at such a moment is like trying to describe the silent scream in a dream that, if heard, would prevent otherwise sure death. I died, but worse, I was

still alive, hopping away in a void of humiliation. My group hopped
back in toward me, and I rejoined the proceedings for the remainder
of the ballet without further trouble. But everyone knew what I had
done: the ballet mistress, the conductor, and 2,800 people in the
audience. And, I found out when the ballet was over, someone else
had been watching in the wings, awaiting his lead role in the last
ballet of the night, *Cortège Hongrois*.

This illegally attractive Dane had recently been imported by Balanchine, as he had imported others from the Royal Danish Ballet, to
shore up the always thin ranks of lead male dancers. Of all the great
classical schools—including English, French, Italian, and Russian—
it was the Danish Bournonville training that Balanchine liked best,
the meticulous, fast, precise footwork, and regal yet subdued attitude
most suited as a base for his own training and aesthetic. This dancer,
however, was not cut from the same cloth as his fellow recruits. Both
physically and egoistically, this one derived from the superstar, pow-
erhouse model of the two great Russian defectors—Nureyev and
Baryshnikov. He was dripping with animal charisma, sex appeal,
serious muscles, and gasp-inducing jumps and turns that begged for
applause mid-solo: the kind of thing Balanchine abhorred. Predictably perhaps, his tenure in Balanchine's world was short-lived. But
not before he cut a small, but notable, path of conquest, and I, for
reasons still unclear, was one who landed on his path.

Barely holding back hysterical tears once the curtain came down
on *Serenade* (those came once I reached the relative privacy of a
bathroom stall), I was gathering up my leg warmers at the backstage bench, and this man, whom I had never spoken to, came up,
his navy terry-cloth backstage robe hanging open over his warm-up
garb, and asked me to dinner after the performance. I was thunder-
struck. I was a virgin who had been kissed just once—the vigor of
it had frightened me—and he was known for his vigorous woman-
izing. Dinner? How insane. I said yes. Of course. Not only had I
just messed up onstage in a royal manner and he had seen it; I was
simply not, in my view, one of the most attractive girls in a company
of stunners. But his blue eyes trapped me, and the curiosity that
compels love ignited in a flash. I called him the Duke in my journal.

I have since always associated my great onstage gaffe—tellingly,
a directional error—with the loss of my virginity. Now, this did not

happen for three more months, during which time he took me to dinner regularly, and put me on the bus home, where I still lived with my parents on the East Side, without so much as ever touching me. But then one night he said, "You know I would be happy to just keep having dinner with you like this, but I don't think it will stay this way." Was he alluding to the unthinkable, what I only knew from books, from Anaïs Nin and D. H. Lawrence? After a short negotiation, over yet another post-performance dinner, I stated my terms. Being realistic and yet prideful—and knowing an adventure was imminent—I had a single requirement, as I detailed in my journal: I needed to know that he did not already know who the girl would be after me. (I was, perhaps naively, assuming there wasn't one already running alongside me.) This amused him greatly and produced the predictable response. He blew out the two tealight candles that were on the restaurant table and, when the melted wax had hardened after a few minutes, pocketed them. I knew why later when they were relit. Once his apartment door was closed, he touched me for the first time. Then kissed me, and everything, everything, happened, and those few hours changed my life forever. And I knew that they had. I noted in my diary that I had "not known that rational human beings could lose all reason in thirty seconds."

This grand, operatic introduction—he had the audacity to play Aram Khachaturian's *Spartacus* for my debut, melodious, gladiator-sized music with one crescendo after another between occasional adagios of alluring sweetness—into the erotic realm, where two bodies and two minds crash into each other, producing a third state, showed me the only other theater, besides Balanchine's, in which I wanted to reside. Both these places were—still are—"real life" to me, the quotidian merely a necessity. This unprecedented power captured me whole. He was the second great astonishment of my life.

While it has been said that the "high" art of Balanchine and the "lower" activity of the sexual self are opposites, to me they are so deeply connected as to emanate from the same source. Balanchine's work portrayed, in endless forms, the erotic and spiritual plastically melded into public art, while the erotic does the same, only privately.

I will never forget walking near Lincoln Center with this man and seeing Mr. B on the other side of the street. It was known that Balanchine didn't like this particular dancer sexually cycling through the ranks of young women. Three months later Balanchine fired him—he stopped being cast—after he insisted on accepting guest appearances with another company without NYCB management's approval. He returned to Europe for a long and successful career—and never came back. So that is how it ended for me with him. But if he hadn't emigrated, he would shortly have just moved on to that next pretty girl. I knew it was doomed from the start—which didn't stop me from airmailing him, for two years, boxes of my homemade almond crescents addressed to various opera-house stage doors around Europe where he was performing. Insistent young love. I never heard a word.

I have always wondered if it was my onstage blooper in *Serenade* that night that made him notice me, ask me to dinner, and then become my first great love, introducing me to romantic suffering within hours of deflowering me. He showed me in a single night a place of profound, ever-ongoing mystery—which, until then, was a purely literary affair for me—thus igniting my lifelong fascination and exploration of the uncertain science of desire. I see now that my first calamitous *Serenade;* my first date; my first man; my first love; my first amorous grief are now, however arbitrarily—but so goes love—intimately linked. *Serenade,* for me, is strangely inseparable (or perhaps not so strangely) from this other corporeal awakening. I will never know if it had not been this particular man—one of outsized magnetism—and the magnificent theatrical drama that was sex for him, but some other, more ordinary, fumbling young lover as equally inexperienced as myself, whether this enduring passion would have emerged in me. I wonder. He showed me not an act but a world. And broke my heart so as to remake me.

Minute 17:56.

18. ANARCHISTS

Soon after all the hopping, we clear offstage. The Waltz Girl and her partner have just rushed in, meeting each other in a sharp, head-to-head forked charge. There ensues a brief, intimate interlude between them. It is only their second time alone since the beginning of the Waltz, almost ten minutes ago—an eternity in dance time. If this is a courtship, it is proceeding glacially, if at all, and is certainly not the ballet's focus, not yet anyway.

His blue costume is far darker than hers and ours, almost navy, and he all but blends into the deep blue cyclorama, appearing at times like little more than a passing silhouette. This is a beautiful mini-interaction, an exposition of one of Balanchine's central subjects: a man's pursuit of an impossible creature, a dancer, a woman ever on the move.

The Waltz Girl jumps in a sauté arabesque away from him, then piqués onto pointe in an arabesque that leans, perilously, away from him while she turns her upper body to look back at him, as if checking that he is following her. He is. But she stays just out of reach. Each time he moves toward her but misses, he kneels, one arm extended to her, his head lifted up in a gesture of respect, even devotion—and perhaps a touch of dignified pleading. Still, he misses, failing four times. Finally, success: as she goes into her leaning arabesque the fifth time, the sixth, and the seventh, he captures her hand—she has finally allowed it, by lessening her distance—and with his counter-pull she stays on pointe longer and can lean even farther away from him, thanks to her connection to him. This seventeen-second pas de deux has all the hallmarks of romance but remains so brief, so unresolved, that Balanchine leaves no time for it to register as "story." It stands simply as exquisite movement. He was sly.

We four Russian dancers come onstage again, soon joined by twelve more. The couple—together and separately—make brief entrances on and off until we are all assembled. And we hop again. But the formation and directions are different this time, and there is now an unmistakable re-creation of a monumental moment from our heritage, from *Giselle*.

Two sets of four girls form two squares—two dancers in front, two in back—on either far side of the stage, while just behind them, centered, are two rows of four girls each. The Waltz Girl takes her place in front of us all, downstage center. The last time she joined our ranks, long ago, in the Sonatina, she had come onstage, lost, and found her place among us, as our seventeenth member—but now she has stepped forward as leader, her evolution distinct, yet also our evolution. "The three women and the corps could be one person," said one dancer. "We're all incorporated into each other."

We were seventeen; now we are sixteen and one. But together we all hop in arabesque toward stage right, then toward stage left, our long skirts each forming a beautiful quarter-circle swoop: hundreds of yards of gathered tulle draping under gravity's downward draw as our arabesque legs counter that pull like living curtain rods. The cumulative effect of these seventeen wheels of soft fabric while we are hopping, hopping, in a kind of two-dimensional Egyptian profile, is a duplication of the same movement, in the same long-skirted bell tutus, by the Wilis in Act II of *Giselle*. But we are not Wilis. Or are we?

The Wilis are the ghosts of dead girls. Their unique manifestation in *Giselle* is, to my mind, the originating archetype of the female classical ballet dancer as ethereal feminine perfection: dedicated, fragile yet agile, an elusive creature of untrammeled purity, a streamlined, winged Madonna veiled in white. Her floating above the ground on her pointes, her sustained, soundless jumps, and her lightning speed confirm her status; she hovers impossibly just above the plinth of salvation.

Virgins all, the Wilis died from the betrayal by their beloveds just before their weddings. The exquisite Romanticism of *Giselle* onstage presents a brilliant paradox, a luring distraction, from a dark and violent tale of mortal female suffering giving birth to immortal, militarized revenge. Spectral anarchists of the first order, the Wilis' pitiless revolution is camouflaged inside the sheer beauty of their dreamy appearance in white veils, pink pointe shoes, and an avalanche of white tulle.

But they are, in fact, fierce fanatics. Kirstein called them a "force as a collective identity," merciless dominators disguised in the robes of angels: their unused bridal trousseaus are now armored vestments in their relentless crusade against men. A war they wage—and win—night after night in time without end.

No longer maidens suffering the debilitation of male duplicity, the Wilis have been reborn as women of purpose, their power deriving from their common cause and indissoluble unity. Their vulnerability is transformed into a blitz of slaughtering rage. Led by their queen, the pitiless Myrtha, their sole aim in their afterlife is to end

Myrtha and the Wilis in their bridal veils, *Giselle,* Act II *(© Ken Stiles)*

the life of men who cross their path—any man will do. And danc-ing itself is the Wilis' hidden-in-plain-sight lethal weapon. Dancing their prey through the night, they exhaust them into their graves.

The origins of this brutal tale—which invokes variously the god-dess Diana and her devoted virgin priestesses, the sexually irresistible femmes fatales of the late nineteenth-century poets, and the furious feminists of the twentieth and twenty-first centuries—resides in the imaginations of four men, three French, one German. Victor Hugo, in his 1829 poem "Fantômes," emphasizes the association between dancing and death, dancing into death, dancing after death, which found its most popular expression in 1949 in the greatest dance film ever made, Michael Powell's *The Red Shoes*. "Why do you want to dance?" the impresario asks. "Why do you want to live?" the dancer responds.

Heinrich Heine, in *De l'Allemagne*, recounts the legend of the Slavic "ghostly female dancers," adding to the dance-and-death link the sensual association, specifically female sexual frustration.

> The Willis are brides who died before being married. The poor young creatures cannot lie calmly in their graves; in their dead hearts and feet the old passion for dancing, which they could not gratify in their lives, still burns. So at mid-night they rise, assemble in troops on the highways, and woe to the young man who meets them! He must dance with them, they surround him in unbridled madness, and he must dance with them without rest or repose till he falls down dead. In their bridal dresses, crowns of flowers, and rib-bons flying from their heads, flashing rings on their fingers, the Willis dance in the moonshine, as do the elves. Their faces though snow white, are young and fair; they laugh so strangely sweet, they nod with such seductive secrecy, so promisingly—these dead Bacchantae are irresistible!

For these "air spirits," this dance to the death is their art. In 1841, the poet Théophile Gautier and the playwright Jules-Henri Vernoy de Saint-Georges collaborated on the libretto for *Giselle*, basing their drama on these two scant references, only slightly downplaying the erotic drive of Heine's fatally "seductive" and "irresistible" Wilis, who "seek after death the joys" deprived to them in life; the story is haunting and surprisingly suggestive.

The Giselle of the libretto is a peasant girl whose "only pleasure" is dance and "only happiness" is Loys, who is in fact Albrecht, an aristocrat, a duke in disguise as her equal. When she finds out that she has been betrayed—Albrecht is already betrothed to a woman of his own high rank—"a horrible and dark delirium seizes her" and she "drops" herself down on the point of her lover's sword. Her mother "pulls her out." Most productions to this day sanitize this phallic suicide, and Giselle simply dies of her "madness."

Act II takes place at night, the "lugubrious hour" when the "Wilis go to their ballroom" and take "their voluptuous poses" in "this fatal place." This "deadly network," this "cruel troop," welcomes Giselle, its newest member, and "her wings are born."

In short order, the Wilis dispatch Hilarion, a jealous paramour, to his death by drowning, and aim for the same with Giselle's beloved Albrecht. But here comes the twist: her love for him, despite his deception, emerges as even greater than her obedience to the Wilis' mission. She begs Myrtha to have mercy on him. As the "bright rays of the sun" rise, the Wilis "bend," "stagger," and "die at the approach of day," but Albrecht remains alive. Giselle returns to her tomb, and as the ballet ends, we see that he, having killed the thing he loved, will mourn her all his days.

Gautier and Saint-Georges, however, did not end their story here, as most productions now do, but added one last scene. Albrecht's royal entourage arrives onstage, and just before Giselle expires in the daylight, she directs her beloved to marry Bathilde, his betrothed, confirming her character as a virgin saint. In his final gesture, as the curtain lowers, Albrecht extends his hand to Bathilde, obedient, in his eternal grief, to his great love. It's a great story.

Giselle premiered in Paris in 1841, with choreography by Jean Corelli and Jules Perrot, to an instant acclaim that has not abated for almost two hundred years, and it remains unique in the classical dance canon. Balanchine hated it. He would refer not infrequently to the ever-rampant balletic virus of "Gisellitis"—easily identified by the earnest brow and oh-so-solemn demeanor of a dancer: "soulfulness." "I'm not interested in dancers who want to show *soul*," he said. "Soul is very difficult to see." It is the rare dancer, like Suzanne Farrell, who dances so deeply, not only spatially but morally, that she does not *show* soul but becomes it.

One day in company class, to my great consternation, Mr. B diagnosed me with this illness, saying, as I extended a leg in an adagio sequence, "You know, dear, if you want to dance *Giselle,* you can go across the plaza." "Across the plaza" meant across Lincoln Center to the Metropolitan Opera, where American Ballet Theatre danced *Giselle,* a staple of their repertory. Total embarrassment.

Perhaps it was my perfect low-lying bun, my pale pink outfit with matching chiffon skirt, short in front but trailing my calves in back. Perhaps it was my furrowed brow. But the master psychologist was right. While I had no desire to dance *Giselle* at ABT, I was still imprinted with the romance, purity, and pathos of seeing Fonteyn and Nureyev dance it long before I ever saw a Balanchine ballet, long before I knew what Balanchine was about, long before I knew to love him.

Unable to allow this impression of me to stand, after class I gathered up my courage and knocked on the door of his office on the fourth floor. He welcomed me in, told me to sit down, and sat himself opposite, looking at me, waiting at full attention to hear what I had to say. How many hundreds of times in his life had he had such meetings with dancers, tending to their myriad questions, and problems, and requests for new or more parts—something I never dared.

"I do not want to dance *Giselle*. I want to dance your ballets."

"Okay, dear. Good. Now I know." That was settled between us right there and then. Things with Mr. B were always simple. And this was how I learned—became conscious—that I did indeed have a split commitment to the classic ballets of my British girlhood and the elongated power of his dances.

We chatted a little longer, and he turned the subject to what else I liked. When I left a few minutes later, he kissed me on the forehead and said with delight, as if it were far more important than my career cri de coeur, "And now I know you like champagne!" He loved champagne.

. . .

Act II of *Giselle* lies on a continuum in the history of dances called "les ballets blancs"—the white ballets, so named simply because the dancers wear white. These dances all take place after dark in a world of mist inhabited by the ephemeral ballerina radiating translucence. A not quite mortal vision, she embodies "the 'Christian' spirit," wrote Lincoln Kirstein, "a virginal paleness, sweet suffering, soulful abnegation"—and she appears only at dusk, alone or with her sisters, their lament matched only by the sheer beauty of their shapes, their shadows: for dancers are but shadows.

Ten years prior to *Giselle*, Giacomo Meyerbeer's grand opera *Robert le diable* presented, in Act III, a ballet interlude set under moonlight in a ruined cloister where "lapsed nuns laid buried," known as the "Ballet of the Nuns." Considered the first ballet blanc, the epitome of Gothic Romanticism, its theme is "passion and death, love beyond the grave," Kirstein wrote. Marie Taglioni—in choreography by her father, Filippo Taglioni—was cast as the Abbess Helena, in charge of nuns who had violated their vows in life with their "unholy thrills." Summoned, they now rise from their tombs and "deliver themselves to voluptuous pleasure," dancing madly like "huge night moths." It is a frequent theme in les ballets blancs—as in *Serenade:* in a world without men, women, literally, soar.

With its subversive undercurrent, its blunt juxtaposition of the sacred and the profane, the ballet was a sensation, the beginning of Taglioni's ascent at the Paris Opera, and what was probably the first time a sizable salary was allotted to a dancer in a notoriously underpaid profession. The scene was painted by Edgar Degas, and Hans Christian Andersen breathlessly described it: "By the hundred [the nuns] rise from the graveyard and drift into the cloister. They seem not to touch the earth. Like vaporous images, they glide past one another . . . Suddenly their shrouds fall to the ground. They stand in all their voluptuous nakedness, and there begins a bacchanal." Despite her success, Taglioni soon gave up the role of the abbess, fearing her participation in this "bacchanal" would curtail her carefully curated image of virtuous perfection.

The "Ballet of the Nuns" inaugurated a new phase in the still young art of classic dance: it introduced depth, an ethical compo-

Ballet of the Nuns, by Edgar Degas, 1871

nent. Until now, ballet had been "an agreeable exercise," a "diver-tissement," explained the Russian critic André Levinson, but now it "clarified matters of the soul. It became a mystery."

Less than four months later, in March 1832, Taglioni debuted in what would become her most famous role: the Sylph in *La Sylphide.* Sylphs, "whose Habitation is Air, are the best-considered Creatures imaginable," wrote Alexander Pope in 1712. In their role as messengers between our world and theirs, "Mortals may enjoy their company . . . with an inviolate Preservation of Chastity." *La Sylphide* defined this apparition, the ballerina, as exotic, wild, supernatural, all but divine: she was virtually canonized, a priestess, the artist as saint, and Taglioni was her avatar.

In the ballet, the Sylph is a flirtatious sprite in love with James, a Scotsman, who, like Albrecht in *Giselle,* is promised to another mortal—sacred and profane again in battle. James's desire to possess his enchanting Sylph results in a witch's giving him a magic scarf by which to secure his beloved—but as he wraps her in his instrument of capture, her wings fall off and she dies. She is carried aloft by her sister sylphs.

Decades later the "Kingdom of Shades" scene in *La Bayadère* and Acts II and IV of *Swan Lake* provided yet more examples of ballets blancs, bringing the genre to the precipice of the twentieth century. Just past the turn, in 1909, when Michel Fokine choreographed *Les Sylphides*, set to Chopin, he carried the white ballets into the multi-colored world of Diaghilev's Ballets Russes. While it was a one-act ballet with no plot, a mere "reverie," the costumes were designed in purposeful tribute to Taglioni in *La Sylphide*—long white bell skirts and little wings mid-back, bouncing more than flapping.

Twenty-five years later, in the wake of the Jazz Age in America, Balanchine made *Serenade*—a ballet blanc in blue, set, like all ballets blancs, "in the light of the moon." But this lineage was not apparent for almost two decades after its premiere, when *Serenade* was still a ballet in search of its final fabric and form.

So while Mr. B protested Gisellitis to rid us of superficial sorrow, false poignancy, and mannered moves, he not only acknowledged our heritage but also incorporated it into our present. While he yanked us dancers out of the dusty trappings of the Romantic ballet, he did not take the ballerina, which Taglioni exemplified, off her pedestal: he elevated us all onto hers. There was, surprisingly, plenty of room.

The nineteenth century saw classical ballet finally established as a serious art form after several hundred years as an extravagant novelty of the aristocracy—and its stars were enchanted women, airborne women. Alongside their dresses of silk and tulle, they were adorned with accessories: veils, scarves, feathers, and wings, wings, wings—these "Light" women flew. Sylphs, swans, sprites, wraiths, seraphs, dryads, shades, phantoms, these are the magical, mythical, mischievous, chaste, and luminous creatures inhabited by ballerinas. They are youthful, often childlike, emanations of grace and delicacy that enchant, evanesce, flirt, charm, drift, hypnotize, disappear, reappear,

haunt, melt, float, and, of course, die—beautifully—only to be resurrected on a higher plane. Embodying the desire to merge with the
divine, these virgin femmes fatales are male dreams: they are angels.
Dying in the prime of their youth and beauty, they live forever, only
ever united with their beloveds in death. And they were very, very
popular.

We, in *Serenade,* are the granddaughters of these women, and
Balanchine makes our connection clear, unbreakable. Our grit,
determination, discipline, beauty, passion, and enigmatic presence
are the same from the moment the audience first sees us in parallel
in rays of blue light, but our motivation is no longer defined in relation to a man, to earthly love. In Balanchine's world, stated from the
outset in *Serenade,* it is the man, not the woman, who is imprisoned
in the ever-thwarted pursuit of the ideal romantic partner while
we—despite dalliance and pleasure and occasional heartbreak—
forever escape his possession. We possess, finally, ourselves.

As young dancers, we were unconscious of this gift, of course,
but as descendants of these specters—creatures transfigured by
death—we are the ghosts of ghosts, deadless. We live in the distant
echo of romantic cause—but never were we more alive than when
breathing, chugging, turning, jumping, and hopping onstage, then
off, in *Serenade.*

We still, like them, dance at midnight under the moon in our long
gowns. But we are no longer naughty nuns, neurasthenic peasants,
trapped harem girls, or cursed swans—all women banded together
in servitude. We are not them. After a century of metamorphoses,
Balanchine smashed the genre wide open and elevated our profile
from these male projections of the Madonna and whore—and their
impossible resolution. But he removed more than just our wings and
stories and interfering relatives. He took away our motivation of
Beloved love, its violence and death, and left us to our own devices.
The Waltz Girl's easy-come, easy-go repartee with her partner early
in the ballet reveals this shift. We are indeed the Wilis of our time,
but we are long past killing men, who are no longer our focus—men
are rendered as elegant background in *Serenade,* our aides-de-camp.

From dead, wronged virgins, we emerge as dancers, just dancers,
autonomous. In *Serenade,* Balanchine pulled our forebears out of the

nineteenth century and gave us a profession other than that of a virgin frustrated by love. He gave us dance—not as a means to achieve a purpose, but as the purpose itself. Balanchine looked at women dancers and found that we were more than enough, so he dispensed with wings, veils, princes, cads, mothers, fiancés, and pending nuptials. While at once tying us tightly, irrevocably, to our foremothers, he released us from their strictures, their froufrou. He pared down our entire complex, gorgeous history—just as he learned to "eliminate" and "clarify" in *Apollo*—to its most essential essence: femininity distilled, two-hundred-proof.

Placing us all onstage, alone together, he freed us from male instigation and interference. Men come—though mainly go—in *Serenade,* but they are transient, neither our raison d'être nor the determinators of our fate. They do not define our existence; they are but stops, some important, some amusing, some utilitarian, along the way. We no longer dance in madness, misery, or revenge. We dance for dance's sake, fate enough.

As the Russian Dance comes to its end, we all swiftly run off together stage right, but though the Waltz Girl heads in the same direction, she breaks from us, whirling in chaîné turns on demi-pointe, fast, too fast with her arms waving about her head in a haphazard, most unclassical manner. Her tight top twist, until now an unmoving small bun crowning her head, loosens, and her long hair is suddenly spinning about her like a dervish. She collapses to the stage floor. It is unsettling to see a ballerina succumb, to witness gravity having its rare triumph over her airborne life. Now, stilled by unknown turmoil, she lies on the barren stage, her face bowed, elongated in a pool of tulle, hair everywhere, a cobweb net.

What happened?

And what of the loose hair that ties this fall to Giselle so clearly? It was not there in 1934 but was added by Balanchine forty-four years later. Critics liked to protest that he should not alter his own work, particularly *Serenade,* which the great critic Arlene Croce anointed "a messianic work." But his view of "critics" was, predictably, low. While at the end of his life, he was sanctioned as "genius," there were many decades when his work was derided or dismissed.

Anna Pavlova in the mad
scene of *Giselle,* Act I,
1903, holding Albrecht's
sword, the instrument of
her suicide

"Critics don't know anything!" he said. "Who is a critic? A person who can write."*

Was Balanchine purposefully, so late in the game, reminding us of Giselle's mad scene here in the ballerina's dramatic fall and her wild, loosened hair? Hardly. And yet.

* Balanchine dramatized the damage inflicted on an artist by critics to demolishing effect in the 1980 *Robert Schumann's "Davidsbündlertänze,"* where five towering figures, head-to-toe in ominous black, enter the stage to torment the artist with their enormous black quills, poised like spears. In rehearsal, and to his undisguised amusement, he went so far as to give each of these ominous figures the name of a current dance critic. "This is Clive, this is Tobi, this is Arlene ..."

19. CUPID'S KISS

S o how is your hair, is it still long?" Mr. B asked Maria Calegari. "Or have you cut it for your boyfriend?"

Mr. B often pronounced the word "boyfriend"—on the rare occasions he said it—with a lingering, amused twang on the "oy." He didn't like them. Why would he? It was so simple: more often than not if a young dancer—and we were always young when we first came into his orbit—got a boyfriend, she would become distracted from her dancing, from class, from performance as her sole purpose for being, and more than one career suffered, halted, or occasionally entirely evaporated as a result of this lost focus. If you put a stallion in the barn with a female champion racehorse, there will be trouble—nature's favorite kind of trouble, perhaps, but trouble nonetheless—and she will lose her next race. Time for a dancer is so short; he wanted us to succeed.

It was the late 1970s and Balanchine had asked for an impromptu rehearsal between matinee and evening shows on a weekend— not the usual union-regulated rehearsal time but always a special request—with the three solo women currently performing *Serenade*. The four of them gathered in the Main Hall studio on the fifth floor of the theater with the pianist. Calegari, having just danced the matinee, was still in stage makeup, the great black wings of her false eyelashes hovering in place.

"Yes, my hair is still long," said Calegari, who, though still in the corps, had been dancing the Dark Angel since she first was cast in the role at age seventeen in the 1974 School of American Ballet year-end Workshop performance. It was the same performance, staged by Suki Schorer, that I also had danced, where we all learned those steps together and entered Mr. B's mystical blue world before ever knowing him.

The truth is, hardly any of us would have cut our long locks for any "boyfriend"—we didn't highlight it, or layer it, and we certainly never wore bangs. We did nothing that would place us in any identifiable place or epoch; ballerinas are timeless and exist only in a moment of music. However, every now and then a rebel came into company class having cut her hair, thus Mr. B's question.

Calegari had that rare, rich, deep-red hair, which, with her pale white skin, large green eyes, high cheekbones, and Italian heritage—via Queens—rendered her a veritable Botticelli by a Pre-Raphaelite. She reached up and started pulling out the endless hairpins holding her bun in place, piling them in one palm. The other two dancers, Karin von Aroldingen, whose hair was dirty blond, and Colleen Neary, whose hair was dark brown, also took their hair clips out. All had long hair, though of varying lengths. Balanchine was delighted. "GREAT!!!!" he said of the three colors: "It looks like a Clairol commercial!!!"

Sometimes in class or rehearsal, he would pause and say, "Ah! We are alone now," meaning we were en famille, the public and critics absent, then he would proceed to make seemingly non sequitur references to current American advertisements and popular television series. Thus he would disarm our ever-present gravity, his constant levity keeping us all very down-to-earth—no "soul" required—particularly while working on a long-established "masterpiece."

For four decades, all the female dancers of *Serenade* had worn their hair tightly smoothed back in either buns or French twists. Balanchine now wanted to see how it would look for the three muses of the Elegy to release their tresses, drastically changing the look of the ballet and the movement itself—their hair joined their tulle skirts in trailing waves, their movements extended.

Balanchine loved long hair on women, and it had a deep significance for him. A few of his earliest works in St. Petersburg even featured unpinned hair—radical in the immediate wake of Petipa's classical mode. Free-flowing hair reappeared periodically throughout his life, right up to the end. A woman's soft, long hair denoted the intimacy of the erotic, the vulnerability of the bedroom, though, of course, he never said as much. But it was evident: on the Sleepwalker in *La Sonnambula* in 1946 (well, after all, she'd been in bed, so her hair likely was down); in the mysterious, ethereal section of *Ivesiana* titled "The Unanswered Question" in 1954, where a solo woman with bare legs and feet and wearing a simple white leotard is partnered by four men and never touches the floor for the entire dance; in 1963, in the yearning, love-torn pas de deux between an older man and a younger woman in *Meditation;* on Dulcinea as she washes the Don's feet like the Madonna in *Don Quixote* in 1965; in the first three of the four movements of *Tschaikovsky Suite #3* in 1970, where the costumes, scenery, and lighting denote a balletic bedroom; in the opening section, the Elysian Fields, of *Chaconne* in 1976. Even his devastating farewell to romantic love, the 1980 *Robert Schumann's "Davidsbündlertänze,"* has the four lead women wearing bouncing ponytails with silk ribbons. Their half-up, half-down hair signals the receding of the Romantic.

That same year in the finale of *Walpurgisnacht,* set to music from Gounod's *Faust,* Balanchine wanted the hair of the entire cast of twenty-four women entirely untethered, and our movements here were anything but restrained. There was so much long hair of all hues flying about onstage that, backstage, we called the ballet "Fire at the Hairdresser's." Balanchine adored it: a world of beautiful, lithe Terpsichores, his goddesses. He our Apollo.

As Balanchine aged, his desire to see this kind of free, open, feminine beauty seemed to only increase. "Love is a very important thing in a man's life, especially toward the end," he told Solomon Volkov from his hospital bed a few months before he died. "More important than art. When you're getting old, it seems that art can wait, but a woman won't. In art, you think you understand a thing or two already. But with a woman, that's not the case, you can't understand her totally—never, ever." When faced with his own end, love took precedence over art; his art done, love remained, wanting and wanted.

And never was Balanchine's love for the mystery of women

more apparent than in *Serenade*'s eight-minute Elegy, involving one man and, yes, three women. He liked what he saw that afternoon in the Main Hall on his ballerinas with their unleashed locks—and so it is danced to this day. This is how a ballet with no story gained yet deeper layers of storylessness.

More than one critic protested, not pleased with him—which amused him—for challenging their long worked-over analysis of the ballet's meaning.

> "People never seem to understand unless they can put their finger into things," he said once. "Like touching dough: when people see bread rising, they smell something and they say, 'Oh, is it going up?' And they poke their finger in it. 'Ah,' they say, 'now I see.' But of course the dough then goes down. They spoil everything by insisting on *touching*."

So very Balanchine, ever teaching by upending assumptions, all the while simply pleasing himself, true to his own compass. But his own direction, so clear, so precise, so vast as to have created not so much a body of work as an entire universe, was not the result of any "personal growth" or line of philosophical pursuit. He said it came from God. This, he said, is what he was given. I, an atheist, have no better answer. No one does.

The Waltz Girl remains grounded and motionless as the last movement, Elegy, begins. By presenting a woman downed, this dance becomes ever more inscrutable. Tipped onto her right side facing the audience, her body hugging the stage floor, she rests her head on her extended right arm. Is she wounded?

A man and a woman quietly enter from the shadows far upstage left and begin walking slowly on a diagonal in her direction. They do not travel side by side, but as one. The woman is the Dark Angel. She has always been called the Dark Angel—Balanchine called her this—though we never knew exactly why she got this name. In Stravinsky's *Orpheus* fourteen years later, Balanchine has another Dark Angel, but he is male. It is rare in a Balanchine ballet to have a "character" defined, though this particular moniker gives her more evocation than specificity. With only a few short entrances and exits in the ballet so far, it is only now that she reveals her mantle. Her hair, like the Waltz Girl's, is also free about her shoulders.

The unnamed man—her second anonymous man in dark blue, not the one who danced with her in the previous movements—walks in front of the Dark Angel. But she is so close behind him that her hips press against his, while his left arm curves low and back, the top of his hand resting on her lower back, their pelvises moving in perfect unison. Her left arm is curved up under his left arm, her hand resting gently on his left shoulder, their torsos now also locked together. Her right hand covers his eyes, her palm his mask, removing his sight. "You are his eyes," Mr. B said to one Dark Angel. A dancer who was there in 1934 asked Mr. B about this unusual coupling and he told her with his classic specificity, "You know, Laskey [Charles Laskey, the male dancer], he is very near-sight. I thought he does not see, so, maybe more comfortable if eyes have cover and Kathryn [Mullowny, the Dark Angel] looks where to go."

He is taller, and as she turns her head to rest her left cheek on his upper back, her head disappears: the two are bonded now, merged into a single body, with one head. They walk forward, two right legs stepping, then two left legs stepping, like a mythical four-legged, one-bodied creature. After a few more paces, they pause and he lifts his right arm straight before them, appearing to point them in a forward direction. But it is she, not he—who cannot see—who leads from behind. In this exquisite, unusual, and yet so very simple formation of a man and woman moving together lies so much of Balanchine: the eroticism of their physical closeness, the visual beauty and symmetry of their walk-as-one, and the manifestation of mystery. What is going on? Who is he? Who is she? Where are they going? Are they even a man and a woman? Or a man and a woman metamorphosed into metaphor? Are they but allegory? But of what? It is glorious.

They proceed magisterially toward the still girl. Ten unified steps later they reach her and stop just behind her, as if he, in his blindness, has encountered a physical impediment. What unfolds next is so very beautiful.

The Dark Angel lifts her right hand from the man's eyes, allowing him to see again in such a way that the power is clearly hers, the decision to restore his sight hers. At the same time, her left arm lifts from her hold about his shoulder, releasing him from her entirely. Her arms float skyward, forming, briefly but distinctly, a V. Both arms stretched upward like this is not one of classical ballet's codified arm positions. Are these the Dark Angel's wings? Of course.

Angels were unique for Balanchine: they were not unreal to him. He called his dancers "angelic messengers"—though never, ever, to us directly—intermediaries between gods and humans, between the divine and the mortal, angels, with their wings, after all, can fly—classical ballet's highest aspiration and occasional illusion. "When Balanchine spoke of angels," wrote Lincoln Kirstein, "as he often did, and of his dancers as angels, he intended confidence in an angelic system that governed the deployment of a corps de ballet." In keeping with ballet's verticality, Balanchine's angels' wings are always raised upward, never folded down, most notably in the massive six-foot-high wings on the angels in the 1980 *Adagio Lamentoso**—two-winged seraphim—and as in one of the two angels on Tschaikovsky's grave, who stands guard, holding the crucifix, protecting and blessing the composer.

The Dark Angel's arms then drop low—are they still wings? or now arms again?—and she and the man lower themselves together on bended knees, she folded over his back, toward the prone, elongated body in front of them. As they descend, they arch their upper bodies over the girl on the stage floor, their arms curved downward to her.

Simultaneously, she moves too—she is revived!—drawing herself up so that her torso is vertical, though she remains sitting on the stage. She lifts her arms, mirroring theirs in an upward arc: four arms reaching down, two arms reaching up in a wide, all but closed, embrace. It is a gesture of intimate greeting, of compassion, of tenderness, the man airily sandwiched between the two women.

Or perhaps he is hovering between a woman he loves and his art, which, inexorably fastened to his being, pulls him elsewhere? How often a man—a woman—is lured by romance, though sense,

---

* The full name of the work is *Symphony No. 6—Pathétique: Fourth Movement, Adagio Lamentoso.*

Tschaikovsky's grave in St. Petersburg
(© *Paul Kolnik*)

and providence, dictate otherwise. This was most certainly the path of Balanchine's own love life: many loves, but his work—celebrating women, expanding women—the constant throughout.

This grouping will be repeated later, closing out the ensuing drama, with broken yearning. But for now, they are together, not quite entwined. Not yet.

This pose is a re-creation of Antonio Canova's voluptuous marble sculpture *Psyche Revived by Cupid's Kiss*. The young Balanchine likely saw it in Paris in the years just before he arrived in America and made *Serenade*.* The statue was commissioned from the Ital-

* A censored rendition, with a fig leaf on Cupid and an oversized drape on Psyche's lower body, is also in the Hermitage museum in St. Petersburg, but it was not there until 1926, two years after Balanchine left Russia.

ian sculptor in 1787 by a young Welsh member of parliament, John Campbell, later the Right Honorable Lord Cawdor. But Campbell never received the piece, having never paid for it, and, for two thousand gold coins, it came into the possession of Napoléon's brother-in-law General Joachim Murat. He was executed in 1815, and the statue was eventually acquired by the Louvre, where it now resides. Canova was in his early thirties when he carved this statue (as was Balanchine when he made *Serenade*) that commemorates, in three dimensions, the birth of Love itself.

The story of Cupid and Psyche is an allegory about the fiery melding of physical desire and spirit. The tale was written in Latin, based on numerous folktales, by Lucius Apuleius, in the second century in his book *The Metamorphosis* (St. Augustine called it *The Golden Ass*). The story is later echoed in "Cinderella," "Beauty and the Beast," *A Midsummer Night's Dream*, and "Orpheus and Eurydice." It is a lengthy, poetic, entertaining, and ribald tale that includes not only a good deal of unsanctioned lovemaking but also what today would be termed the kidnap and rape of a woman by an anonymous captor, who impregnates her and with whom she falls in love. Despite these untoward doings, the mischievous Lord Byron wrote, "The story of Cupid and Psyche is not only one uniform piece of loveliness, but is so delicate that it might be read at school by a class of young ladies."

The story is set in motion by the wrath of one very jealous woman, Venus, the goddess of love, beauty, and desire. "The earth had produced another Venus," wrote Apuleius about the young and human Psyche, who is "endued with virgin-like flower," such that the disciples of Venus divert their "celestial honors to worship a mortal virgin." Psyche's beauty is so great that her despairing father can find her no willing husband—she is worshipped but not loved—while he easily dispatches her two (also madly jealous) sisters into wedlock.

Venus plans her revenge, conscripting her son, the capricious Cupid, who, with his "depraved manners" runs "through other men's houses at night," "corrupting the matrimony of all," and inciting "pernicious desires." She orders him to arrange, with a prick of his arrow, for Psyche to awaken and fall in love with "a miserable son of

Antonio Canova's *Psyche Revived by Cupid's Kiss* *(Jean-Pol Grandmont/*
Wikimedia Commons)

the vulgar." But upon viewing the beauty of Psyche, Cupid himself is
so enraptured by her that he defies his mother—a Freudian field day.

There ensues a sequence of misadventures: Cupid captures
Psyche in a paradise where her every wish is met, and he comes to
her each night, incognito, and ravishes her, eventually impregnating
her. Disobeying his order never to look upon him, one night Psyche
shines the light of an oil lamp on Cupid, and discovers that he is not
the monster she feared but the god of love himself, with "wings of
shining whiteness." Examining his arrows, she inadvertently pricks
herself and falls "in love with Love."

But a drop of the boiling lamp oil burns Cupid and he springs
"on his pinions" to Mount Olympus to convalesce in the "bedcham-
ber of his mother," while Psyche begins her arduous quest to locate

The Canova moment: Darci Kistler and Kip Houston, with Valentina Kozlova as the Dark Angel behind them *(© Paul Kolnik)*

her beloved. Her "desire of finding him," wrote Apuleius, describing one of love's great truths, increased "in proportion to the difficulty of the search."

Venus, meanwhile, resorts to the "consolation of revenge," and appoints Mercury to find her rival. Soon enslaved by her, Psyche is given four increasingly dangerous trials. The last requires her to travel to the underworld to retrieve from Proserpina (also known as Persephone), queen of the underworld, a box of beauty for Venus. Though counseled not to open the box, once again, Psyche cannot resist knowing the forbidden. But Proserpina has tricked Venus, and when Psyche opens the box "it contained no beauty, nor indeed anything but an infernal and truly Stygian sleep, which being freed from its confinement, immediately invades her . . . so that she lay motionless, and nothing else than a sleeping corpse."

Once recovered from his injury, Cupid flies to Psyche and rouses her with "an innoxious touch of one of his arrows." It is this very moment when the lovers are reunited after a long separation and

much suffering that Canova chose for his commission—and which
Balanchine, in turn, replicated in the Elegy of *Serenade*. It is a tableau of such beauty, such tenderness, such erotic promise. While his
arrows and quiver rest on his hip, Cupid cups Psyche's right breast
with one hand while cradling her head with the other as he leans in
close to her, his slim, nubile body carried by the magisterial wings of
an archangel. Their two faces are poised only inches apart, the kiss
imminent.

Apuleius ends the tale with the god of all the gods, Jupiter, for
whom Cupid has supplied "many a virgin," ordering Mercury "to
bring Psyche to heaven." Upon her arrival, Jupiter gives her a cup
of ambrosia: "Take this, Psyche," he says, "and be immortal." Thus
Psyche becomes one of the few women in mythology to become a
goddess, and thus Soul attains its desire: immortality. The lovers are
wed. The daughter of Soul and Eros is named Pleasure.

Aside from breathing life into Canova's moment of divine uni-

Psyche's marble mane (© *Sailko/
Wikimedia Commons*)

son, what has the tale of Cupid and Psyche to do with *Serenade*? Balanchine repeatedly refuted all conjecture about his work: "There are no hidden meanings in my ballets." Indeed, the links to the myth of the birth of Love itself weren't hidden at all, but there in layers, in levels, both explicit and muted. He never acknowledged any connection of this myth about the unification of Psyche and Cupid with *Serenade*. He didn't need to.

One might recall that it was in his debut onstage at the Maryinsky, as Cupid, that young Georgi was first entranced by the theater, igniting his passion for dance, and heralding the early deliverance of his destiny. And Canova's Psyche displays an astounding, luscious, truly mad, marble mane.

20. MARIA'S ARABESQUE

The gentle embrace of the Canova-esque Cupid and Psyche pose shifts when the Dark Angel and her wings break from the triune. As she rises up from them, she splits from the man, to whom, until now, she was integral, leaving him and the Waltz Girl alone in their intimacy. Taking five large, considered steps around the couple—she passes carefully outside the Waltz Girl's elongated legs—she moves from behind them to in front of them and, extending her right leg forward, piqués into an arabesque in precise profile to the audience. This is not, however, a transitional arabesque, or the arabesque of a sequence; this arabesque is the defining leitmotif of the Dark Angel, not only her signature but her core, her essence: her reach is vast.

The man, crouching behind the Waltz Girl, places both his hands under the Dark Angel's long tulle skirt and around her leg, above the knee, holding her ramrod straight in place. Because the man is now invisibly supporting her, the Dark Angel can sustain her arabesque far beyond her own balancing abilities—though it is still a tricky situation. As if this magical arabesque on pointe were not enough, the man then rotates her supporting leg clockwise while she maintains her position. It is a magnificent event. While she is revolving, she not only holds her arabesque leg high behind her, perpendicular to her torso, but holds her head high too, as if balancing a crown, and her eyes face constantly forward—unlike "spotting" in pirouettes, where we keep our eyes on a single point in front of us and then quickly whip our heads back to that same point.

Rotating thus as a single entity, the Dark Angel magisterially maps the globe. She is sister incarnate to Augustus Saint-Gaudens's weather vane of Diana, virgin goddess of women, slaves, nature, and the moon, who twirled for three decades at the turn of the twentieth century atop Madison Square Garden in New York, where her gilded body caught the sunlight and glittered for miles around.

The "Lady Higher Up," as the writer O. Henry called Saint-Gaudens's golden goddess, was commissioned by architect Stanford White in 1891 for his new design of Madison Square Garden, and White was infamously shot dead on the rooftop, just beneath Diana, fifteen years later amid a love triangle involving the beautiful young model Evelyn Nesbit. This Diana did not sport her usual tunic and boots but—scandalously in 1894—was nude. And she is slim, leggy, small-breasted, narrow-hipped, her hair gathered in a high bun, presaging not only what became known as a "Balanchine dancer" but more specifically his revolving Dark Angel in *Serenade,* as Diana balances in arabesque on a single demi-pointe, her scarf trailing, her bow drawn before her, like Cupid's crossbow of love.

Saint-Gaudens's Diana was, at the time, the highest point in New York's skyline—forty-two feet taller than Lady Liberty. She was removed from her perch in 1925, and nine years later Balanchine echoed her in *Serenade*—probably unknowingly, as Diana had been taken down eight years before he arrived in New York. He reincarnated her revolution in the flesh.

The Dark Angel makes her full 360-degree inscription in space not just once, but then again, with increased risk, a second time—in case you missed round one. Repeats in ballet, as in music, are frequent and purposeful and often arrive in threes, but here it's just two.

For the man and the Dark Angel, this arabesque double rotation is a tricky choreographic moment that can be fraught with trouble—mostly due to the fact that as he pivots her, however carefully he proceeds, the endless yards of tulle of her skirt will wrap into his hands, loosening his secure grip on her leg while also pulling on her skirt and threatening her already perilous balancing act on her right toe tips.

Balanchine did a version of this movement eight years earlier, in 1926, in a ballet for Diaghilev called *La Pastorale*, starring the elegant, endlessly leggy Felia Doubrovska. But for her—and in pre-1952 versions of *Serenade*—the skirt was short, so the audience could see the man's hands turning her. Easier for the dancers, but not so mysterious as it is when his hands are hidden by tulle. This precarious turn is usually rehearsed a lot. A lot.

Minute 24:12.

Over the decades there have been some memorable Dark Angels, including Mimi Paul, Yvonne Mounsey, and Jillana. Maria Calegari was the reigning Dark Angel of Balanchine's last years—my own time dancing the ballet. Her presence in our midst onstage was particularly felt in the amplified grandeur of her quiet authority. After Balanchine's death, she continued dancing the role for yet another decade, during the fragile, transitional years of the company, during which his ballets became, for us, even more literally him. By the time Calegari retired, she had danced the Dark Angel almost one hundred times: it was imprinted in her DNA.

Born in Bayside, Queens, Maria is of Italian heritage, and like so many thousands of little girls, started classes at a local ballet school at age five. But this girl, unlike 99.9 percent of young ballet students, actually became a great ballerina.

Maria entered the big-league School of American Ballet in Manhattan at age fourteen and was invited by Balanchine to join the company at age seventeen, in 1974. She was promoted to soloist six years later, and became a lead dancer in 1983, the year of his death.

While this may sound like a smooth, steady rise to stardom, it was not, and Maria's stall-stop-start struggle is illustrative of a certain alchemy wrought by Balanchine. He could make a ballerina out of a merely graceful, talented dancer. But he could not do it alone. A real ballerina is magic, but to become one, the dancer, the very rare one, must rise to the occasion and incarnate that tenuous entity called "promise." Most of us, beautiful and accomplished as we were to even be chosen by Mr. B for the company, did not, could not, would not, go as far as Maria did.

Within two years of joining the company, she was cast by Mr. B

Maria Calegari, age five, in her first tutu and ballet slippers, before a recital
(© *Richard Calegari*)

in a few solo roles—the fierce and fast-spinning Dewdrop in *The Nutcracker;* the lead in the sultry, soft Elegy section of *Tschaikovsky Suite No. 3;* a tight, fiendish solo in *Divertimento No. 15*—and the Dark Angel in *Serenade*. It was an unusual, but not unprecedented, occurrence for a young dancer, fresh out of the School, to be singled out, but when Balanchine liked something, he abided by no rules of seniority, even less so any notion of "fairness." He knew that budding talent needed immediate attention, how quickly a flower can blossom—or wilt. And he loved her name; Maria was his mother's name. But soon after being showcased, she faltered and went into what she calls her "hibernation," her "rest period." Calegari says, "I wanted results without the work. I couldn't handle the jealousy from other dancers. I also couldn't handle his attention, so I gained twenty pounds." Weight gain was often a sign in a ballet dancer, as it would be in an athlete whose profession resides in their body, that she was troubled, conflicted—a way, unconsciously, to put forward movement on hold. "I had a lot to work out," she explains. "I was so insecure, and I hated the thought of being by myself on the stage. It was just too scary."

Balanchine was frustrated with Maria's inability to handle her own talent and its attendant pressures, and he stopped scheduling her in her various solos. Casting for Balanchine always told the real story, as he once said: "It's all in the programs." Maria went to Mr. B's office for an explanation of his apparent withdrawal of interest.

"He really let me have it," she says. "He told me the truth, is what he did. He said that dancing was 99 percent skill, not art. He told me I was too 'fancy-schmancy.' That I was trying to elaborate without getting to the nitty-gritty. 'You have to work,' he said. 'You have to get in a room and you have to work. I can't do it for you. You have to do it. You have to be able to jump; you have to be able to turn.' Then he said, 'You have no aura,' which really killed me because

Maria Calegari as the Dark Angel in 1974, age seventeen *(Martha Swope © The New York Public Library for the Performing Arts)*

that was the one thing I thought I had. He said, 'If you want to do a matinee for your mother, I'll give it to you. Or you can go to Ballet Theater and become a soloist.' It was brilliant, saying everything that was against my real nature. He took a chance: I could react to this by going either straight up—or straight down. I started to cry, those sobs where you can't control what you're doing. As I cried, he said, 'Now, dear, grown-up people do not get hysterical.' Well, that just lifted me straight into reality. I remember leaving that room and that conversation and I began to change my life."

Maria bit the bullet and started the real work Balanchine had referred to—with demonic focus. "I stuck it out. I lost the weight and I asked to reaudition for him for Dewdrop. He made me go through every entrance without a break—in actual performance there is time to recover between entrances. But he cast me again and started giving me my parts back."

Maria Calegari as the Dark Angel in 1984 (© *Paul Kolnik*)

And so the butterfly was born of the chrysalis. How many dancers over Balanchine's sixty years of teaching, of overseeing, encouraging the development of individual dancers, had such a life-altering talk with him? Many. But who among us could match the challenge to go even further than we already had? Maria.

In a telling visual, one can even view Calegari's ascension to greatness from goodness, to beauty from sweetness, in two photographs of that same moment where she is the Dark Angel who circles the world. At age seventeen in the Workshop performance her position is precise and pretty, her clear lines resting on the space about her, a lovely lithograph. A decade later her limbs are amplified, cutting into the air, bending it, pushing it aside; her body is carving out space, commanding it, thus searing the sculpted dimensions into a viewer's subconscious so that they remain there over time, perhaps forever. I can see her now before me. This kind of depth of movement—virtue embodied, fueled by soul rather than youthful duty—becomes, somehow, instantly identifiable as the gift of an utterly unique person, as if you have entered into their world rather than their passing through your own. It is the way one identifies the voice of Frank Sinatra or Elvis Presley so instantaneously: we don't just recognize them, we *know* them.

Despite the death of Balanchine midway through her career, Calegari managed, against many odds, to push through. He was gone just as she was entering that delicate realm where a beautiful dancer becomes a true ballerina, no longer a promising presence, a reliable soloist, or a dazzling technician, but a full-blown, engaged creature whose femininity so ascends as to attain unsurpassed dominion—and all of us onstage reside, with delight, in her monarchy. Others were not so able to proceed after he was gone and their careers halted, stalled, or occasionally regressed after his death, so essential was his daily vigilance, his mere presence providing the inside of the theater with an unavoidable, pervasive, silent oversight.

Even with Maria, we will never know how much farther, or in what directions, she might have traveled had he lived longer: her particular mysticism suggests a distinct loss. But, somehow, she inserted her sorrow into the abyss of his absence, and there she danced each night on the edge of the volcano, her beauty distilled by fragility, yet so sustained. And by then she was doing it entirely alone, so well had she—and her body—absorbed what he taught her. Her commitment was manifest, and she became the last of his ballerinas with true gravitas—and the glamour of a 1940s movie star. I see him giving that rare, barely discernible, nod of approval.

Ave Maria, gratia plena, Dominus tecum.

21. VITRUVIAN MAN

Balanchine at a seminar, illustrating the vertical body,
1962 *(© Nancy Lassalle/Eakins Press Foundation)*

After her two rotations, the Dark Angel extends even farther her already plush arabesque—four limbs reaching ever more out, up—before she descends forward onto one knee, body and head low and down, as if after such a display of her own authority she knows to bow to the yet higher one, the invisible one. Humility at the summit is as rare as it is beautiful.

She and the pair behind her rise from their grouping and reassemble again toward the back of the stage, where they form a sandwich, all facing forward on a diagonal together. Their bodies are pressed tight, the man in the middle, securing each woman to him with an arm—the Dark Angel by the waist behind him, the Waltz Girl over her shoulder before him—and thus they walk forward as one. Right foot, left foot, right foot, left foot ... Their intimacy is building.

After eight steps, they stop and turn to face the audience directly. They keep close, but the dynamic changes. Until now, the man has been blind, dependent, led, perhaps dominated, by the Dark Angel: even his apparent romantic interest in the fallen Waltz Girl takes place under her aegis. But now he shifts and becomes their center and, with his legs parted at shoulder width for stability, he takes in each hand the outer hand of each woman while they wedge their respective two feet together against the side of one of his feet for leverage. Each woman's entire body weight is now secured against one of his legs. His arms are in a classic muscleman biceps flex and he slowly, slowly begins to lower their upright, barely bending bodies as he opens the right angle of his arms. And down they both go, one to his left, one to his right—down, down to the stage floor, each woman's body tracing the soft lines of a protractor's curve, each a side of the moon.

The man has become Leonardo da Vinci's Vitruvian Man, his body the axis of symmetry, while the two women now mirror each other in a parity previously unclear. The dynamic of the Dark Angel leading him has given way to a different prospect.

This schema is dangerous and wondrous. The delicate nature of the triad is reflected in its physical tenuousness. Once elongated on the stage floor, the two women are in close proximity, and the two great pillows of tulle that amass about them as they descend are slippery, causing the risk of mishap when yet more women—yes, more, and soon—fly toward the man. In the late 1970s, Mr. B said at one rehearsal, to everyone's astonishment, "I'm changing it!" (There had been too much skidding on the rogue tulle.) He then adjusted this Herculean display of coordination and male strength—particularly the biceps leverage—so that after only a brief leaning outward, each woman rescinds her dependence on the man and completes her own descent by lunging forward to one knee, lowering herself softly to the floor, tucking her skirt in close.

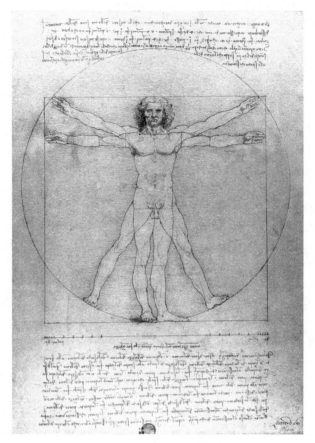

Vitruvian Man, by Leonardo da Vinci, 1490

This seemed a particular loss. But was it? One of the few moments in the entire ballet, in this land of women, where a man is unquestionably holding the center, the world, in his hands, was now gone. But Balanchine was ever serving the cause of the practical, knowing that the scaffolding of *Serenade* was indestructible by any single shift.

Suddenly a girl appears from the downstage-right wing (your left from the audience) and runs fast toward the man, who has just lost hold of his two consorts. She jumps over one floored dancer and her skirt, and he catches her by the waist as she leaps into a tour jeté, both legs kicked alternately skyward behind her as her body turns in space. He lifts her so high above him, over him, that she looks down upon him directly, like an angel floating. He lowers her down and she continues her diagonal trajectory offstage as if her brief conjoining with him was but chance, a mere detour while en route elsewhere. Another girl does exactly the same thing, though she enters from the opposite downstage wing. These two interjections are so swift and seamless that the airborne tulle of the dancers' skirts wafts by, up, down, around, a mirage of blue smoke. This sole man is only beginning his negotiation of a steady bombardment of women coming at him—though we all are just passing through. Or is it he who is just passing by, like Albrecht searching for Giselle in the land of Balanchine's Wilis?

Now the Russian Girl runs on, her loose hair trailing, and leaps madly toward the man in a large arabesque, pivoting in midair. He catches her as she flips forward. Drama is building here, through both surprise and risk. After the catch, he continues the momentum, carrying them both around yet again. Now facing you in the audience, she pirouettes, arms rising above her head as she turns twice. Remaining on pointe, held by the man at her waist, she extends her right leg into a high penché arabesque while reaching her left arm down to join hands with the Waltz Girl, who reaches her right hand upward toward her, though her body remains on the stage floor. The man extends his left arm across the front of the Russian Girl's waist and similarly joins his hand to the Dark Angel's right hand on the other side: all four dancers are now linked in several draping garlands of arms, an open figure eight of arms.

Minute 25:41.

There are only seven minutes and eight seconds left before the ballet ends. It is remarkable how much has yet to happen in this ballet of no story with plot to spare.

Six hands release, and the four dancers unwind; the Dark Angel and the Waltz Girl rise up, and the Russian Girl slips offstage yet again. The three are alone once more. But the women's brief equality alters yet again, as each, from opposite sides of the stage, runs at the man alternately, while he stands center stage. As they approach him and he catches them about the waist, they swoop dangerously low in a plié on pointe with one leg, while the other is in attitude derrière. He carries one woman around in two fast circles in reverse before he releases her into fast, spinning chaîné turns back to her side of

Draping garlands of arms (from left: Maria Calegari, Kyra Nichols, Leonid
Kozlov, and Merrill Ashley) *(© Paul Kolnik)*

the stage. Then the other dancer repeats the same sequence with
him. Then again one and again the other. This is no longer sisterly
cooperation between the Dark Angel and the Waltz Girl, nor is the
Dark Angel in charge: this is now all but open warfare, unveiled
competition between the women for the man. But he receives each
in succession with grace—choosing neither, accepting both.

Then, in another shift, the women parallel each other again in
united purpose, each taking one of his arms and pulling him to the
back of the stage on a diagonal, clearly restraining him as he looks
to escape. He pushes forward as they attempt to hold him back,
and just as they release his hands for a moment, two more dancers run toward him. He lifts the second in a high arabesque before
she continues her speedy exit offstage. I was one of these who was
lifted, and it felt like a surreptitious interruption of the adults in
the midst of their grown-up complications. And then all this again:
the restraining of him, the letting go of him, his brief interaction
with two other women passing through. The Russian Girl reappears

and the Waltz Girl and Dark Angel clear the stage for her, assembling close together upstage right. But this is no ordinary entrance.

She runs in fast from the downstage-front wing, Mr. B's wing, toward the man, and leaps. Shooting her right leg straight skyward in a large, lush développé. As she starts to tip behind herself, he leans forward, legs wide, and lands her on his lower back, his right arm reaching behind him to secure her waist. It is an extraordinary leap-and-catch, resulting in her right leg pointing up, past perpendicular, her left leg extending in opposition. Splayed in 180 degrees, she is upside down, her hair spilling to the stage floor. And then the man lets go with his right arm (not all dancers manage this last release), extending both his arms to the sides: free. Her entire body is now balanced, her lower back over his lower back like a seesaw, her lever to his fulcrum. My God.

During my era, a particularly passionate Russian Girl was a dancer whom Balanchine would have called one of his "nuts and raisins"; these were dancers who defied the parameters of the so-called "Balanchine dancer"—though he always denied there was such a thing. As he would have it, the single criterion for a Balanchine dancer was that he liked her—liked her dancing, found her beautiful. Thus there were dancers who were more voluptuous—like the glorious Gloria Govrin—or spikier, like the chiseled Wilhelmina Frankfurt. Or smaller and more classically romantic in demeanor like the pale, brunette Nichol Hlinka, our Russian Girl. Short by the usual company standards, she was a strong dancer, with a huge jump and the Carla Fracci–like femininity of a nineteenth-century Giselle. Her trajectory to principal dancer was full of pit stops and time-outs, and it took some years for her to bloom. Mr. B said dancers were like flowers, and not only did we all blossom on different schedules but some opened more fully than others, lasted longer than others. Most remained only buds—still beautiful, but not a dominant bloom. I was one of these.

Mr. B focused intensely on Nichol during her first years in the company—but it was not her time. She had rebellion to spare and was not always able to follow his lead. But she remained dancing in the corps throughout, and pressed forward after his death, becoming only then a leading light in the company. This put her, like Maria

Nichol Hlinka and Kip Houston *(© Paul Kolnik)*

Calegari, in the unique category of what, to me, a true Balanchine dancer came to mean—dancing as he taught, as he loved, long after his death. Once Nichol did find her way, she was fiery and fearless, the rebellion utterly intact but focused into onstage power. When she leapt as the Russian Girl in *Serenade* from too far away, both legs splayed upward, her abandon had a wildness that always made me see his love for this gorgeous woman made visible—as was her love for him. And because he was not in the wings to see it, her leap of faith was not only literal, physical, but true.

The Russian Girl is swung back upright, steps into an arabesque on pointe, runs around, and spins about in the man's arms, before he slides her back and then forward on her pointe tip, holding her in an extravagantly lunging penché . . . the movements are relentless and full and fast. Now, unlike in her previous entrance, when the Waltz

Girl and the Dark Angel presided, the Russian Girl does not leave the stage; she stays. They are a man and three women, a neat quartet.

I have wondered if this could be the exact gathering Mr. B was referring to when I visited him in the hospital at the end of his life when he suggested I write about a "man and three women." I must doubt it. *Apollo* is also the story of a man and three women, and there are numerous other moments, groupings, dances in his ballets where a man and more than one woman dance together. I think he was speaking to me that day of the story that interested him most—an artist and his muses—the story that was his life, his only story. I see his ballets as but the outpouring, the shedding, the emanation, and the elucidation of his enduring, all-consuming devotion to the mystery of the female sex. Their beauty his engine.

22. CHARLIE'S ANGELS

Of the many dynamics that a man and three women could manifest, how does Balanchine place them here, now, in *Serenade*? In perfect harmony, in civilized parity, in consecutive accord. But only briefly. All is temporary in Balanchine.

The Russian Girl parts from the man, running toward the other two women, who have remained together, all but huddled, on stage right. As she approaches, the Dark Angel separates, runs by her, to him, just past. She turns, faces him, pauses, breathing in, her loose hair still unsettled from her speed, and then, in a sudden, most unexpected show of ardor, she flings one arm about his neck and the other about his waist and buries her face in his shoulder, as if he is a lost lover finally found, and not to be lost again, like Eurydice if reborn to Orpheus. She grasps him almost aggressively, and yet her vulnerability surfaces too, as if she is looking for protection, for solace, for a safe harbor. But most of all her gesture is one of possession: "You are *mine*." This is startling. It is the first show of such a very human emotion in the ballet, breaking the classical mode of aristocratic etiquette into something far more personal, potentially problematic.

She lifts her arm from about his neck, and it flies loose and high as she turns her face, her whole torso, away from him, twisting deeply out from her waist while her hips and legs stay beside him:

her claim made, her body opens wide to you, the audience, announcing her victory.

Her triumph is short-lived. Balanchine never stops anywhere: dancing's only permanence, only stability, is progression. But if any notion of coupledom or resolution appears imminent, he muddies the waters immediately.

In succession, the Waltz Girl and then the Russian Girl run to the man and perform the identical sequence of passion and possession, each dancer layering herself upon the last until they are all upon one another, all grasping his waist, their bodies opened outward: three heads turned sideways, three right arms hanging down, three pointed toes peeking in succession from beneath their dresses.

Are these the three Muses of Apollo, taking over—or making cameos—in *Serenade*? The Olympian Graces summoned by Tschaikovsky? A romantic triad? Balanchine never spoke of, much less explained, the suggestive dynamics he created here. But while rehearsing this pileup in the Main Hall studio one day in the late 1970s, he did say one thing: he told the three women to run to the man "like Charlie's Angels," referencing the eponymous television show that starred three feisty, female private investigators whose benign boss is the never-seen, omnipresent "Charlie." He just loved that show, with its unlikely premise of sexy women with big hair and serious lipstick as serious crime fighters.

"I think he felt very close to that part," Calegari has said. "He was good at demonstrating that boy. It was Balanchine himself. No one could do that part the way he did it, wheeling around with those three girls." Despite this ambush, the man holds firm, accepting the triplicate embrace, as all three women fold in, then out from him. He looks upon them. Each has chosen him. Lucky chap—though it must be remembered that Balanchine had a real deficit of adequate male dancers in 1934 during the making of *Serenade:* the one-to-three ratio here might have been more about necessity and ingenuity than romance. Or not.

Where does the man go from here? Outnumbered, he wisely lets the women lead—and lead they do. In Esther Williams–like synchronization, they lift their right arms upward and fold them gently over the air in a soft curve above his head, their own hands each atop the other, as if enclosing him, blessing him. He raises his

"A man and three women..." (Valentina Kozlova, Darci Kistler, Kyra Nichols, and Leonid Kozlov) *(© Paul Kolnik)*

left arm yet higher and rounds it over theirs: sheltering their sheltering, blessing their blessing, uniting them all.

Turning inward to one another, the four dancers begin moving slowly counterclockwise with small shuffles on demi-pointe; having joined their eight hands together like the spokes of a wheel, they start whirling, faster and faster, around and around as they lean out. The women's left arms rise vertically, pulled by the upward force, and after three more ever-widening circles, the force pulls all four from the center hub. Their hands break apart, and each dancer flies backward to one of the far corners of the stage: a Balanchine centrifuge, dispersing their intimacy upward, outward, around. The three-minute-fifty-two-second streak of close-ups since the Waltz Girl was first left alone on the stage floor is now broken as the four fly out wide into space.

From their corners, they run toward center stage, jump high in a grand jeté, and quickly exit, each to a different wing. As they leap in opposing directions, their already-enigmatic intimacy evaporates. Poof!

Minute 27:43.

Eight girls are in various wings now, watching, ready for an entrance—as a Russian Girl, I am one of them. We come onstage in two lines of four, followed by four men dressed in simple dark blue leotard costumes, their only decoration being a gold-embossed infinity chain encircling the necklines of their tops—we call these dancers the "Blueberries." But these men have never appeared before, and are appearing only now in the last few minutes of the ballet. As Balanchine told it, one afternoon in 1934 in the Madison Avenue studio, four men actually showed up together; he pounced.

Each man proceeds to partner two dancers in succession, in a lovely demonstration of classic adagio moves. First we each développe the right leg to the front, then rond de jambe the leg high to the side and high to the back into attitude. Then we double pirouette to arabesque times two, followed by a great lunge arabesque on pointe times two. Finally, the inside four of us run to center stage facing one another, close, and a man comes to each of us, bends low, and wraps us tightly at mid-thigh, and lifts us so we rise very high. After raising our arms, rounded above our heads, we are almost nine feet tall, operating with our partner as a single solid structure. The last four girls approach us, and we reach down, each girl partnering another girl, hand to hand, as she pivots on pointe into an enormous wide and open arabesque enabled by the support we can give her from our great height. We are now four entities joined in a common pursuit: each a man and two women—again. The men set us down, and as swiftly as we entered we all run offstage. We have been onstage for fifty-four seconds.

A few months after Mr. B died, the company went on a long-planned, six-week tour of Europe to London, Copenhagen, and Paris. During the two weeks at Covent Garden, many of us got sick with the flu: during rehearsals we all wore our leg warmers around our necks like scarves to try to keep ourselves warm in the British damp. In theater, the show always goes on, and in our case, with few understudies, there was no question of taking to our beds: we all performed right through the aches, fatigue, and runny noses. We were young, resilient, and on a mission.

Our next stop was at the Concert Hall in Tivoli Gardens, a very old, truly charming amusement park in Copenhagen. We loved dancing in Denmark, home of Bournonville, and Balanchine had a lifelong association with the Royal Danish Ballet, dating from his earliest European years. As we descended from the plane onto the tarmac at the airport, there was a band of young boys in red uniforms marching and drumming, official greetings, and generous shots of aquavit all around. At ten-thirty in the morning.

One night, a week into our two-week season, the curtain rose on *Serenade* and there I was standing in parallel at the front of the left diamond. Then came that first high kick of the right leg to the side and a stabbing pain deep in my right hip joint. I kept going, of course, and all was fine until the adagio section on the big rond de jambe of the right leg that requires a full, high rotation in the hip socket. I was almost unable to do the movement, not so much because it hurt but, worse for a dancer, because there was a terrible weakness, a disconnection between the mind and the body. This had never happened to me before.

As soon as the ballet ended, I went to visit our in-house physical therapist, Marika Molnar—given our profession, she was family.

She noted, with some dismay, as I lay on her portable examination table in her minuscule backstage room, that my right hip was literally hot, burning to the touch, as if with its own isolated fever. I could not dance for the remaining weeks of the tour. I could barely walk. Some nights I watched from the wings or the back of the audience as Copenhagen and then Paris received the company in both mourning and celebration in the wake of Balanchine's death. The company had never danced better, his teachings still so recent, and we knew our best tribute to him was to dance full force. The company was dancing for the love of him. All the while, I wondered why my body had turned on me. So suddenly, so completely, four months after he died. At least it was after.

Back home in New York, I had X-rays of my right hip. Dr. William Hamilton, our company physician and good friend of Mr. B's, told me to "sit down," never good words for a dancer to hear from a doctor. He explained that I had severe damage and loss of cartilage in my right hip socket. Even I could see it in the X-rays. Of all the many, many injuries a dancer can sustain, this—a form of isolated, fast-moving, advanced arthritis—was the worst, incurable. My career was over. I was twenty-five years old.

Ever defiant, I wasn't, of course, going to take a doctor's word for this, but I did have to go to bed for three months until the inflammation subsided. Slowly, very, very slowly, I began walking again, though now with a slight limp that I disguised well to all but the trained eye, as my body accommodated the pain and weakness in my joint. I eventually began taking beginner ballet classes at a studio outside the theater, at first just fifteen minutes at the barre, then slowly more.

My turnout on the right side was now rigid at 45 degrees, while my left side remained at 90 degrees. I had to coax that right hip socket back out centimeter by centimeter. X-rays a year later showed that all this work had done some more damage to the socket. But a dancer, especially when so young, does everything—everything— she can in order to dance.

A year later I finally danced again onstage. With the aid of anti-inflammatories and several daily adjustments of my unstable pelvis by Marika, I danced for just over another year. A victory of sorts. At least over the doctor's prediction. Perhaps unsurprisingly, I danced better than I ever had, for now it was truly, finally, life or death for me. The "fuego," the "fire," Balanchine sometimes referred to in class was lit—though, for me, too late to hope for a much longer career, much less one where I might excel my way out of the corps de ballet. I had never, ever, dared to entertain the thought that I might be a dancer of solo quality. But what I did know for sure was that I was capable of more glow, more definition, than I ever actually attained: my fears ruled before my hip rebelled, and after—when I was, as Mr. B might say, finally truly "awake" to "now"—it was physically, anatomically, too late.

Eventually, inevitably, due to the localized damage in that hip, injuries started appearing in other places until finally the choice was made for me. I retired from the stage having just turned twenty-seven, young even for a ballet dancer. Such was my fate, and to this day no one has been able to accurately diagnose why my hip joint went from healthy to destroyed in what felt like one week, a process of degeneration that in natural aging takes decades. Possibly the virus so many of us caught in London had entered that vulnerable hip joint and just ate away my cartilage at an unusually rapid rate. I will never know.

For years after, I still thought that just the right combination of rest, Pilates, therapy, vitamins, teas, drugs, willpower, sleep, meditation, even prayer, would heal my hip, which now dominated every day of my life with its unrelenting demands. Surely I could conquer this, perhaps even dance again. I was still so young. Decades of denial later I surrendered, and agreed to have my hip replaced. The day before the surgery I walked up Madison Avenue thirty blocks, just to prove to myself that I could still walk unaided: a dancer's determination does not abate.

I required two conditions from my surgeon before I would go under the knife: that I have a short, straight, smooth scar and that he give me the bone joint he would take out of my body when he replaced it with a titanium one. The scar is clean and straight, if an inch longer than he promised. Though he raised his eyebrows at my other request, he arranged it with the pathology department, where all body parts go for testing upon excision.

Two weeks after the surgery I retrieved my extirpated hip bone, and the many surrounding chips of bone and calcium formations

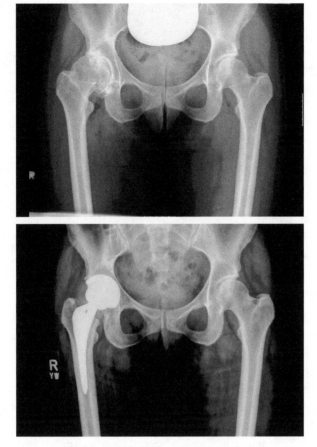

Before and after *(Courtesy of the author)*

that had accrued and been removed along with it. There it all was, my career and the end of it, the work of decades, floating in murky formaldehyde. This was not at all the Georgia O'Keeffe white bone I was expecting.

As advised by a lab assistant, I called a taxidermist, to treat the bones for dry land. After explaining that he could not perform the job himself—it was illegal to have human bones on his premises— he jovially offered me the recipe. As when making chicken broth, boil the bones in water for forty minutes; drain in a colander; soak in a solution of half water, half bleach for a few hours; and then place outside in the sun to dry. But he warned me to not leave the bones

Box painted by Mr. B *(Courtesy of the author)*

out at night in the garden as raccoons would make off with them. I performed this multistep curation ceremony with a certain good humor—as the daughter and sister of scientists, I found it a strange but not impossible endeavor. Day in, day out, I sunned my hip bone and her adjoining pieces, though, to my disappointment, they never did turn starch white but rather became a pale, golden honey color.

Finally, now I could touch and hold, without cringing, what I really wanted to see: tangible physical evidence of the loss of my onstage life. The clean, dried bone, separated from me, the crime, now visible, outside my pelvis. The round ball of my right hip joint was missing more than three-quarters of its cartilage, the strong flexible connective tissue that covers joint bones to smooth and ease their interaction, allowing them to produce movement smoothly, seamlessly. When the cartilage is worn away, bone grinds on bone, causing pain and severely limiting movement. And cartilage does not have a direct blood supply, so once it is damaged or lost, unlike other body tissues, it does not regrow itself: if the finite amount given is lost, it is lost. This is why my particular trouble ended my dancing while most dancers' injuries can be surmounted. An arthritic hip for a dancer is a done deal.

The smooth bone in my hand was like veined beige marble, and smooth as marble too. It was this beautiful smoothness—bone without cartilage—that caused my increasingly limited rotation. There, finally, I saw that this hip that had taken over my life for years and years was not my fault. It was truly damaged. I could now *see* it.

I put the joint and numerous small strangely shaped bone pieces—how all these had fit inside me in any sort of order was a puzzle never to be solved—in a small wooden box given to me by Father Adrian, the Russian Orthodox priest who had befriended Balanchine in the hospital and then buried him. The box had been painted by Mr. B in black, with small red flowers and green trellises. And now it is the casket of my career. What enabled me disabled me.

23. DESTINY

The cordial but jarring sudden shift from the drama of the man and three women to a short, almost academic demonstration of adagio partnering by multiple couples (as may be found in a ballet classroom) seems curious, but for Tschaikovsky's music appearing to dictate it. And likely, again, the necessities of circumstance too: Balanchine in 1934 certainly wanted to teach his young dancers partnering. This platonic classical interlude calms the apparent romantic turmoil. But the disarray is not over.

The man now enters from stage right; the Dark Angel and Waltz Girl enter together from stage left (the Russian Girl stays gone). Each again, in turn, runs to him several times and flings herself about his neck and retreats. *Mine. No, mine. No, mine* . . . The Waltz Girl stays after her last possession, performs six or seven fast spins in front of him, falls to one side as he catches her on a low horizontal diagonal. She spins in his hold yet one more time, her long hair now wound about her like a veil. Slowly, he gently lowers her to the stage, flat on her back, and then rolls her gently onto her right side facing you in the audience. She is lying exactly as she did before, at the Elegy's start.

The Dark Angel approaches just behind him, ceremoniously leaning over him while he is still kneeling over the Waltz Girl. As

Darci Kistler, Leonid Kozlov, and Valentina Kozlova *(© Paul Kolnik)*

the Dark Angel rises, he rises with her, pulled invisibly by her. It is a return to the Canova pose. Their end, their beginning. But romance has intervened, and even as the man rises, he grasps the Waltz Girl's hand and presses her palm over his heart. Bonded, they look into each other's eyes, he looking down, she looking up.

He does not want to let her go. He loves her.

The Dark Angel then does something astonishing. In an impetuous, almost warlike declaration, she reasserts her dominance. Menacingly, unballetically, she flaps her arms—her great wings—up and down, up and down, six times. Her arms remain straight; only her wrists bend back and forth, back and forth, creating a wave, like the wings of the swans in *Swan Lake*, but with more muscle. All attention is on her. With unwavering conviction, she takes the man's right shoulder with her left hand and places her right hand over his eyes, removing his sight, returning to their entrance stance. She leads him forward offstage, continuing the stage-dividing tangent they had

Kip Houston, Maria Calegari, and Merrill Ashley *(© Steven Caras)*

begun so long ago, but, due to diversion, never completed. She has steered him back to his original course, proceeding in the direction that she, not he, dictates.

As they walk on, he can no longer see the Waltz Girl, who remains on the stage floor. She watches him pass by her, beyond her, while reaching, reaching out toward him, yearning, but he is focused onward, inward. She is already, now, his past.

The evident emotional scenario here has been subject to more analysis over the decades than any other single section of *Serenade*— including by the dancers themselves. And for the only time in this particularly female ballet, the conjecture inevitably revolves around the significance, the symbolism, of the different women, as experienced by the single man who contends with them. The Elegy presents a definite drama, though still of nebulous plot, within the parameters of the full ballet. Thus Balanchine's "there is no story" insistence strains credulity while forever begging interpretation: he got exactly what he wanted.

Alexandra Danilova, who danced the Waltz Girl for the Ballet Russe de Monte Carlo in the early 1940s, said that Balanchine, at that time, actually suggested this scenario: "She [the Dark Angel] is his wife and together, he said, they pass down the road of life. I, the girl on the floor [the Waltz Girl], was pitied by the man, but I was a frivolous girl who had one affair after another. Then I was left alone." The "wife" reference is startling. This from a man who said you cannot dance family relations much less actual relatives. Curiously, this explanation was given to his most recent ex-wife, Danilova herself—whom he cast in the role of the "frivolous girl."

In contrast, Colleen Neary, who danced both the Russian Girl and the Dark Angel in the 1970s, remembers the very opposite: "Balanchine said about the Elegy that the girl on the floor was the wife, the Dark Angel was the mistress, and the Russian Girl, passing through, was the lover."

Ryuji Yamamoto, who learned the Elegy male role from Patricia Neary (Colleen's sister, who also danced the ballet), gave me his version, which is similar to Danilova's: "The [male] role is Balanchine himself. The girl behind him [the Dark Angel] is the wife; the other girl [the Waltz Girl] is the girlfriend. And the Russian Girl is also a girlfriend. He has relationships with all the girls."

Kumiko Matada, who performed in the same production with Yamamoto, says of her role as the Russian Girl: "Too much worry for nothing. I was just a girl for a love affair. Why do I have to work so hard, but not be rewarded?"

Edwin Denby kept things simple, writing in 1944, "There seems to be a girl who meets a boy; he comes on with another girl and for a while all three are together; then at the end, the first girl is left alone."

On and on go the interpretations. Balanchine would be pleased: their variance guarantees no determination. Is the Elegy autobiographical? Is this man George Balanchine? Of course! Mind was made physical; every role he ever created, male and female, solo and corps, was him. And even he, speaking in 1960 after a performance of *Serenade,* told a friend: "It's like fate. Each man going through the world with his destiny on his back [the Dark Angel]. He sees a woman [the Waltz Girl]—he cares for her—but his destiny [the Dark Angel] has other plans."

Balanchine's destiny did, indeed, involve many women, with little division between private and professional: ballerinas were his great loves, five of them becoming his wives, his love life so full that the Russian Orthodox Church Synod in New York City protested burying him (the counterprotest both astonished and overwhelmed them, and they agreed to allow the ceremony). During the final decade or so of his life, Karin von Aroldingen, a lead dancer, became his last deep attachment, one that carried over into his legacy. Balanchine's will, made as late as 1978, is a curiously simple document of eighteen pages with a two-page codicil, clarifying a previous detail. He showed consistently little interest in preserving his ballets, his art, per se: "I can see no need for preservation. A ballet is a movement in time and space, a living moment. Like a hothouse flower, it blooms, and dies. . . . This is as it should be." He divided his main assets among, yes, three women.

The first seven entries disposed of his relatively modest worldly property: his two checking account balances and the royalties on a book to Tanaquil Le Clercq, his last wife; a co-op apartment near Lincoln Center and his Mercedes-Benz to von Aroldingen; a condominium on Long Island and a savings account balance to Barbara Horgan, his longtime personal assistant; and to his brother Andrei, he left two gold watches given to him by Lincoln Kirstein. Starting with the eighth entry on page three, and through the next eleven pages, he allocated the "rights, title and interest"—copyrights, and domestic and foreign royalties—to his only significant assets: his ballets.*

While Balanchine's catalogue documents close to four hundred and fifty works, his will lists a total of 113 ballets, the ones either remembered or still in repertoires around the world (not including the seventeen he made after the will was written).† Until the drawing up of this document, his ballets were, for him, things he made that existed only in performance, and he gave them away at minimal cost to those ballet companies around the world who asked and

---

* With no precedent in the modern tax code for so massive a body of copyrighted works with no tangible, or fileable, existence, the Internal Revenue Service was baffled as to how to assess their value in order to tax Balanchine's estate. Eventually, they settled on an algorithm that left his estate in debt.
† Of the three-hundred-plus other works, most are lost to history, with perhaps, at best, a photograph or two remaining.

showed capability. But upon his death, his work suddenly became a very complicated business.

Shock reverberated when it was realized that he had left no rights—zero—to any of his ballets to the New York City Ballet, his company, his home for thirty-five years where many of these ballets were first made. The company would need to acquire and pay for performance rights like any other company in the world, though with a favorable arrangement. It is not precisely known why he did this, but most likely it was simple, practical: he wanted to take financial care of people whom he loved, and this was the way to do it, especially since he died with relatively little cash.

He had left his ballets to people, a small assortment of individuals, with the greatest responsibilities and financial worth going to the same three women. Tanaquil Le Clercq, whom he had divorced in 1969, was a beloved and exquisite ballerina who contracted polio at age twenty-seven while on tour in Europe in 1956. Balanchine was devastated, and she spent the remainder of her life, more than forty years, in a wheelchair. Balanchine adored her and always saw to her well-being; she was left the rights that would generate the most income. And again he named Horgan, whose many decades of devotion kept his complicated life running in good order, and von Aroldingen.

The first ballet mentioned by name in the will—though they are by no means listed chronologically*—happens to be *Serenade,* which, along with five other works including four made on her, he left to von Aroldingen. Like many dancers, she had danced several different roles in the ballet over time: a corps dancer, the Dark Angel, finally the Waltz Girl. After her retirement in 1984, she went on to stage *Serenade* for companies around the world.

Karin was very much one of Mr. B's "nuts and raisins." One of three sisters, she was born in a small town in Czechoslovakia and trained as a dancer in Germany in a slower, heavier, old-Russian style, very different from Balanchine's School. When he invited her to join NYCB in 1962, she was the very rare, perhaps only, woman he hired for the company who had not trained as a young dancer at

---

* The Balanchine catalogue lists *Serenade* as his 141st work.

EIGHTH: I give and bequeath to KARIN ANNY HANNELORE GEWIRTZ, all my rights, title and interests in the following ballets, including any and all of my statutory and renewal copyrights pertaining to such ballets, my media, U.S.A., European and foreign royalty rights from such ballets, and all rights under any contracts with respect to such ballets:

Year	Ballet
1935	Serenade (Tschaikovsky)
1960	Liebeslieder Walzer (Brahms)
1972	Stravinsky Violin Concerto
1974	Variations Pour Une Porte et Un Soupir (Pierre Henry)
1977	Vienna Waltzes (Johan Strauss Jr., Franz Lehar, Richard Strauss)
1978	Kammermusik No. 2 (Hindemith)

Balanchine's will, from page three. (Gewirtz was Karin von Aroldingen's married name.)

the School for, by then, it was producing a steady crop of us trained to dance as he wanted.*

Karin had wide shoulders, muscular legs, and a beautiful, aristocratic, sculpted face above a long neck. Her dedication and determination, at the very late age (for a ballet dancer) of twenty-one, to retrain her body and relearn technique as Balanchine wanted were extraordinary. Also out of the norm, she both married and had a child shortly after joining the company—two things Balanchine did not advocate for a ballet dancer as they could so easily interfere with a dancer's career. Over time, Karin became not only Mr. B's constant companion—one assumes a love affair—but also something more. He was godfather to her daughter, friendly with her husband, and spent holidays with her family. No one quite understood this configuration, but it lasted through Balanchine's death, giving him

---

* He hired foreign-trained male dancers until the end, given the continued scarcity of good male dancers to partner his ballerinas.

solace. Thus Karin became an heir, and a guardian of his work: her devotion to him was absolute.

Karin had never known her father—he was a German scientist who had disappeared without a trace during World War II when she was only two or three years old. (Coincidentally, his surname bears a strong resemblance to that of Balanchine's mother's possible father, Nikolai von Almedingen—who was also German.)

When asked to describe her connection to Mr. B, Karin said, speaking for so many of us who arrived in his world: "Balanchine was the father I never had."

With the Dark Angel behind him, leading him, the man exits the front-right wing, Mr. B's wing. He is gone. The Waltz Girl folds. Her small collapsed body is the only thing on the entire stage—exactly where she had first fallen as the Elegy began, full circle. What just happened? Love happened. And departed. Perhaps her whole life happened? Or was the Elegy all her dream, and his story inside hers? She lies still. Is she dead?

Minute 30:39.

The Waltz Girl (Darci Kistler) *(© Paul Kolnik)*

CURTAIN DOWN

||||||||||||||||||||||||||||||||||||||||||||||||||||||||||||||||||||||||||||||||||||||||||||||||||||||||||||

I t is thirty-three minutes since I vaselined my teeth, sewed my toe shoe ribbon tips into themselves, rubbed my pointe shoes in rosin, smoothed out any creases from my tulle skirt, and suctioned my feet into parallel as the curtain rose and the rhythms of Tschaikovsky's sweet sorrow became my pulse. My costume and skin are both warm and moist; adrenaline is making my heart race. High from exertion, I have no sense of how I feel. I am just there, doing it. I am with five other dancers in the downstage-front-left wing—the one directly across the stage from where Mr. B is watching. We can see him, chin up, taking his kaleidoscope view down the aquiline nose.

The first wing is shallow, and we huddle close so not a trace of a head or tip of tulle is glimpsed from out front—though you are most likely looking at the Waltz Girl, lying there on the stage to the right—your left—of center. We are, in reality, already onstage, but the shallow, thin, tall black sheet of wing covers us until our entrance, the last one, from which we do not depart.

Two by two, we run swiftly, quietly, toward her, each pair doing in succession what the previous has done. I and my friend are second, me downstage, she upstage, to my right. On cue, we scuttle onstage into a diagonal in fast little demi-pointe runs, arms moving up before us, and line ourselves up behind our two predecessors, who have stopped just short of her body. As we reach our places, we rise—as did they and as the pair after us will—onto pointe, in parallel, feet tight together. We are in our opening stance, but higher. Staying in place, we lift each toe alternately in tiny steps—stationary bourrées, sweet and small—while raising both arms forward and up, parallel to each other, parallel to our toes, extending out, palms softly facing down, on a diagonal toward the Waltz Girl's body, but far above her, up.

We are reaching as if toward an undefined summit in the direction of high upstage right and far beyond the reaches of the theater walls, our upper bodies, our faces all reaching too. The light no longer comes from the audience as when our dance started but beckons now from somewhere past the upstage-right-back wing. We lower our arms and our faces and settle our feet flat down, parallel again. The last pair of girls does as we did and settles behind us. The six of us, together, rise again and repeat the reaching forward as a sixsome, a unified homage to the upper space. Then all feet down, arms down, face down.

Are we mourning the fallen sister in front of us like female elephants gathering around their dead?

No one moves. All is quiet.

The Waltz Girl has already been lost and found, alone and joined, several times over since the ballet's start; she has fallen and risen, but now she is down again, lying there on the stage in front of us, a heap of unmoving tulle, soft arms about her face, eyes closed. Is this a final fall? No! She raises her head slowly, her long hair a tangled web. Awakened, but disoriented.

She is not dead. Or perhaps she is; perhaps we are all ghosts and are now elsewhere? In some afterworld? Nothing is clear, but everything is definite.

She looks around, rises a little, then all the way, and she whirls, looking back, arms wide. She runs backward: there is nothing there. She pivots again toward us and suddenly she sees us, and past us; from inside her confusion, she appears to at last recognize something and starts toward it, down the center aisle of us six, parting the way furiously with her arms. Instigated by her forward force we each lunge outward to our respective sides, allowing her space, collect ourselves up, each in a tight, stationary circle of our own, and bourrée around and around and around—as many as nine or ten full turns—like the swirling transition in a film passing from one state to another, or one time zone to another, before re-collecting back in our same lineup, in the same diagonal formation, feet flat, head and arms again lowered.

At the end of our group, downstage near the wing from whence we came, a very tall girl has appeared silently standing, reaching forward toward the Waltz Girl. It is she whom the fallen girl has seen with such passion. "Look at her like she's your mother," Mr. B said enough times that this dancer became known to us in rehearsal simply as Mother. The Waltz Girl runs, madly—like Giselle to her mother, upon discovering the betrayal of her lover—and falls into Mother's arms, rising on pointe to reach about her neck. But here, with Balanchine, it is not *Giselle*. While human love appears to have come and gone, sorrow's aftermath does not wreak revenge on men but solidifies a world of women: his world, a matriarchy.

Mother stands strong, upright, holding the girl's entire body weight, and then scoots backward from her while still supporting her, thus lowering the girl to her knees, her body draping over backward from the waist until she is deeply arched, her face reversed, her hair gathering on the stage floor behind her. She appears to have lost all, so gives all. Mother steps away. Her brief job is finished, her consolation only momentary.

Slowly the exhausted girl pulls her arced body upright and looks up. Mother is gone and a man in blue stands before her. As she pulls all the way up to standing, she sees him. Lowering her face, she turns around and sees two more men before her. She waits in parallel. She accepts. She is ready.

The three men crouch low together and two reach under her skirt and take hold of her legs, high above her knees. She fixes her body taut. In one smooth swoop, they lift her vertically, placing her feet on the third man's shoulders. She is now very high. Higher than everyone else by the length of a man, higher than she has ever been. Alone again, but among us, she is no longer lost. Now she leads. Or does she follow?

This maneuver takes a lot of rehearsal: the dancer and the three men have to work in perfect precision, trust, and harmony for it to

Karin von Aroldingen, in 1983, just after Balanchine's death. In defiance of the usual prohibition against personal jewelry onstage, she is wearing a gold chain with a single diamond that many of us thought Balanchine had given her. Not a word was said. (© *Paul Kolnik)*

be safe and smooth. It is both surprising and magnificent—she rises solidified like a statue hoisted by a crane—and the symbolism is so physically manifested that it feels daring, sacred.

Mother rises onto her parallel tips and with tiny little toe steps starts to follow upstage what is now quickly becoming a cortège. As Mother passes between us, we six rise on pointe and follow on tiny tiptoe in courtly parallel. The men walk slowly forward, and the Waltz Girl travels perched upon them like Cleopatra at the helm of her barge. She raises her rounded arms slowly before her as she begins to lean forward into her thighs, legs straight—two men supporting her legs underneath her costume—and her back arches slightly, then deeply, then completely, as her arms reach past the peak and break backward. She offers herself entirely, surrendering to divination.*

We, her sisters, her handmaidens, her ladies-in-waiting, follow her at a close distance, answering her, arms rising, rounded upward, and then, finally, we bend our backs too, while still on pointe, arms breaking open softly at the elbow just as hers have done—just as we all did at the ballet's opening, the orbit complete, but this time we are on pointe, risen. As I lean back, my face is now flat up and I see past the shadowed outlines of the truss pipes, cables, lights, and the bottom edges of scenery, hoisted high above the proscenium, ready to be "flown in" for other ballets, right up to the top of the roof of the stage, almost a hundred feet above me. A little farther back, I can even see the top edge, upside down, of the fourth ring of the theater and the bright specks of its red emergency exit lights.

No longer mortal girls evading the light we shielded at curtain's rise, during the eons that comprised the last thirty-two minutes and

The final diagonal (© *Paul Kolnik*)

* After Mr. B died, Karin von Aroldingen placed her hands into a rising prayer for him before opening her arms wide in surrender.

thirteen seconds we are become spirit and bring our mission to a close as we enter the light that is now home. The curtain falls as we tiptoe into the inferno of female freedom.

Who is this girl on high? Is she a mortal woman, like Psyche, transformed into a goddess, a woman becoming an artist, an American girl become royalty?

Whoever she is, she is us and we are her, plural. Though backstage she is simply the Waltz Girl, she has been given many monikers over the years, none of them by Balanchine—the Beloved, the Affair, the Initiate, the Student, the Sacrifice, the Heroine, Joan of Arc, and by a wife, "the wife," even a Butterfly.

But for us, onstage, the Waltz Girl is not some lofty symbol—there is no dancing such a static concept—she is just another one of us, who takes a more circuitous route to join our common destiny. But we have each traveled similarly before her, or will do so later. She is our prototype: a dancer. Her pathway, though, is uniquely cut. Giving her, the Waltz Girl, no tiara and no name, Balanchine set his revolution in motion. She is our past and our future, and we, now, already onstage, are her present, one she comes to join, then lead, so deep is her experience—which is each of ours too. She is our innocence, our Giselle, a virgin suicide betrayed in love, resurrected from the nineteenth century, transformed into a twentieth-century hero who is a woman: men come and go, but no longer do they break her. Her purpose is no longer love, or self, but beauty. Only through her art does she become free.

Balanchine deified democracy in *Serenade*. And it is, for a dancer, his most definite, most ritualized, architecturalized rite of passage. The apotheosis as the curtain is lowered remains his overt declaration: "Ballet is a Woman. And all my life I have dedicated my art to her." For him, the World is Woman. He told one dancer that *Serenade* could simply be called "Ballerina."

But where have we all gone at curtain's close?

I am reminded of a rare time that Balanchine explained, sort of, his work. In 1981, almost fifty years after making *Serenade* and only two years before he died, he spoke of his staging of Tschaikovsky's

Adagio Lamentoso. It was music, Balanchine believed, that the composer wrote as his own requiem before committing suicide. "I have poured my whole self into this symphony," wrote Tschaikovsky of the *Pathéthique*. "It is intensely personal. But its meaning will be an enigma. Let people guess it for themselves. It has a lot to say about the judgment, the punishment, and the vengeance of God!!!"

When Balanchine choreographed this music for the final night of the 1981 Tschaikovsky Festival at Lincoln Center, he had a little boy enter at the end of the spectacle in a simple white tunic, holding a lit taper. The boy stood alone center stage. The single flame was the only light in the entire black cave of the New York State Theater: at Balanchine's insistence even the red "Exit" signs were, illegally, extinguished. The little boy blew out the candle. Black. Pitch. The audience gasped. No longer observing a performance, they were inside one. No applause. In that moment of total darkness, Balanchine gave his audience the ability to really see. Just for one barely bearable moment. The audience filed out in silence, assaulted and blessed by a glimpse of their own transience.

Balanchine intended this piece to be performed only once, ever. But, unscheduled, it did happen one more time. The first time there were still a few stray lights left on in the theater when the boy blew out the candle; Balanchine wanted to do it again, to get it right. I saw this performance from the back of the first ring, where dancers not performing often go to watch. This time not a single light was on in the theater, and the whole massive space was lit by the flame of a short white candle in the young boy's hand. He blew it out. I remember the rehearsal where Mr. B talked quietly on one side of the stage with the little boy. I wonder what he said to him. Probably just "Blow out the candle." Echoing his beloved Tschaikovsky, Balanchine had staged his own death—not dust to dust, but light to light.

Balanchine said in an interview that he derived this rite—it was hardly a dance—from a Sufi parable. "A small boy enters with a candle," Balanchine explained. "A man asks him, 'Tell me where this light comes from.' The boy blows out the candle and replies, 'If you tell me where this light went, I will tell you where it comes from.'" Then Mr. B said, "The wonderful pure soul, still innocent, is this little boy." Little Georgi from St. Petersburg.

. . .

So where do we go in *Serenade*'s final diagonal? To where the light goes. To where it comes from. And the beauty, our plebeian princess, who was thrice lost, takes us there. This is, after all, where we all first stood. Where I stood when I was sixteen. The cycle completes, continues. We began the ballet shielding ourselves from the light and end by going into that light, becoming light. The journey of the dancer. The story of woman. All women, any woman. Mr. B gave us that. "A little thing like that," he called it.

Freed, in our final incarnation, from the exigencies of romance as our central drama—the men come, the men go, we remain, we press forward—we dance for dance's sake: we are but artists, first and last. Balanchine released us into the great wide fullness of female anarchy—our highest expression. His revolution was total, if lightly disguised inside a disciplined, aristocratic art that brings us back to its birth father, Louis XIV. Radical to the core, Balanchine was that fearless in his love for us, for woman.

You may or may not believe in heaven. I doubt I do. But I went there once. In *Serenade,* we are dancing for Mr. B at the pearly gates, his angels, ghosts, fairies, sylphs, Psyche reunited with her beloved Cupid. We are American girls learning to dance, recapitulating the origins of the very art we practice. We are not in a metaphorical heaven, but a real one. The only real heaven is the one that is here. Now. We dance it here, for you, while we dance it there, with him watching, leaning as he did night after night after night on his right elbow, in the front wing of eternity, of the vast here and now, overseeing a dance in the moonlight.

And Mr. B made this dance, manifesting here his own afterlife, his own heaven, when he was just thirty. "I had a dream," he said, "that it could be like this." And we, the hundreds of dancers of *Serenade* over the fifty years of his life that followed, lived there, with him.

A Balanchine dancer is defined not by her elongated legs and neck, her slim body, her small head, her quick mind, her fleet feet, or her devotion to tendus, but rather by a single binding, unblinding, passion. We all just wanted, you see, only one thing: to dance with him across the shadowed land of the eternal present. *Serenade* is a dance of rapture, of crushing beauty: a single mortal man spinning generations of mortal women into visible immortality, swirling, swooning, running, running, running into unending time with him.

Minute 32:49.

CODA

||||||||||||||||||||||||||||||||||||||||||||||||||||||||||||||||||||||||||||||||||||||||

September 22, 1982

Dear Mr. Balanchine,

My name is Jennifer Poerio, and I am in the sixth grade at the West Middle Island School. In social studies we were talking about the people who influence other people. My teacher, Mr. Schmidt, said that people who have influence over other people are the most powerful people in the world and they have an obligation to use that power for the good of the world. He used you as an example. He said you have a lot of influence over a lot of people and therefore you are a powerful person. Our class would like to ask you some questions. My teacher doesn't think you have the time to write to me but I got your address out of a book in the library and I want to try.

1. When you were my age, did you want to be powerful?
2. At what point did you realize that you had influence over other people?
3. Have you misused your power either by accident or on purpose?
4. What accomplishment are you most proud of?

5. Is there anything you really want to do but you aren't powerful enough to do it?
6. Who do you think is really powerful?
7. Who influenced you when you were my age?
8. Who do you think doesn't use their power well?

Please write back to me. I know I'll get extra credit in Social Studies if you do. Thank you very much.

Your friend . . .
Jennifer Poerio

Balanchine replied to this letter nine days later, on October 1, 1982, one month before he entered the hospital where he would die.

Dear Miss Poerio,

In reply to your letter of September 22, 1982.
I do not think of myself as a "powerful" man. I choreograph ballets, because that is what I do. God made me a choreographer. Only God is powerful and we are his servants.
I hope that this answers your questions.

Sincerely,
George Balanchine

EPILOGUE

At the now sadly dilapidated Warburg estate in upstate New York where the first performance of *Serenade* took place outdoors, in 1934, under the threat of rain, resides a small, all but obscured rectangular iron plaque, half hidden by struggling strands of grass and stained by the elements to resemble a map of America. It lies under what was the elevated stage, while the surrounding area is mostly barren, according to Eddie Warburg, from that performance almost nine decades ago.

> We invited some two hundred guests and erected a platform on a stretch of lawn (which, incidentally, never recovered from the shock). With rather primitive spotlight facilities and a piano hidden in the bushes, we introduced the American Ballet to a rather astonished group of friends. The first scene was 'Serenade,' ... With the music of Tchaikovsky, the lights went up on the assembled group of dancers, each one standing with arm outstretched, looking towards the heavens. It was a moving moment ... No sooner had the dancers become visible when, as if in answer to their raised arms, the heavens opened up, and it poured!

Plaque commemorating the location of the outdoor stage for the first performance of *Serenade* in 1934 *(Courtesy of the author)*

"On June 10 of 1934 students of the School of American Ballet under the direction of George Balanchine first performed 'Serenade' choreographed especially for them and based on the music of Tchaikovsky's 'Serenade for Strings.' Mr. and Mrs. Felix Warburg sponsored this performance as a twenty-sixth birthday present to Edward, their youngest son who, along with his friend Lincoln Kirstein, had founded the school and later the company. This was the beginning of what eventually became the New York City Ballet with its permanent home at Lincoln Center. 'Serenade' has for many years been performed as part of that company's regular repertoire."

A ruined lawn, a sacred place, the American soil that begot "a hymn to ward off sin." Or sun.

Closer to the sun, so close that seventeen shading hands would ward off little, there is another, far larger, memorial ground, where Balanchine and *Serenade* lie embedded together. This one is deep and wide and resides 96 million miles from the small forgotten plaque on the sloping lawn in New York. On Mercury, a planet so close to the sun that the daily temperature reaches 800 degrees Fahrenheit, lies "Balanchine," the crater.

Named in 2012 by Brett W. Denevi, a geophysicist and planetary scientist at NASA (she had studied ballet and danced *Serenade* as a student), the crater's location was first identified from images sent back to earth by the *Messenger* spaceship, on its first historic orbit of the planet. Balanchine is huge: over twenty-three miles wide and over two miles deep. Given that Mercury is about 4.6 billion years old, Balanchine, at less than 100 million years old, is termed a "young" crater: this is "why it's still so pretty," says Denevi.

Balanchine was immediately notable to her as it spewed beautiful ejecta particles in asymmetric, ray-like streaks of aquamarine light that reminded her of the *Serenade* tutus. This light show is called by NASA "Balanchine's Blues."

Perhaps Mercury is where Mr. B landed—as a comet—when he left us down here, forming this crater that now emits the celestial beams of *Serenade*. Geologically, Balanchine will probably exist for "at least two billion years," explains Denevi, but "in human terms" that is, technically speaking, "forever"—long past humankind's exis-

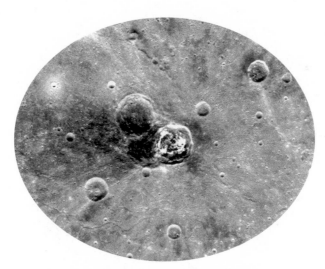

Balanchine crater and its northwestern blue rays on Mercury *(NASA/Johns Hopkins University Applied Physics Laboratory/Carnegie Institution of Washington)*

tence. What a heavenly paradox of permanence for the master of the most transient art.

In a mercurial, elegiac stroke, Balanchine's blue rays radiate in the very same northwest direction as the final diagonal processional of *Serenade*. I'd like to tell him of his crater. I can see him holding up that gentle forefinger of wisdom with delight, and saying, again, "You *see!*"

ACKNOWLEDGMENTS

I want to extend my gratitude to the following for graciously giving me interviews: the late Karin von Aroldingen and Elyse Borne; Maria Calegari, Brett W. Denevi, Rosemary Dunleavy, Allegra Kent, Kumiko Matada, Lauren Lovette, Ryuji Yamamoto, Suki Schorer, and Perry Silvey.

Much gratitude to photographers Steven Caras and Paul Kolnik, and to the Eakins Press Foundation for their generosity.

At Pantheon, my thanks to a truly first-rate team: Emily Mahon for the beautiful jacket design; Soonyoung Kwon for the elegant interior design; Nicole Pedersen and Altie Karper, who expertly kept the trains running on time; Romeo Enriquez and Melanie Muto for their expertise; publisher Lisa Lucas; editorial director Denise Oswald; and the terrific publicity and marketing team of Michiko Clark, Andreia Wardlaw, Morgan Fenton, and Matthew Sciarappa.

Many thanks to Sibylle Kazeroid for copyediting.

And a very special thanks to Todd Portnowitz, a man of many talents and a support throughout.

The following all contributed in a myriad of ways for which I am grateful: David Bentley, Jonathan Bentley, Karin Bentley, Liliane Bentley, Clayton Cubitt, Robert Gottlieb, Julia Gruen, Barbara Horgan, Nicholas Jenkins, Anna-Sophie Keller, Judy Kinberg, Tracy Kinell, Susan Freedman Londoner, David Mellon, Sara Miller, Emma Paltrow, Claudia Roth Pierpont, Tamara Pkhakadze, Judith Regan, Margaret Roberts, Bob Roth, Lance Spiro, Alice Truax, Binky Urban, Katie Wedlund, and Emily Wells. And a special thanks to Linda Murray, Curator, Jerome Robbins Dance Division, and Associate Director, Collections & Research, the New York Public Library of the Performing Arts.

I appreciate the generosity of the Guggenheim Foundation. And at New York City Ballet, the support of Wendy Whelan, Jonathan Stafford, Kina Poon, Rob Daniels, Erin Hestvik, and Laura Raucher.

Great thanks to the kind and indulgent staff at the Petit Ermitage, Le Sirenuse, and Hotel Welcome.

To Markus Hoffmann, a superb agent who truly went the extra mile for this book, my lasting gratitude.

And a very particular warm thank-you to Jonathan Brent for being the first to believe in this book.

To John Donatich at Yale University Press for his graceful forbearance.

To Martin Garbus for solid advice and deep friendship.

A very special thanks to Alix Freedman, always.

To Allison White for her unfailing wisdom.

For my beloved editor, Deborah Garrison, I have no words to describe the unprecedented pleasure of working together, and my gratitude and respect for her kindness, warmth, sanity, expertise, and attention to detail while keeping the big picture afloat. Thank you, Deb.

My love to Scott, and to the great Edith Wharton for her magnificent company during the isolation.

NOTES

In addition to the sources in the bibliography, I have relied on interviews I conducted with dancers and others close to Balanchine; the interviewees are listed among the abbreviations below, followed by the date of each interview. In the source notes that follow, I identify the interviewees by initials, and do the same for radio interviews with Balanchine conducted by Patricia Marx and Bob Sherman on WNYC, as well as for the privately printed booklet *By George Balanchine,* which remains one of the best sources in the choreographer's own words, and for the ample and well-organized website Tchaikovsky Research (both also listed in the bibliography). Abbreviations used are as follows:

AK: Allegra Kent, January 18, 2008
BD: Brett W. Denevi, October 7, 2020
BGB: By George Balanchine
BH: Barbara Horgan, December 5, 2020
BS: Bob Sherman Balanchine interview, June 11, 1977
KM: Kumiko Matada, February 15, 2008
KVA: Karin von Aroldingen, January 17, 2008
MC: Maria Calegari, September 27, 2007
PM: Patricia Marx Balanchine interview, September 17, 1963
PS: Perry Silvey, June 22, 2007
RY: Ryuji Yamamoto, February 15, 2008
SS: Suki Schorer, October 1, 2007
TR: Tchaikovsky Research

Additionally, my references to Alastair Macaulay's impressive *Serenade* compendium (whose publication in *Ballet Review* is listed in the bibliography) are from an updated version (2016.viii.04) that he graciously emailed to me on August 4, 2016. I identify the source by his name and the number he assigned to the relevant entry. Last, I would like to commend the scholarship of Emily Beeny, Kathryn Kane Hansen, and Sarah Curtis Lysgaard, whose excellent theses all live on the Internet, where I was grateful to find them, and to add my special thanks to Elizabeth Kendall for her detailed research on Balanchine's childhood, the most thorough we have to date.

INTRODUCTION

xx   "If you set out": *BGB,* 17.

xx   "If a ballet is decent": PM.

xx   "his imperial talent": Sontag, "Mr. Balanchine," 71.

xxi   What I know now: Bentley, *Winter Season,* xvi.

xxi   "Too fancy!": Taper, *Balanchine,* 157.

xxi   "Why do Americans": Kirstein diary, March 2, 1935, Macaulay #68A.

xxii   "I don't have": *BGB,* 9.

xxiii   "nostalgia is pure": Bentley, *Winter Season,* xvii.

xxiv   "a dance in": Balanchine and Mason, *101 Stories,* 391.

1. AUDIENCE

8   "a continuous present": *BGB,* 5.

11   What orange grove?: Kisselgoff, "Ballet as a Balm."

11   "a string of pearls": Balanchine, "Notes on Choreography," 26.

12   stage light RF961: PS.

12   "If I had only": Steichen, "Stories of Serenade," 10.

3. MR. B

23   "He stands in the hoop": Volynsky, *Ballet's Magic Kingdom,* xxxiii.

26   "There is no future": PM.

4. SIXTEEN

36   "dancer's being": Levinson, *André Levinson on Dance,* 45–46.

5. 1934

40   "the light of God": Homans, "Hail Balanchine."

40   "He said his head": Kirstein diary, March 14, 1934, Macaulay #1.

41   "He tried two": Kirstein diary, March 14, 1934, Macaulay #1.

41 "first night": Balanchine and Mason, *101 Stories*, 531–32.

41 "One Sunday": Tracy, *Balanchine's Ballerinas*, 66.

42 "I didn't look": Tracy, 66.

42 "He excused": Mason, *I Remember Balanchine*, 160.

43 "I was there": Mason, 160.

44 "I still didn't know": Mason, 160.

44 "very ragged": Kirstein diary, April 7, 1934, Macaulay #45.

44 "dark blue uniform": Kirstein diary, April 24, 1934, Macaulay #45.

45 "Hunted for bathing": Kirstein diary, June 5, 1934, Macaulay #47.

45 "at last at Abercrombies": Kirstein diary, June 8, 1934, Macaulay #47.

45 "The Warburg mansion": Kirstein diary, June 8, 1947, Macaulay #47.

46 "I made myself": Kirstein diary, June 9, 1934, Macaulay #47.

46 "With the music": Macaulay #48; Dunning, *"But First a School,"* 64.

47 "A more agonizing": Chujoy, *The New York City Ballet*, 30.

47 "A little sun": Kirstein diary, June 10, 1934, Macaulay #48.

47 "red pants": Kirstein diary, June 10, 1934, Macaulay #48.

48 "Without an implicit": Kirstein, *Program Notes*, 17.

48 "Alan Blackburn": Kirstein diary, June 10, 1934, Macaulay #48.

48 "The Ballet had": Kirstein diary, August 19, 1934, Macaulay #70B.

6. TURNOUT

53 "It was simplicity": Taper, *Balanchine*, 169.

54 approximately two hundred: Beeny, "Poussin," 33.

54 "There is a great difference": Beeny, 33.

54 "the Author of the Universe": Beeny, 36.

54 "God creates": *BGB*, 32.

54 "for a young": Lysgaard, "Ballet de la Nuit," 47.

54 "After having": Lysgaard, 45, note 139.

56 rehearsed for just: Lysgaard, 10.

56 "You'd never seen": Burden and Thorp, *Ballet de la Nuit*, 4.

57 *The company of:* Lysgaard, "Ballet de la Nuit," 67.

57 The sun appeared: Beeny, "Poussin," 250.

57 "The king's costume": Lysgaard, "Ballet de la Nuit," 64.

58 "desire for glory": Lysgaard, 7, note 59.

58 The Lettres Patentes: Needham, "Louis XIV," 174.

59 "each violation": Needham, 180, 181, 187.

60 "The Art of Dance": Needham, 180.

60 "This Academy": Kunzle, "Pierre Beauchamp," part I, 34.

61 Born in Paris: Kunzle, part II, 44.

61 Beauchamps debuted: Kunzle, part II, 42.

61 At age nineteen: Hansen, "Dancing for Distinction," 27.

61 proceeded to teach: Powell, "Pierre Beauchamps," 169.

61 "damsels": Arbeau, *Orchesography*, 17.

62 Delivered to the: Hansen, "Dancing for Distinction," 42.

62 "What is termed": Rameau, *Dancing Master*, 5.

62 *"Hence o'er the"*: Jenyns, *Art of Dancing*, Canto II, 156–57.

64 ninety-four forms: Karl-Johnson, "From the Page," 274.

64 "When I came to": Powell, "Pierre Beauchamps," 186, note 91.

64 often stated as: Kunzle, "Pierre Beauchamp," part II, 43.

64 He left no: Beeny, "Poussin," 54.

64 The single lithograph: Kunzle, "Pierre Beauchamp," part I, 32.

7. POINTE

67 "the most famous": McCarthy, "History," 119.

68 "find with surprise": Willis, "La Jolie Bayadère."

68 "abandon their soft": Homans, *Apollo's Angels*, 162.

69 "During these six": Goldschmidt, "Marie Taglioni," 108–10.

70 "by loosening the": Goldschmidt, 108–10.

70 "We do thousands": Goldschmidt, 108–10.

70 "Ill-made": Homans, *Apollo's Angels*, 137.

70 "When one has": Goldschmidt, "Marie Taglioni," 108–10.

71 "vertical culture": Volynsky, *Ballet's Magic Kingdom*, 84–85.

71 "provocative smiles": Goldschmidt, "Marie Taglioni," 119.

71 "He demanded a": Goldschmidt, 108–10.

72 "all the past": Goldschmidt, 107.

72 In addition to: Brusegan, *I palazzi di Venezia*, 91.

8. THE GREAT RUN

78 "In order to make": KVA.

78 "had to leave": SS.

80 "Ballet is a lot": Taper, *Balanchine*, 169.

9. JOHN'S GEOMETRY

86 "apotheosis of verticality": Rabinowitz, "Against the Grain," 11.

86 "a lamentable fiasco": Volynsky, *Ballet's Magic Kingdom*, 197.

86 "pirouette requires": Volynsky, 193.

89   "couldn't get there": Lobenthal, *Wilde Times,* Kindle edition, loc. 2642.

10. STONEHENGE

91   program from 1957: Balanchine, *Balanchine: New York City Ballet in Montreal.*
91   "A ballerina is": *BGB,* 7.
92   these three solo girls: Kirstein, *Thirty Years,* 39.
92   "I assemble": Massie, "Mr B: 'God Creates, I Assemble.'"
92   "The leg thrown": Volynsky, *Ballet's Magic Kingdom,* 56.
95   "After Jillana's": Taras Collection.
97   A 1940 film clip: Macaulay #87.
97   According to witnesses: Macaulay #29; Balanchine and Mason, *101 Stories,* 390–92.
98   "I am made": *BGB,* 30, 31.
99   "I felt I was": Macaulay #31.
101   "When he walks": Hunt, "Encounters," 55.

11. WALTZ

103   "It would be easier": *BGB,* 6.

12. LITTLE GEORGI

110   "It's all in the": Taper, *Balanchine,* 366.
110   He would close: Kendall, *Balanchine,* 31.
110   conduct High Mass: Buckle, *George Balanchine,* 34.
110   Another child who: Kendall, *Balanchine,* 248, note 22.
111   *I am Ba:* Taper, *Balanchine,* 44.
111   His favorite subjects: Volkov, *Balanchine's Tchaikovsky,* 63.
111   "The music passes": Taper, *Balanchine,* 16.
112   "I am often asked": Volkov, *Balanchine's Tchaikovsky,* 71.
112   Meliton Balanchivadze: Kendall, *Balanchine,* 248, note 17.
112   the von Almedingens: Kendall, 22.
112   Balanchine's mother remains: Kendall, 21.
112   "closed in, and dry": Kendall, 249, note 45.
112   "Everyone wants to": Kendall, 29; Volkov, *Balanchine's Tchaikovsky,* 39.
113   There are three existing: Kendall, 24, 27, 28.

113 though it also: Kendall, 27, note 4, 247; BH.

113 Balanchivadze had a: Kendall, 18.

113 were likely forged: Kendall, 259, note 44.

114 By 1911, when: Kendall, 28–45.

114 Balanchine's paternal: Kendall, 16, 19.

114 Before the altar: Kendall, 31.

114 Balanchine's parents: Kendall, 38.

114 Founded in 1738: Kendall, 47, 49.

115 taught Russian, French, arithmetic: Kendall, 39.

115 "felt like a dog": Taper, *Balanchine*, notes, September 19, 1961; Kendall, 40.

115 His first glimpse: Kendall, 83–84.

115 "I was Cupid": Volkov, *Balanchine's Tchaikovsky*, 31.

115 An elaborate production: Slonimsky, "Balanchine," 6.

115 They also would: Taper, *Balanchine*, 40; Kendall, *Balanchine*, 52.

116 Balanchivadze memorized: Kendall, 135.

116 detective stories: Volkov, *Balanchine's Tchaikovsky*, 42–43.

116 the German UFA: Volkov, 70.

116 "This was a court": Volkov, 60–62.

117 "very thin, pale": Kendall, *Balanchine*, 90.

117 While the Theatre: Kendall, 89.

117 His father escaped: Taper, *Balanchine*, 46; Kendall, 100–102.

117 received exit visas: Kendall, 125.

117 There is evidence: Kendall, 158.

117 Georgi went to work: Slonimsky, "Balanchine," 20; Kendall, 118.

117 "The worst part": Volkov, *Balanchine's Tchaikovsky*, 66–67.

117 "We did a Hindu": Volkov, 69.

117 Typhus, lice: Kendall, *Balanchine*, 131.

118 "They smoked": Volkov, *Balanchine's Tchaikovsky*, 68.

118 "Balanchine possessed an": Slonimsky, "Balanchine," 23.

119 "I trembled with": Slonimsky, "Balanchine," 24–25.

119 "the Rubicon": Slonimsky, "Balanchine," 24–25.

119 "especially reliable": Slonimsky, "Balanchine," 30.

119 The previous year: Kendall, *Balanchine*, 135.

119 "sexy number": Danilova, *Choura*, 44.

119 "tender transitions": Kendall, *Balanchine*, 140.

119 "reproached for indecency": Slonimsky, "Balanchine," 52; Taper, *Balanchine*, 53.

120 "accidental brain child": Slonimsky, "Balanchine," 46.

120   Within a year: Kendall, *Balanchine*, 186.

120   The group met: Kendall, 186.

120   "This evening has": Slonimsky, "Balanchine," 55.

120   "Balanchine is bold": Slonimsky, "Balanchine," 61.

120   St. Petersburg cabaret: Slonimsky, "Balanchine," 60.

121   playing piano for: Kendall, *Balanchine*, 157.

121   He said yes: Kendall, 204.

121   on the cover of *Teatp:* Slonimsky, "Balanchine," 61.

121   "His whole presence": Buckle, *George Balanchine*, 20.

121   seventeen and eighteen: Kendall, *Balanchine*, 160, 181.

122   The family lived: Volkov, *Balanchine's Tchaikovsky*, 58.

122   "Principal Dancers": Simmonds, *Choreography by George Balanchine*, 24.

122   on June 16: Kendall, *Balanchine*, 217–19.

122   Her death, never: Volkov, *Balanchine's Tchaikovsky*, 147.

122   "We paid no attention": Volkov, 99.

122   They quickly hustled: Kendall, *Balanchine*, 230.

13. THE AMERICAN

125   "I don't get": Volkov, *Balanchine's Tchaikovsky*, 212–13.

125   "somehow not of": Reynolds, "Apollon Musagète."

125   "it demands goddesses": Danilova, *Choura*, 100.

125   "*Apollo* is about": Denby, *Looking at the Dance*, 124–125.

125   "It seemed to tell": Balanchine, "Dance Element," 254.

126   "morbid interest": Taper, *Balanchine*, 92.

126   "the most important": Taper, 117.

126   "Their thrilling dances": Kirstein, *Flesh is Heir*, 188.

126   "This gathering was": Kirstein, *Flesh is Heir*, 220–21.

127   He refused surgery: Taper, *Balanchine*, 135.

127   "I knew I must": Kirstein, *Mosaic*, 257.

127   Through Romola Nijinsky: Kirstein, *Mosaic*, 242.

128   "I asked Balanchine": Chujoy, *The New York City Ballet*, 20.

128   On July 16: Kirstein, *Mosaic*, 249.

129   "Dear Chick": Grunwald and Adler, *Letters of the Century*, 212–15.

129   "I began to sense": Kirstein, *Mosaic*, 255.

130   the "Black Pearl": Gregory, "Obituary: Tamara Toumanova."

130   "All the ladies": Mason, *I Remember Balanchine*, 99–103.

130   "They didn't want": Volkov, *Balanchine's Tchaikovsky*, 107.

130   "I became a choreographer": Haggin, *Discovering Balanchine*, 35.

130   kept all the letters: Homans, "Unknown Young Balanchine."

14. THE COMPOSER

133   the occasional phone call: Dunning, "Whimsical Balanchine."

133   "I didn't like it": Volkov, *Balanchine's Tchaikovsky*, 214.

133   condemned by critics of the day: Sokolov-Kaminsky, "Mikhail Fokine," 53–58.

134   After deciding on: Taper, *Balanchine*, 371.

134   "I was born in": Volkov, *Balanchine's Tchaikovsky*, 51–52.

134   "Russian European": Volkov, 56.

134   "I don't quite understand": Volkov, 73.

134   "Tchaikovsky is Pushkin": Volkov, 95.

134   "Tchaikovsky was convinced": Volkov, 145.

135   "The stage, with all": letter to von Meck, TR #2791.

135   "If it were not": Kisselgoff, "Balanchine and Tchaikovsky."

135   "I couldn't move": *BGB*, 8.

135   "I can't understand": *BGB*, 22.

135   Bach, Mozart, Stravinsky: Simmonds, *Choreography by George Balanchine*.

136   "I not only love": letter to von Meck, TR #790.

136   two brief flirtations: February 16, 1931, Simmonds, 101.

137   "merely a talented person": Alberge, "Tchaikovsky."

137   "What a giftless bastard!": letter to von Meck, TR #3439.

137   "a conceited mediocrity": diary entry, September 21, 1886, Nilsen, "A Conceited Mediocrity."

138   "I love fame": letter to Sergei Taneyev, TR #1544.

138   "The SEED of a future": letter to von Meck, TR #763.

138   "I consider it": Brown, *Tchaikovsky: The Man and His Music*, 209.

139   "I am silence": *BGB*, 30.

139   "Tchaikovsky loved his mother": Volkov, *Balanchine's Tchaikovsky*, 39–40.

139   he decided, at age: Poznansky, *Tchaikovsky*, 5.

141   "I find that our": letter to Modest Tschaikovsky, TR #494.

141   "I am dying": Brown, *Tchaikovsky: The Man and His Music*, 135.

141   "I have decided": letter to Modest Tschaikovsky, TR #492.

141   what she could expect: letter to von Meck, TR #574.

141   "Why did I": letter to von Meck, July 15, 1877, in Brown, *Tchaikovsky: The Man and His Music*, 135–36.

142 one of the two: Poznansky, *Tchaikovsky*, 107.

142 he cried when asked: Brown, *Tchaikovsky: The Man and His Music*, 139.

142 *"intolerable spiritual torments":* Brown, 139.

142 *"totally repugnant":* Brown, 139.

142 "It appeared to me": letter to von Meck, TR #592.

142 He found his wife: Poznansky, *Tchaikovsky*, 107.

142 "an unbearable encumbrance": Brown, *Tchaikovsky: The Man and His Music*, 139.

142 "a terrible wound": letter to von Meck, TR #592.

142 The couple separated: Poznansky, *Tchaikovsky*, 107.

142 Though she twice refused: Poznansky, 109 and 293, note 29.

142 *"paranoia chronica":* Poznansky, 110 and 283, note 28.

142 Her grave has: Poznansky, 110.

142 adopt her youngest, a girl: Poznansky, 109 and 283, note 29.

143 "You know how I": Brown, *Tchaikovsky: The Man and His Music*, 171–72.

143 "Every note that will": "The von Meck Family History," www.von-meck.info.

143 "my own Providence": letter to von Meck, TR #590.

143 "You are the only": Tommasini, "Patroness."

144 "Music puts me": von Meck letter to Tschaikovsky, November 29, 1877, in Lobanova, 1.

144 "My ideal man": Tommasini, "Patroness."

144 "The more I am": Brown, *Tchaikovsky: The Man and His Music*, 133.

144 "Of my imaginary": Brown, *Tchaikovsky: The Man and His Music*, 132.

145 "that disenchantment": Brown, *Tchaikovsky: The Man and His Music*, 133–34.

145 "I am very unsympathetic": Poznansky, *Tchaikovsky*, 197.

145 "the thought of you": Tommasini, "Patroness."

145 "what [delighted him] not": letter to Jurgenson, TR #1525.

145 "My dear chap!": letter to Jurgenson, TR #1517.

146 "from the heart": letter to Jurgenson, TR, #1517.

146 little more than four days: letter to von Meck, TR #1601.

146 "Imagine, my dear": letter to von Meck, TR #1609.

146 "Pyotr Ivanovich!": letter to Jurgenson, TR #1619.

148 "This piece [*Serenade*]": letter to von Meck, TR #1632.

148 The great Russian pianist: Brown, *Tchaikovsky: The Man and His Music*, 226.

148   would "always be": letter to von Meck, TR #584.

149   "the anchor of": letter to von Meck, TR #4221.

149   "I believe that he": Volkov, *Balanchine's Tchaikovsky*, 225–26.

149   "She did not endure": Holden, *Tchaikovsky*, 401.

15. TRANSITIONS

150   *"ces affreux trompettes!"*: Kirstein letter to Muriel Draper, February 28, 1935, Macaulay #66.

151   "took me a long": BS.

151   "pink Latex which tears": Kirstein diary, November 25, 1934, Macaulay #55.

151   The *Serenade* blue: Kirstein diary, March 20, 1934, Macaulay #6.

151   It was never: Macaulay #56.

151   "the sky over": Kirstein in "The American Ballet in Brazil" (1941), Macaulay #88.

151   A quixotic Paris Opera: Macaulay #99.

152   Eventually the scenery: PS email to author, September 9, 2021.

152   "After the Waltz": PS.

154   "Nobody cared about": PM.

16. THE OTHER BALLETMASTER

155   (he claimed 105 works): Petipa, "The Diaries," 47.

156   "Russian Ballet": Meisner, *Marius Petipa*, 2.

156   retain his French: Wiley, "A Context," 45–46.

156   every ruble: Petipa, "The Diaries," 1–79.

156   "All my relatives": Petipa, "The Diaries," 69.

156   unreliable memoirs: Meisner, *Marius Petipa*, 11.

156   never properly: Meisner, 160.

157   brief, bankrupting tour: Moore, "The Petipa Family," 77.

157   like his father: Meisner, *Marius Petipa*, 79.

157   *Psyché et l'Amour:* Meisner, 84.

157   Lucien, age eight: Moore, "The Petipa Family," 73.

158   "How devoted": Meisner, *Marius Petipa*, 39–40.

158   apparently off: Meisner, 39.

158   He debuted: Meisner, 47.

158   daughter of: Meisner, 52.

158   Count de Gabriac: Meisner, 51.

158   "I thought that": Meisner, 52.

158   Petipa challenged: Petipa, *Russian Ballet Master*, 18; Meisner, 51.

158   in her pointe shoes: Meisner, *Marius Petipa*, 80 and 363, note 49.

159   he denied: Petipa, *Russian Ballet Master*, 20.

159   Laura Hormigón: Hormigón, *Marius Petipa;* Hormignón, "La apasionante fuga de España de Marius Petipa."

159   German newspaper: Meisner, *Marius Petipa*, 51.

159   pursuing his lover: Meisner, 53.

159   missing from: Meisner, 52.

159   "kidnapper," was: Meisner, 52.

159   "she cited": Meisner, 52.

159   Carmen was arrested: Meisner, 53.

159   possibly obtained: Meisner, 53.

160   As director of: Slonimsky, "Marius Petipa," 106.

160   seeing a decline: Wiley, *A Century*, 351.

160   "whom fate": Rabinowitz, "Against the Grain," 21.

160   "The chart of": Slonimsky, "Marius Petipa," 107.

160   made in only: Meisner, *Marius Petipa*, 100.

160   "tendency to monumentality": Slonimsky, "Marius Petipa," 105.

160   "there are so many": Slonimsky, "Marius Petipa," 103.

160   "crowned with glory": Slonimsky, "Marius Petipa," 105.

160   fifty ballets: Meisner, *Marius Petipa*, 3.

161   "It is particularly": Rabinowitz, "The House That Petipa Built," 60.

162   "Petipa turned the art": Rabinowitz, "Against the Grain," 26.

162   "Repeated mewing": Slonimsky, "Marius Petipa," 133.

163   "Madame Petipa is": Meisner, *Marius Petipa*, 97 and notes 142, 143.

163   "In the duration": Meisner, 125–26.

164   Petipa serving time: Meisner, 126.

164   Perhaps due to: Meisner, 126–27.

164   "My work is wasted": Petipa, "The Diaries," 29–30.

165   "choreographic death agony": Wiley, "A Context," 48.

166   two outside girls: Macaulay #81.

18. ANARCHISTS

177   "The three women": Hunt, "Encounters," 54.

178   "force as a collective": Kirstein, *Four Centuries*, 151.

179   1829 poem "Fantômes": Hugo, *Les Orientales*.

179   "The Willis are brides": Heine, *The Works*, 138–40.

181   "I'm not interested": *BGB*, 13.

182   "the 'Christian' spirit": Kirstein, *Four Centuries*, 142.

182   "lapsed nuns laid buried": Kirstein, *Four Centuries*, 142.

182   "unholy thrills": Kirstein, *Four Centuries*, 142.

182   "deliver themselves to": Kirstein, *Four Centuries*, 142.

182   "huge night moths": Kirstein, *Four Centuries*, 143.

182   "By the hundred [the nuns]: Stoneley, *A Queer History*, 24–25.

183   "an agreeable exercise": Kirstein, *Four Centuries*, 143.

183   "whose Habitation is": from "The Rape of the Lock" by Alexander Pope, 1712, quoted in Kirstein, *Four Centuries*, 146.

184   "Light" women : from "The Rape of the Lock" by Alexander Pope, 1712, quoted in Kirstein, *Four Centuries*, 146.

186   "a messianic work": Strauss, *Dance Criticism*, 35.

187   "Critics don't know anything!": PM.

19. CUPID'S KISS

188   "So how is your": MC.

189   "GREAT!!!!" he said: Macaulay #126.

190   "More important than art": Volkov, *Balanchine's Tchaikovsky*, 88.

191   "People never seem": Taper, *Balanchine*, 7.

192   "You are his eyes": Colleen Neary email, July 14, 2016, Macaulay #37.

192   "You know, Laskey": Gottlieb, *Reading Dance*, 1069.

192   The Dark Angel lifts: SS.

193   "When Balanchine spoke": Kirstein, "Beliefs of a Master."

195   "The story of Cupid": Wilson, *Cupid and Psyche*, vii.

199   "There are no hidden": *BGB*, 15.

20. MARIA'S ARABESQUE

202   Balanchine did a version: Tracy, *Balanchine's Ballerinas*, 42.

204   "It's all in": Taper, *Balanchine*, 308.

21. VITRUVIAN MAN

209   "I'm changing it!": MC email to author, December 11, 2019.

22. CHARLIE'S ANGELS

217   "like Charlie's Angels": Macaulay #126.

217   "I think he felt": Hunt, "Encounters," 57.

23. DESTINY

228 "She [the Dark Angel]": Mason, *I Remember Balanchine*, 7.

229 "Balanchine said about": Colleen Neary email, April 28, 2015, Macaulay #128.

229 "The [male] role is": RY.

229 "Too much worry": KM.

229 "There seems to be": Denby, *Looking at the Dance*, 75.

229 "It's like fate": Taper, *Balanchine*, 172.

230 "I can see no": *BGB*, 11.

233 "Balanchine was the father": KVA.

CURTAIN DOWN

236 "Look at her": Lobenthal, *Wilde Times*, Kindle edition, loc. 3413.

239 the Initiate: Daniels, "Academy," 5.

239 the Student: Daniels, 2.

239 the Heroine: Daniels, 3.

239 "the wife": Danilova, *Choura*, 161.

239 a Butterfly: Danilova, 162.

239 Joan of Arc: Goldner, *Balanchine Variations*, 23.

239 virgin suicide: Volkov, *Balanchine's Tchaikovsky*, 225.

239 "Ballet is a Woman": *BGB*, 22.

239 He told one dancer: KVA.

240 "I have poured": This passage was read aloud in the BBC documentary *Who Killed Tchaikovsky?* at minute 6:18.

240 "The wonderful pure": Kisselgoff, "City Ballet."

241 "A little thing": Homans, "Balanchine."

EPILOGUE

245 "We invited some two hundred": Dunning, *"But First a School,"* 64.

247 "why it's still so pretty": BD email to author, September 7, 2021.

247 Balanchine was immediately: BD.

247 This light show is called: Talbert, "Balanchine's Blues."

247 "at least two billion years": BD email to author, September 9, 2021.

BIBLIOGRAPHY

Acocella, Joan. "The Diaries of Marius Petipa." Edited, translated, and introduced by Lynn Garafola. *Dance Research: The Journal of the Society for Dance Research* 12, no. 1 (Summer 1994): 78–84.

———. "Souls in Single File." *New York Review of Books,* December 19, 2019.

Alberge, Dalya. "Tchaikovsky and the Secret Gay Loves Censors Tried to Hide." *Observer,* February 6, 2018.

Arbeau, Thoinot. *Orchesography: 16th-Century French Dance from Court to Countryside.* Translated by Mary Stewart Evans. New York: Dover, 1967.

Balanchine, George. *By George Balanchine.* Edited by Thomas W. Schoff. New York: San Marco Press, 1984.

———. "The Dance Element in Stravinsky's Music." *Dance Index* 6, nos. 10–12 (October–December 1947): 250–56.

———. "Notes on Choreography." *Dance Index* 4, nos. 2–3 (February–March 1945): 20–31.

———, and Francis Mason. *Balanchine's Complete Stories of the Great Ballets.* Garden City, N.Y.: Doubleday, 1977.

———, and Francis Mason. *101 Stories of the Great Ballets.* New York: Anchor, 1975.

———, Jerome Robbins, Paul Hindemoth, et al. *Balanchine: New York City Ballet in Montreal: Vol. 1: Orpheus and Serenade.* Performed 1957, 1960. Pleasantville, N.Y.: Video Artists International, April 29, 2014. DVD, 59 min.

Beeny, Emily A. "Poussin, Ballet, and the Birth of French Classicism." PhD diss., Columbia University, 2016. https://academiccommons.columbia.edu/doi/10.7916/D8KD1XV6.

Bentley, Toni. *Winter Season: A Dancer's Journal.* New York: Random House, 1982.

Brown, David. *Tchaikovsky: The Man and His Music*. New York: Pegasus Books, 2007.

———. *Tchaikovsky: The Years of Fame 1878–1893*. London: Victor Gollancz Ltd., 1992.

Brusegan, Marcello. *I palazzi di Venezia* [The Palaces of Venice]. Rome: Newton Compton, 2007.

Buckle, Richard, in collaboration with John Taras. *George Balanchine: Ballet Master*. New York: Random House, 1988.

Burden, Michael, and Jennifer Thorp, eds. *Ballet de la Nuit*. Hillsdale, N.Y.: Pendragon Press, 2010.

Chujoy, Anatole. *The New York City Ballet*. New York: Alfred A. Knopf, 1953.

Croce, Arlene. "Balanchine Said." *New Yorker,* January 26, 2006.

———. "On 'Beauty' Bare." *New York Review of Books,* August 12, 1999.

Daniels, Don. "Academy: The New World of *Serenade*." *Ballet Review* 5, no. 1 (1975–76): 1–12.

Danilova, Alexandra, and Holly Brubach. *Choura: The Memoirs of Alexandra Danilova*. New York: Alfred A. Knopf, 1986.

Denby, Edwin. *Looking at the Dance*. Introduction by B. H. Haggin. New York: Popular Library, 1968.

Dunning, Jennifer. *"But First a School": The First Fifty Years of the School of American Ballet*. New York: Viking, 1985.

———. "Fifty Years Ago: The Beginning of the School of American Ballet," *Playbill* (Winter Season 1983–84), 8–9.

———. "A Whimsical Balanchine Maps June Tchaikovsky Festival." *New York Times,* February 10, 1981.

Feuillet, Raoul-Auger. *Chorégraphie ou l'art de décrire la dance*. Paris: Chez l'Auteur et Michel Brunet, 1701. https://publicdomainreview.org.

Goldner, Nancy. *Balanchine Variations*. Gainsville: University Press of Florida, 2008.

Goldschmidt, Hubert. "Marie Taglioni." *Ballet Review* 46, no. 2 (Summer 2018): 101–24.

Gottlieb, Robert. *George Balanchine: The Ballet Master.* New York: Harper-Collins, 2004.

———, ed. *Reading Dance: A Gathering of Memoirs, Reportage, Criticism, Profiles, Interviews, and Some Uncategorizable Extras.* New York: Pantheon Books, 2008.

Gregory, John. "Obituary: Tamara Toumanova." *The Independent,* May 31, 1996.

Grunwald, Lisa, and Stephen J. Adler, eds. *Letters of the Century: 1900–1999.* New York: Random House, 1999.

Haggin, B. H. *Discovering Balanchine.* New York: Horizon Press, 1981.

Hansen, Kathryn Kane. "Dancing for Distinction: Pierre Beauchamps and the Social Dynamics of Seventeenth-Century France." Undergraduate honors thesis, College of William and Mary, 2010, Paper 344.

Heine, Heinrich. *The Works of Heinrich Heine, Vol. VI, Elementary Spirits.* 1834. Translated by Charles Godfrey Leland, 1891. Reprint. New York: E. P. Dutton and Co., 1906.

Holden, Anthony. *Tchaikovsky: A Biography.* New York: Random House, 1996.

Homans, Jennifer. *Apollo's Angels: A History of Ballet.* New York: Random House, 2010.

———. "Balanchine: Making and Being Don Quixote." *New York Review of Books,* June 4, 2015.

———. "Hail Balanchine." *New York Review of Books,* December 21, 2017.

———. "The Unknown Young Balanchine." *New York Review of Books,* October 24, 2013.

Hormigón, Laura. "La apasionante fuga de España de Marius Petipa. Una cuestión de estado." *ADE Teatro* 169 (January–March 2018): 8–19.

———. *Marius Petipa en España, 1844–1847: Memorias y Otros Materiales.* Madrid: Danzarte Ballet, S.L., 2010.

Hugo, Victor. *Les Orientales.* Paris: J. Hetzel, 1829.

Hunt, Marilyn. "Encounters with Poetry: *Serenade* at Fifty." *Dance Magazine,* June 1985: 52–57.

———. "Joseph Duell: Coming of Age." *Dance Magazine,* June 1985: 57–61.

Jenyns, Soame. *The Art of Dancing: A Poem, in Three Canto's.* 1729. Reprint, London: Forgotten Books, 2018.

Jerome Robbins Dance Division, the New York Public Library. *Balanchine in America.* Film of *Serenade* in the New York Public Library Digital Collections, 1990. Telecast on WNET/Thirteen's *Great Performances: Dance in America* series.

Karl-Johnson, Gabriella. "From the Page to the Floor: Baroque Dance Notation and Kellom Tomlinson's 'The Art of Dancing Explained.'" *Signs and Society* 5, no. 2 (Fall 2017). Semiosis Research Center.

Kendall, Elizabeth. *Balanchine and the Lost Muse: Revolution and the Making of a Choreographer.* New York: Oxford University Press, 2013.

Kirstein, Lincoln. "Beliefs of a Master." *New York Review of Books,* March 15, 1984.

————. Diaries (unpublished), 1934. Writings by Lincoln Kirstein are held at the New York Public Library (Astor, Lenox and Tilden Foundations).

————. *Flesh is Heir: An Historical Romance*. New York: Brewer, Warren & Putnam, 1932.

————. *Four Centuries of Ballet: Fifty Ballet Masterworks*. New York: Dover Publications: 1984.

————. *Lincoln Kirstein: Program Notes*. Edited by Randall Bourscheidt. New York: Eakins Press Foundation, 2009.

————. *Mosaic: Memoirs*. New York: Farrar, Straus & Giroux, 1994.

————. *Portrait of Mr. B: Photographs of George Balanchine*. New York: Viking Press, 1984.

————. *Thirty Years: Lincoln Kirstein's The New York City Ballet*. New York: Alfred A. Knopf, 1978.

Kisselgoff, Anna. "Balanchine and Tchaikovsky." New York City Ballet *Playbill,* June 1981.

————. "City Ballet: 'Pathétique' with Balanchine 'Adagio.'" *New York Times,* June 2, 1981.

————. "Ballet as Balm in a Tribute to a City on the Mend." *New York Times,* November 22, 2001.

Kunzle, Régine. "Pierre Beauchamp: The Illustrious Unknown Choreographer," parts I and II. *Dance Scope* 8, no. 2 (Spring/Summer 1974): 32–42, and 9, no. 1 (Winter 1974–75): 30–45.

Levinson, André. *André Levinson on Dance: Writings from Paris in the Twenties.* Edited by Joan Acocella and Lynn Garafola. Middletown, Conn.: Wesleyan University Press, 1991.

Lobanova, Marina. "Nadeshda von Meck." MuGI (Musik und Gender im Internet), July 12, 2009. https://mugi.hfmt-hamburg.de.

Lobenthal, Joel. *Wilde Times: Patricia Wilde, George Balanchine, and the Rise of New York City Ballet.* Lebanon, N.H.: University Press of New England/ForeEdge, 2016.

Lysgaard, Sarah Curtis. "Ballet de la Nuit: Staging the Absolute Monarchy of Louis XIV." PhD diss., San Jose State University, 2019.

Macaulay, Alastair. "Serenade: Evolutionary Changes." *Ballet Review* 44, no. 4 (Winter 2016–17): 74–119.

The Marius Petipa Society. Amy Growcott, founder. https://petipasociety .com.

Mason, Francis. *I Remember Balanchine: Recollections of the Ballet Master by Those Who Knew Him.* New York: Doubleday, 1991.

Massie, Suzanne. "Mr B: 'God Creates, I Assemble.'" *Saturday Evening Post,* October 23, 1965.

McCarthy, Justin. "History of Our Own Times." *Dance Index* 3, nos. 7–8 (July–August 1944): 119.

Meisner, Nadine. *Marius Petipa: The Emperor's Ballet Master.* New York: Oxford University Press, 2019.

Moore, Lillian. "The Petipa Family in Europe and America." *Dance Index* 1, no. 5 (May 1942): 71–84.

Needham, Maureen. "Louis XIV and the Académie Royale de Danse, 1661: A Commentary and Translation." *Dance Chronicle* 20, no. 2 (1997): 173–90.

Nilsen, Richard. "A Conceited Mediocrity: The Story of Tchaikovsky and Brahms." *Imaginative Conservative,* May 6, 2017.

Petipa, Marius. "The Diaries of Marius Petipa." Edited, translated, and introduced by Lynn Garafola. *Studies in Dance History: The Journal of the Society of Dance History Scholars* 3, no. 1 (Spring 1992): vi–103.

———. *Russian Ballet Master: The Memoirs of Marius Petipa.* Edited by Lillian Moore. Translated by Helen Whittaker. London: Dance Books, 1958.

Petrov, Oleg. "Russian Ballet and Its Place in Russian Artistic Culture of the Second Half of the Nineteenth Century: The Age of Petipa." Translated by Tim Scholl. *Dance Chronicle* 15, no. 1 (1992): 40–55.

Powell, John S. "Pierre Beauchamps, Choreographer to Molière's Troupe du Roy." *Music and Letters* 76, no. 2 (May 1995): 168–86.

Poznansky, Alexander, ed. *Tchaikovsky: Through Others' Eyes.* Translated by Ralph C. Burr, Jr., and Robert Bird. Bloomington and Indianapolis: Indiana University Press, 1999.

Pruiksma, Rose A. "Generational Conflict and the Foundation of the Académie Royale de Danse: A Reexamination." *Dance Chronicle* 26, no. 2 (2003): 169–87.

Rabinowitz, Stanley J. "Against the Grain: Akim Volynskii and the Russian Ballet." *Dance Research: The Journal of the Society for Dance Research* 14, no. 1 (Summer 1996): 3–41.

———. "The House That Petipa Built: Visions and Villains of Akim Volynsky." *Dance Research: The Journal of the Society for Dance Research* 16, no. 1 (Summer 1998): 26–66.

Rameau, Pierre. *The Dancing Master.* 1725. Reprint, translated by Cyril Beaumont. London: C. W. Beaumont, 1931.

Reynolds, Nancy. "Apollon Musagète." *The Routledge Encyclopedia of Mod-*

ernism. London: Taylor & Francis, 2016. https://www.rem.routledge.com.

———. *Repertory in Review: 40 Years of the New York City Ballet.* New York: Dial Press, 1977.

Simmonds, Harvey, ed. *Choreography by George Balanchine: A Catalogue of Works.* New York: Eakins Press Foundation, 1983.

Slonimsky, Yuri. "Balanchine: The Early Years." Translated by John Andrews. *Ballet Review* 5, no. 3 (1975–76): 1–64.

———. "Marius Petipa." Translated by Anatole Chujoy. *Dance Index* 6, nos. 5–6 (May–June 1947): 99–144.

Sokolov-Kaminsky, Arkady. "Mikhail Fokine in St. Petersburg 1912–18." *Dance Research: The Journal of the Society for Dance Research* 10, no. 1 (1992): 53–58.

Sontag, Susan. "Mr. Balanchine." *Vanity Fair,* July 1983: 71–74.

Steichen, James. *Balanchine and Kirstein's American Enterprise.* New York: Oxford University Press, 2018.

———. "The Stories of Serenade: Nonprofit History and George Balanchine's 'First Ballet in America.'" Working Paper #46, Spring 2012.

Stoneley, Peter. *A Queer History of the Ballet.* London: Routledge, 2007.

Strauss, Marc Raymond. *The Dance Criticism of Arlene Croce: Articulating a Vision of Artistry, 1973–1987.* Jefferson, N.C.: McFarland & Company, 2005.

Talbert, Tricia. "Balanchine's Blues," May 24, 2013. https://www.nasa.gov.

Taper, Bernard. *Balanchine: A Biography.* Berkeley: University of California Press, 1984, 1996.

Taras Collection, New York City Ballet Archives.

Tchaikovsky, Modeste. *The Life and Letters of Peter Ilich Tchaikovsky.* Edited from the Russian and with an introduction by Rosa Newmache. New York: John Lane Company, 1906. Project Gutenberg ebook, 2014.

Tchaikovsky Research. https://en.tchaikovsky-research.net.

Tommasini, Anthony. "The Patroness Who Made Tchaikovsky Tchaikovksy." *New York Times,* September 2, 1998.

Tracy, Robert. *Balanchine's Ballerinas: Conversations with the Muses.* New York: Simon & Schuster, 1983.

Volkov, Solomon. *Balanchine's Tchaikovsky: Interviews with George Balanchine.* Translated by Antonia W. Bouis. New York: Simon & Schuster, 1985.

Volynsky, Akim. *Ballet's Magic Kingdom: Selected Writings on Dance in Russia 1911–1925.* Edited and with an introduction by Stanley J. Rabinowitz. New Haven, Conn.: Yale University Press, 2008.

von Meck, Galina. *As I Remember Them.* London: Dobson Books Ltd., 1973.

"The von Meck Family History." https://www.von-meck.info.

Wiley, Roland John. *A Century of Russian Ballet, Documents and Eyewitness Accounts, 1810–1910.* Oxford: Clarendon Press, 1990.

———. "A Context for Petipa." *Dance Research: The Journal of the Society for Dance Research* 21, no. 1 (Summer 2003): 42–52.

Willis, N. P., "La Jolie Bayadère de 1832: 'Pencillings by the Way.'" *Dance Index* 3, nos. 7–8 (July–August 1944): 118.

Wilson, John Lyde. *Cupid and Psyche: A Mythological Tale, from the "Golden Ass" of Apuleius.* Charleston, S.C.: B. B. Hussey, 1842.

Wood, Ralph W. "Miscellaneous Orchestral Works." In *The Music of Tchaikovsky,* edited by Gerald Abraham, 74–103. New York: Norton, 1946.

INDEX

Page numbers in *italics* refer to captions.

A NOTE ABOUT THE AUTHOR

Toni Bentley danced with George Balanchine's New York City Ballet for ten years. She is the author of five previous books, all named "Notable" by *The New York Times: Winter Season: A Dancer's Journal, Holding On to the Air* (the autobiography of Suzanne Farrell, coauthored with Farrell), *Costumes by Karinska, Sisters of Salome,* and *The Surrender: An Erotic Memoir*. Bentley is the recipient of a Guggenheim Fellowship, and her work has appeared in *Best American Essays,* as well as in many periodicals, among them, *The New York Times Book Review, The New Yorker, The Wall Street Journal, The New York Review of Books, The New Republic, The Daily Beast, Vogue,* and *Vanity Fair.*

A NOTE ON THE TYPE

This book was set in a modern adaptation of a type designed by the first William Caslon (1692–1766). The Caslon face, an artistic, easily read type, has enjoyed more than two centuries of popularity in our own country. It is of interest to note that the first copies of the Declaration of Independence and the first paper currency distributed to the citizens of the newborn nation were printed in this typeface.

Composed by North Market Street Graphics
Lancaster, Pennsylvania

Printed and bound by Berryville Graphics
Berryville, Virginia

Designed by Soonyoung Kwon